Microsoft®
OFFICE 97
VISUAL BASIC®

Step by Step

Other titles in the *Step by Step* series:

Microsoft Access 97 Step by Step

Microsoft Excel 97 Step by Step

Microsoft Excel 97 Step by Step, Advanced Topics

Microsoft FrontPage 97 Step by Step

Microsoft Internet Explorer 3.0 Step by Step

Microsoft Office 97 Integration Step by Step

Microsoft Outlook 97 Step by Step

Microsoft PowerPoint 97 Step by Step

Microsoft Team Manager 97 Step by Step

Microsoft Windows 95 Step by Step

Microsoft Windows NT Workstation version 4.0 Step by Step

Microsoft Word 97 Step by Step

Microsoft Word 97 Step by Step, Advanced Topics

Step by Step books are also available for the Microsoft Office 95 programs.

Microsoft®
OFFICE 97
VISUAL BASIC®

Step by Step

Microsoft Press

PUBLISHED BY
Microsoft Press
A Division of Microsoft Corporation
One Microsoft Way
Redmond, Washington 98052-6399

Copyright © 1997 by David S. Boctor

Library of Congress Cataloging-in-Publication Data
Boctor, David S., 1972–
    Microsoft Office 97/Visual Basic Step by Step / David S. Boctor.
        p.   cm.
    Includes index.
    ISBN 1-57231-389-7
    1. Microsoft Office.   2. Microsoft Visual Basic for applications.
    3. Business--Computer programs.   4. World Wide Web (Information
    retrieval system)   I. Title.
    HF5548.4.M525B63   1997
    005.369--dc21   97-8039
                                                                 CIP

Printed and bound in the United States of America.

1 2 3 4 5 6 7 8 9   WCWC   2 1 0 9 8 7

Distributed to the book trade in Canada by Macmillan of Canada, a division of
Canada Publishing Corporation.

A CIP catalogue record for this book is available from the British Library.

Microsoft Press books are available through booksellers and distributors
worldwide. For further information about international editions, contact your
local Microsoft Corporation office. Or contact Microsoft Press International
directly at fax (425) 936-7329.

Microsoft, Microsoft Press, the Microsoft Press logo, Microsoft QuickBasic, MS-DOS,
PowerPoint, Visual Basic, Visual C++, Windows, and Windows NT are registered
trademarks and ActiveMovie, ActiveX, AutoSum, MSN, and Outlook are trademarks of
Microsoft Corporation.

For WASSER*Studio*
Project Manager: Marcelle Amelia
Print Production Manager: Mary C. Gutierrez
Desktop Publishing Lead: Kim Tapia
Manuscript Editor: Jennifer Jurcik
Copy Editor: Debbie Uyeshiro
Technical Editor: Mike Brown

For Microsoft Press
Acquisitions Editor: Casey D. Doyle
Project Editor: Stuart J. Stuple

About the Author

David Boctor works for Microsoft Corporation in the Microsoft Office product unit, where he designs programming features and product functionality for Office. He first used the Microsoft QuickBasic programming language, the predecessor to Visual Basic, in research systems that collect atmospheric environmental data. He then started working with Microsoft Visual Basic in 1993, when designing programs for engineering companies. David joined Microsoft in 1995, and has been working with Visual Basic for Applications ever since. He received a B.A.Sc in Mechanical Engineering from the University of Waterloo, Waterloo, Canada.

Acknowledgments

Many accomplishments, I have come to realize, result from the talents, efforts, and experiences of a group of people. The following people are part of this realization. At Microsoft Press, I would like to thank Casey Doyle, acquisitions editor, for providing me with the opportunity to write this book and for his early guidance and support in getting me started; and Stuart Stuple, project editor, for his valuable feedback, contributions, patience, and motivation.

At Wasser, Inc., I thank Marcelle Amelia and Mary Gutierrez, project managers, for keeping us on track; Kim Tapia, principal desktop publisher, for type, layout, and design; Debbie Uyeshiro, copyeditor, and John Hillburg, proofreader, for putting on the finishing touches. I am especially grateful to Jennifer Jurcik, editor, and Michael A. Brown, technical editor, for the dedicated time and contributions they made to this book.

I will always appreciate the perseverance of Robert Parker, software design engineer at Microsoft, for opening many doors and opportunities. Additional thanks go to Murph, Michelle, and Cillian *beag,* for inviting me to dinner and brunch after long days and nights of writing; and to John Tafoya, Liam Patel, and Ralph Barker. And to Mimi, for being there from the beginning.

To my Dad, for direction; Karen; and little sister Jennifer.

To my Mom and sister Sylvia, for their support throughout.

Table of Contents

Table of Contents

Learn the tools provided by the Visual Basic Editor, see "Examining the Visual Basic Editor," page 12 (Lesson 1)

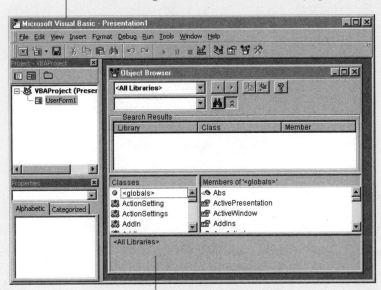

Use the Object Browser to learn about Microsoft Office objects, see "Learning the Members of the Object Model," page 37 (Lesson 2)

Declare and use variables, see "Variables and Constants," page 53 (Lesson 3)

Control program flow, see "Making Decisions with Condition Blocks," page 59 (Lesson 3)

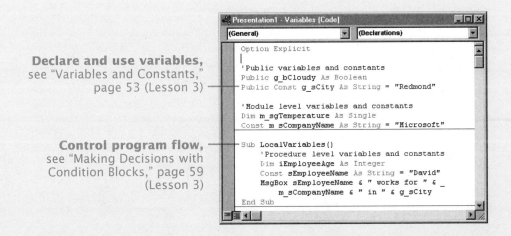

Set control properties, see
"Set the properties of controls,"
page 80 (Lesson 4)

**Building UserForms
in the Visual
Basic Editor,** see
"Constructing Custom
UserForms," page 78
(Lesson 4)

**Use the Toolbox in the Visual
Basic Editor,** see "Using the
Controls in the Toolbox,"
page 83 (Lesson 4)

**Display icons in the
Assistant balloon,** see "Add
icons and bitmaps to
balloons," page 162 (Lesson 7)

**Customize the Office
Assistant balloon,** see
"Create Assistant balloons
to display information,"
page 159 (Lesson 7)

**Display a numbered list
in the Assistant balloon,**
see "Add Label and Checkbox
controls to balloons," page
161 (Lesson 7)

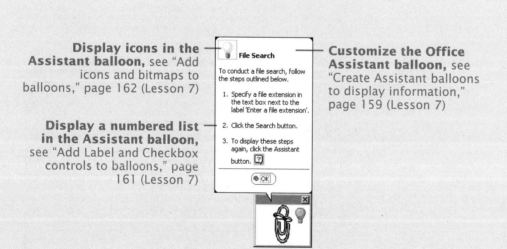

Add code to create Microsoft Office documents from a Microsoft Access database, see "Add code to the database to create an Office document," page 178 (Lesson 8)

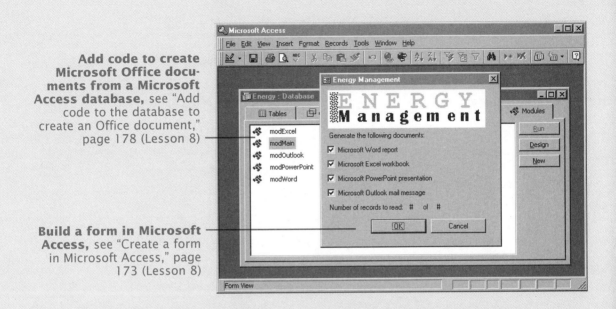

Build a form in Microsoft Access, see "Create a form in Microsoft Access," page 173 (Lesson 8)

Make your Wizards available through the New dialog box, see "Adding Wizards to the New Dialog Box," page 270 (Lesson 11)

Create the new look and style of Microsoft Office Wizards, see "Wizard Look and Style," page 242 (Lesson 11)

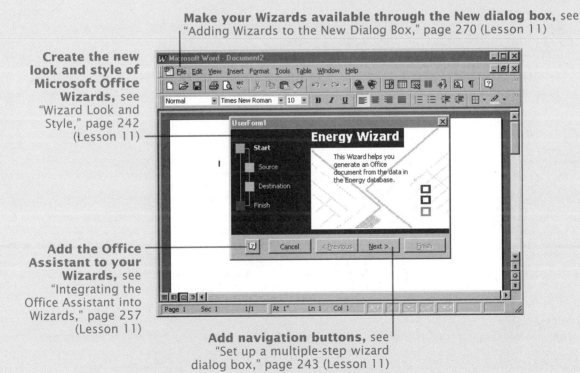

Add the Office Assistant to your Wizards, see "Integrating the Office Assistant into Wizards," page 257 (Lesson 11)

Add navigation buttons, see "Set up a multiple-step wizard dialog box," page 243 (Lesson 11)

Create custom toolbars, see "Create a simple toolbar with Visual Basic," page 124 (Lesson 6)

Search for text in a document, see "Find text in an Excel worksheet," page 282 (Lesson 12)

Add hyperlinks to text in a document, see "Search for Text in an Excel workbook and add a hyperlink," page 279 (Lesson 12)

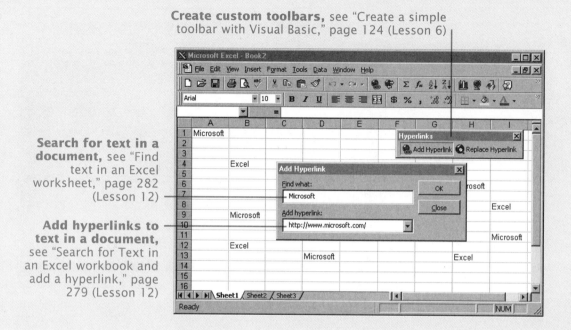

Use the Forms Designer in Microsoft Outlook, see "Display the Outlook Forms Designer," page 300 (Lesson 13)

Add Visual Basic, Scripting Edition, code to a custom form, see "Add code to a custom Outlook form," page 311 (Lesson 13)

Make custom forms available to others, see "Saving, Publishing, and Managing Custom Forms," page 318 (Lesson 13)

Add controls to a custom form, see "Customizing Forms with Controls," page 303 (Lesson 13)

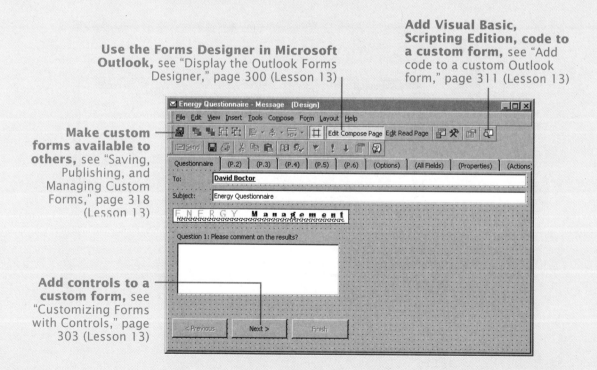

Finding Your Best Starting Point

Building integrated solutions with Microsoft Office has never been easier. The introduction of a number of new programming tools allows you to easily learn and use the Visual Basic for Applications programming language to automate Microsoft Office. You can develop new functionality for Office applications or you can extend existing functionality, taking features leaps beyond their original design to address the specific needs of your customers or your company. *Microsoft Office 97/Visual Basic Step by Step* provides a hands-on experience through self-paced lessons that use Visual Basic for Applications in Office 97 solutions.

 IMPORTANT This book is designed for use with Microsoft Office 97, Professional Edition, for the Windows 95 and Windows NT 4.0 or later operating systems. Office 97, Professional Edition, includes Microsoft Word 97, Excel 97, PowerPoint 97, Access 97, and Outlook 97. If you do not have Microsoft Access 97, you can still do all of the lessons in this book that do not use Access 97. To find out what software you're running, you can check the product package, or you can start Word, Excel, PowerPoint, Access, or Outlook, click the Help menu, and click About Microsoft <product> (where <product> represents the application you started). If your software is not compatible with this book, a Step by Step book for your software is probably available. Many of the Step by Step titles are listed on the second page of this book. If the book you want isn't listed, please visit our World Wide Web site at http://mspress.microsoft.com/ or call 1-800-MSPRESS for more information.

Finding Your Best Starting Point in This Book

This book is designed for Microsoft Office users who are learning Visual Basic for Applications, and for programmers experienced with Microsoft Visual Basic who want to use Office as a development platform for solutions. Use the following table to find your best starting point in this book.

If you are **Follow these steps**

New...

to Microsoft Visual Basic for "Installing and Using the Practice Files."

1 Install the practice files as described in Applications and programming

2 Learn the fundamentals of Visual Basic for Applications by working through Lessons 1 to 4 sequentially.

3 Complete Lesson 5 to learn how to use Visual Basic for Applications to communicate between the different applications in Microsoft Office.

4 Work through Lessons 6 through 13 to learn how to use Microsoft Office objects to build integrated solutions.

If you are **Follow these steps**

Switching...

to Microsoft Office Visual Basic for Applications from Microsoft Visual Basic

1 Install the practice files as described in "Installing and Using the Practice Files."

2 Work through Lessons 6 and 7 to become familiar with the common Office objects. Work through Lesson 8 to create an integrated Office solution that combines Word, Excel, PowerPoint, Access, and Out look. Complete Lessons 9 and 10 to learn how to create add-ins for Word, Excel, and PowerPoint, and complete Lesson 11 to create wizard add-ins.

3 Complete Lesson 13 to create custom Microsoft Outlook forms.

If you are	Follow these steps

Referencing...

this book after working
through the lessons

1 Use the index to find information about a specific topic. Use the table of contents and the *Quick*Look Guide to locate information about general topics.

2 Read the Lesson Summary at the end of each lesson for a review of the major tasks in the lesson.

Corrections, Comments, and Help

Every effort has been made to ensure the accuracy of this book and the contents of the practice files disc. Microsoft Press provides corrections and additional content for its books through the World Wide Web at:

> http://mspress.microsoft.com/MSPRESS/Updates/

If you have comments, questions, or ideas regarding this book or the practice files disc, please send them to us.

Send e-mail to:

> mspinput@microsoft.com

Or send postal mail to:

> Microsoft Press
>
> Attn: Step by Step Series Editor
>
> One Microsoft Way
>
> Redmond, WA 98052-6399

Please note that support for Office 97/Visual Basic is not offered through the above addresses. For help using Visual Basic for Applications, you can call Microsoft Technical Support Services at (800) 936-5700.

Visit Our World Wide Web Site

We invite you to visit the Microsoft Press World Wide Web site. You can visit us at the following location:

http://mspress.microsoft.com/

You'll find descriptions for all of our books, information about ordering titles, notice of special features and events, additional content for Microsoft Press books, and much more.

You can also find out the latest in software developments and news from Microsoft Corporation by visiting the following World Wide Web site:

http://www.microsoft.com/

We look forward to your visit on the Web!

Installing and Using the Practice Files

The disc inside the back cover of this book contains practice files that you'll use as you perform the exercises in the book. By using the practice files, you won't spend time creating the samples used in the lessons—instead, you can concentrate on learning how to become proficient at using Visual Basic for Applications in Microsoft Office. With the files and the step-by-step instructions in the lessons, you'll also learn by doing, which is an easy and effective way to acquire and remember new skills.

 IMPORTANT Before you break the seal on the practice disc package, be sure that this book matches your version of the software. This book is designed for use with Microsoft Office 97 for the Windows 95 and Windows NT version 4.0 or later operating systems. To find out what software you're running, you can check the product package or you can start Word, Excel, PowerPoint, Access, or Outlook, and then on the Help menu click About Microsoft <product> (where <product> represents the application you started). If your program is not compatible with this book, a Step by Step book matching your software is probably available. Many of the Step by Step titles are listed on the second page of this book. If the book you want isn't listed, please visit our World Wide Web site at http://mspress.microsoft.com/ or call 1-800-MSPRESS for more information.

Install the practice files on your computer

Follow these steps to install the practice files on your computer's hard disk so that you can use them with the exercises in this book.

1   Remove the disc from the package inside the back cover of this book and insert it in your CD-ROM drive.

2   On the taskbar at the bottom of your screen, click the Start button, and then click Run.

    The Run dialog box appears.

3   In the Open box, type **d:setup** (or, if your CD-ROM drive uses a drive letter other than "d," substitute the correct drive letter).

4   Click OK, and then follow the directions on the screen.

    The setup program window appears with recommended options preselected for you. For best results in using the practice files with this book, accept these preselected settings.

5   When the files have been installed, remove the disc from your drive and replace it in the package inside the back cover of the book.

    A folder called Office VBA Practice has been created on your hard disk, and the practice files have been placed in that folder. A shortcut named Office VBA Practice has also been added to your Favorites folder, to make it easy to switch to the practice files.

NOTE   In addition to installing the practice files, the Setup program created a shortcut to the Microsoft Press World Wide Web site on your Desktop. If your computer is set up to connect to the Internet, you can double-click the shortcut to visit the Microsoft Press Web site. You can also connect to the Web site directly at http://mspress.microsoft.com/.

Using the Practice Files

Each lesson in this book explains when and how to use any practice files for that lesson. When it's time to use a practice file, the book will list instructions for how to open the file. You should always save the practice file with a new name (as directed in the lesson) so that the original practice file will be available if you want to go back and redo any of the lessons.

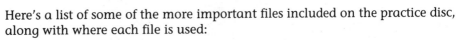

Here's a list of some of the more important files included on the practice disc, along with where each file is used:

Lesson	Filename	Description
1	ExpSales.bas, Q2Sales.xls	Contains Visual Basic code that extracts data from an Excel worksheet and creates a Word document.
	NumBlts.ppa	Sequentially numbers the bullets within a selected shape in a Microsoft PowerPoint slide.
3	Basics.ppt	Reveals the fundamentals of the Visual Basic programming language.
4	Lesson4.xls	Provides a set of custom UserForms showing the use of buttons, list boxes, drop-down lists, and other common controls in dialog boxes.
5	CreatePP.doc	Creates a PowerPoint presentation from the headings in a Word document.
6	CmdBars.ppt	Contains Visual Basic code to customize, add, or delete menu commands and toolbars in Word, Excel, PowerPoint, or Access.
7	FileSrch.xls	Displays a custom file search UserForm to search for specified files on your system.
	DocProps.ppt	Displays the collection of document properties for a PowerPoint presentation.
8	Energy.mdb	Microsoft Access database containing data used to automatically generate a Word document based on a pre-built template, an Excel workbook, a PowerPoint presentation, and an Outlook mail message.
	LabEnerg.txt	A text file containing data generated by a hypothetical digital meter connected to a computer.
	EnerRpt.dot	A template that determines what the report that Energy.mdb creates will look like.
9	Energy.dot	Microsoft Word add-in that generates a Word document based on the data in the Energy database in Lesson 8.
	modMenu.bas	Reusable code to add or remove menu items in Word, Excel, PowerPoint, or Access.

Lesson	Filename	Description
10	Energy.xls, Energy.ppt	Microsoft Excel and PowerPoint add-ins that generate an Excel workbook and PowerPoint presentation, respectively, based on the data in the Energy database in Lesson 8.
11	EnerWiz.dot, EnerWiz.xls, EnerWiz.ppt	Each file displays an Energy Wizard in Word, Excel, and PowerPoint respectively, based on the same look and style as the Fax Wizard in Word, that reveals how to create wizards in Office based on common code.
	modAsst.bas	Contains code to display tips in the Assistant balloon, as well as to close the Assistant bal loon whenever necessary.
	frmBasic.frm, frmAsst.frm, frmSubwy.frm	Provides a UserForm template for the different stages of creating a Microsoft Office wizard.
12	HyprLink.dot, HyprLink.xls, HyprLink.ppt	Add-ins that search for text in a document and add a hyperlink to the text. Also replace an existing hyperlink with a new hyperlink destination.
	FileLink.dot	Searches for a specific text style in a Word document and creates a relative hyperlink to the path of the graphic file specified in text.
13	Energy.oft	Displays a custom Microsoft Outlook form that provides a questionnaire.

Uninstalling the practice files

Use the following steps to delete the practice files added to your hard drive by the Step by Step program.

1 Click the Start button, point to Settings, and then click Control Panel.

2 Double-click the Add/Remove Programs icon.

3 Select Microsoft Office 97/Visual Basic Step by Step from the list, and then click Add/Remove.

A confirmation message appears.

4 Click Yes.

The practice files are uninstalled.

5 Click OK to close the Add/Remove Programs Properties dialog box.

6 Close the Control Panel window.

Need Help with the Practice Files?

Every effort has been made to ensure the accuracy of this book and the contents of the CD-ROM. If you do run into a problem, Microsoft Press provides corrections for its books through the World Wide Web at:

> http://mspress.microsoft.com/MSPRESS/Updates/

We also invite you to visit our main Web page at:

> http://mspress.microsoft.com

You'll find descriptions for all of our books, information about ordering titles, notices of special features and events, additional content for Microsoft Press books, and much more.

Using Shortcuts

Microsoft Office has several different ways of accomplishing almost any action. For most actions, you can select a command from a menu, press a shortcut key, click a toolbar button, and so forth. Different people prefer different techniques. To minimize confusion, for most actions the body of the text describes only a single method. You may find that you prefer a different method than the one described in the text.

Resolving Possible Configuration Differences

This book assumes that Office is configured the way it would be immediately after installing it. You may, however, have customized Office to your preferences. In most cases, customizing Office will not affect the way you can use this book. In some cases, however, you could customize Office in such a way that what you see on the screen may not match the illustrations in the text, or the steps in this book may not work properly.

 IMPORTANT This book requires that you install the optional Visual Basic for Applications Help file for each Microsoft Office 97 application. If you have not installed them, run the Office Setup program. Click Add/Remove, select Microsoft Word, Excel, PowerPoint, Access, or Outlook, click Change Option, select the Help item, click Change Option, and click Select All. Repeat this procedure to install the other Visual Basic for Application Help files. Click OK twice and then click Continue. Once installed, click OK to end the Setup program.

Conventions and Features Used in This Book

When you use this book, you can save time by understanding, before you start the lessons, how the instructions, keys to press, and so on are shown in the book. Please take a moment to read the following list, which also points out other helpful features of the book.

Procedural Conventions

- Hands-on exercises for you to follow are given in numbered lists of steps (1, 2, and so on). An arrowhead bullet (▶) indicates an exercise that has only one step.

Typographic Conventions

- Text that you are to type appears in **boldface**.
- New terms and the titles of books appear in *italic*.
- Names of keyboard keys for you to press appear in SMALL CAPITAL LETTERS. A plus sign (+) between two key names means that you must press those keys at the same time. For example, "Press ALT+TAB" means that you hold down the ALT key while you press TAB.
- Program code appears in monospace type (`monospace type`).

Supplementary Features

The following icons identify the different types of supplementary material:

	Notes labeled	Alert you to
	Note	Additional information
	Tip	Alternatives for a step or programming practice
	Important	Essential information that you should check before continuing with the lesson

Other Features of This Book

Run Macro

- You can perform many operations in Microsoft Office by clicking a button on a toolbar or a tool in a toolbox. When the instructions in this book tell you to click a toolbar button, a picture of the button is shown in the left margin next to the instructions. The Run Macro button in the margin next to this paragraph is an example.

- Screen capture illustrations show sample user interfaces and the results of your completed steps.

- Sidebars—short sections printed on a shaded background—introduce background information or features related to the information being discussed.

- You can get a quick reminder of how to perform the tasks you learned by reading the Lesson Summary at the end of a lesson.

- You can quickly determine what online Help topics are available for additional information by referring to the Help topics listed at the end of each lesson.

Getting to Know Visual Basic for Applications

Part 1

The Basics of Visual Basic for Applications

Estimated time
40 min.

In this lesson you will learn how to:

- Add a control and import prewritten code to a form.
- Record a macro that formats items on PowerPoint slides.
- Load an add-in into an Office application.

Today, we gather and display more information than ever before because we have more dynamic and prolific ways of expressing ideas. Graphical applications such as those in Microsoft Office give people tools with which they can easily organize, present, and share ideas and information. The suite of features and functionality found in Microsoft Office addresses user needs ranging from the basic, such as font formatting, to the advanced, such as automatic grammar checking, charting, and animation.

But, just as one car model does not satisfy all drivers, providing features to satisfy all computing needs of all people is often not possible. With Visual Basic for Applications, however, Microsoft Office gives you the tools you need to customize the graphical interface. You can even develop your own tools so that you can process information and present your ideas in the way that's most efficient and effective for you.

Along with tools to create your own graphical interface, Visual Basic for Applications brings to the table a programming environment and language that allow your custom programs to communicate and interact with the same set of tools that Microsoft Office provides through its graphical interface. Thus, custom programs can take full advantage of the functionality and services provided by Microsoft Office applications, and even expand their usefulness.

Moving Data from Excel to Word

For example, Microsoft Excel contains a number of tools that manipulate and analyze data, including formulas and sorting functions. If you need to develop a program in Microsoft Word that requires Excel data analysis functionality, you can create a Visual Basic program in Word that taps into the data analysis tools of Excel.

Add a control to a worksheet

If you have not yet installed the practice files that come with this book, work through "Getting Ready," earlier in this book. Then return to this lesson.

If, for example, you want to take the latest sales figures, which your book-keeper tracks in Excel, and generate your quarterly report in Word for the board of directors, you can easily do so with a few lines of Visual Basic code and a click of a button.

1 Start Microsoft Excel.

2 In cell A1 of the active worksheet, type **Sales Report: Q2, 1997** and set the font size to 14.

3 In cells A2 through A6, type **Northeast**, **Northwest**, **Southeast**, **Southwest**, and **Total**, respectively.

4 Type the numbers in cells B2 through B5 as shown in the following illustration:

	A	B	C	D
1	Sales Report: Q2, 1997			
2	Northeast	1000000		
3	Northwest	60000		
4	Southeast	800000		
5	Southwest	550000		
6	Total			
7				

AutoSum

5 Select cell B6, click the AutoSum button, and press ENTER.

6 Select cells B2 through B6, and on the Format menu, click Cells. In the Number tab, select Currency in the Category list box and click OK.

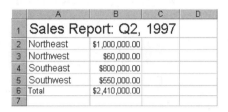

7 If the Control Toolbox toolbar is not displayed in Microsoft Excel, then on the View menu, point to Toolbars, and then select Control Toolbox.

8 In the Control Toolbox, click the Command Button control, and then, in the worksheet, click to the right of the total value in cell B6.

Command Button control

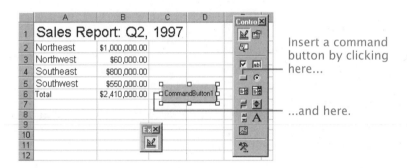

Insert a command button by clicking here...

...and here.

9 Right-click the new command button, and then select Properties on the shortcut menu.

This displays the Properties window for controls in the Control Toolbox.

10 In the Properties window, select the value for the Caption property and type **Export** in the right column.

The Caption and all other properties are listed on the left side of the Properties window, and the property values are listed on the right side.

Close Window

11 Close the Properties window by clicking the small Close Window button in the upper-right corner of the Properties window.

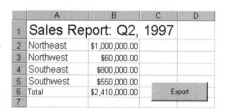

You are now ready to add code that will extract the total sales figure from the quarterly sales worksheet and insert the number into a Word document.

The Visual Basic Editor

Each document, workbook, presentation, or database you open in Microsoft Word, Excel, PowerPoint, or Access, respectively, has an associated Visual Basic for Applications project. When you open a workbook in Excel, for example, an associated Visual Basic project is listed in the Project Explorer window of the Visual Basic Editor. To write Visual Basic code in the Excel workbook's Visual Basic for Applications project, you must display the Visual Basic Editor. One way to display the Editor is to point to Macro on the Tools menu, and then click Visual Basic Editor on the submenu.

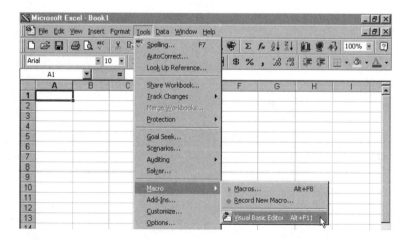

You can also open the Editor by double-clicking an ActiveX control in a document, workbook, or presentation. The command button you selected from the Control Toolbox and added to your worksheet is an ActiveX control, as are the other controls in the Control Toolbox.

Add Visual Basic Code

1   Start the Visual Basic Editor by double-clicking the Export command button.

    This takes you directly to the place where you can add code that runs when the button is clicked later. In the Visual Basic Editor, you see a line that defines a procedure:

    ```
    Private Sub CommandButton1_Click()
    ```

    The line is displayed in a Visual Basic code module. This procedure is the Click event handler for the command button.

The Click event handler is a procedure that runs when you click the command button.

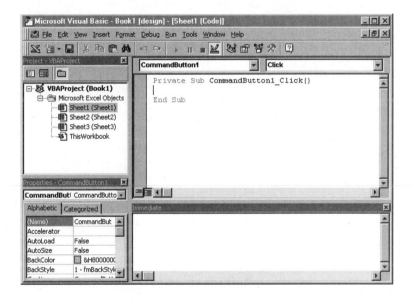

 NOTE   Your Editor may display different windows and title bars than those shown in the illustration.

2   Between `Private Sub CommandButton1_Click()` and `End Sub`, press the TAB key once, and then type **Call ExpSales.ExportFiguresToReport**.

    This code calls a procedure that extracts the values in the Excel worksheet and creates a Word document.

3   In the Editor, on the File menu, click Import File.

    The Import File dialog box appears.

4   Change to the folder C:\VBA Practice\Lesson1.

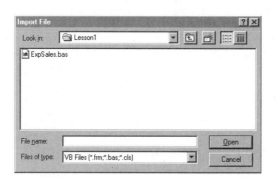

5   Select the file ExpSales.bas and click Open.

The ExpSales.bas file you just imported contains the Visual Basic code that will extract the data from the Excel worksheet and create a Word document, which will be your quarterly sales report. Now you are ready to run the program and see the results. Do not worry about the details of the Visual Basic code for now—where it is or how it works— you will learn about using Office objects in the next lesson.

Add a reference to Word from Excel

The code in the ExpSales.bas file uses the objects from Microsoft Word to create the document. For Visual Basic to understand where these objects come from and how they "look," you need to add a reference to the Microsoft Word 8.0 Object Library. Visual Basic uses the object library to check the syntax of the code within the code module to make sure Word actually *exposes* (makes available) the functionality you added in your code. You will learn more about references in the next lesson as well.

1   In the Visual Basic Editor, on the Tools menu, click References.

The References dialog is displayed. It lists all available references registered on your system.

2   In the Available References list box, scroll down until you find the entry "Microsoft Word 8.0 Object Library."

3   Click the check box next to this item and click OK.

A reference to the Word object library has now been established for the current Visual Basic project you are working in.

Run the program

While you were setting up your program, Microsoft Excel was in *design modè*. This means that when you add controls and code to your worksheet, no code is run when you click ActiveX controls, such as your command button. When you click the command button in design mode, selection handles are displayed around it. You need to change the worksheet to *run mode* so that the code assigned to the command button runs when you click the button.

View Microsoft Excel

Exit Design Mode

1   In the Visual Basic Editor, click the View Microsoft Excel button to switch to the Excel application window, and then click the Exit Design Mode button in the Control Toolbox.

Excel is now in run mode.

2   Click the Export button on the sales worksheet.

Microsoft Word is displayed first and then you see lines of text being added to the newly opened Word document.

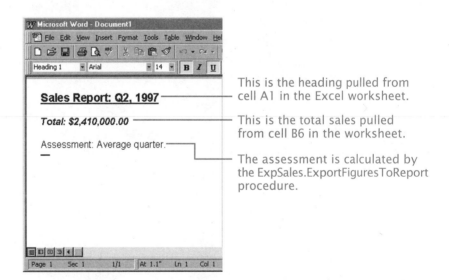

This is the heading pulled from cell A1 in the Excel worksheet.

This is the total sales pulled from cell B6 in the worksheet.

The assessment is calculated by the ExpSales.ExportFiguresToReport procedure.

In ExpSales.bas, a function was added that assesses the total value of sales and provides feedback regarding the sales performance for the quarter. Three ranges were added: less than 2 million; between 2 million and 3 million, inclusive; and greater than 3 million. Type different values in the sales worksheet in Excel, and then click the Export button to export the results to Word and see the different assessments.

3   Exit Word without saving changes, and then switch to Excel.

4   Save the workbook as MyQ2Sales in the Lesson 1 practice folder, and then exit Excel.

You can come back to this workbook and look through it in more detail once you have progressed through the remaining lessons.

The Microsoft Office/Visual Basic Relationship

Visual Basic for Applications is a combination of an integrated programming environment called the Visual Basic Editor and the Visual Basic programming language. The combination of the two allows you to easily design and develop Visual Basic programs. The term "for Applications" refers to the fact that the Visual Basic programming language and development tools in the Visual Basic Editor are seamlessly integrated with applications such as Microsoft Word, Excel, PowerPoint, and Access so you can develop custom functionality and feature solutions using these applications.

How Does Visual Basic for Applications Relate to Visual Basic 5.0?

Visual Basic for Applications (also known as Visual Basic, Applications Edition) is not the same and should not be confused with Microsoft Visual Basic 5.0. Microsoft Office features the Visual Basic language and exposes a set of objects through its object models. Using the Visual Basic Editor and the different objects exposed by Office, which are integrated with Word, Excel, and PowerPoint, you can create specialized programs for Office. These programs can be stored within an Office document or in a separate file called an *add-in*.

The tools and graphical user interface provided by the Editor are consistent with the Microsoft Visual Basic programming system version 5.0 development environment. Visual Basic 5.0, however, provides much more advanced programming tools and functionality, so you can create advanced programs for the Microsoft Windows operating system and components for other Windows programs. You can develop executables (.exe files) and application extensions (.dll files) for Microsoft Office using the tools in the Visual Basic 5.0 programming system.

Microsoft Word, Excel, and PowerPoint all provide the same integrated development environment. The Visual Basic Editor contains all of the programming tools you need to write Visual Basic code and create custom solutions. For example, you can switch to the Visual Basic Editor window from PowerPoint the same way you do from Excel (from the Tools menu, point to Macro, and then click Visual Basic Editor).

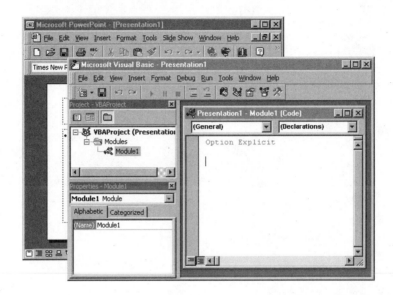

The Editor is a separate window from Microsoft Word, Microsoft Excel, and Microsoft PowerPoint, but it looks and functions the same in each application. Thus, you can potentially have three Visual Basic Editor windows open at one time, each one being associated with a separate application. When a given application is closed, its associated Visual Basic Editor window closes automatically.

Microsoft Visual Basic, Scripting Edition, often referred to as VBScript, is a subset of the Visual Basic programming language that allows you to develop programs for Web-based HTML documents and Web server solutions. You cannot use VBScript in the Visual Basic Editor in Microsoft Word, Excel, PowerPoint, or in Access; however, Microsoft Outlook does enable VBScript programming. For more information, see Lesson 13, "Designing Custom Microsoft Outlook Forms."

What About Visual Basic in Microsoft Access and Outlook?

Although Microsoft Access provides the same rich set of development tools, the development environment is not the same as in Word, Excel, and PowerPoint. All the tools provided within the Visual Basic Editor window, which is separate from the Word, Excel, and PowerPoint application windows, are provided within the Microsoft Access application window itself. However, the concepts and examples you will learn throughout this book can be applied to all of these applications; any differences will be discussed as necessary.

Microsoft Outlook does not provide any of the advanced Visual Basic development tools or environments that Word, Excel, PowerPoint, or Access provides. You can use the mail, scheduling, and other desktop information management services provided by Outlook through Visual Basic from within any of the other Microsoft Office applications. Microsoft Outlook does, however, provide Microsoft Visual Basic, Scripting Edition along with powerful form design capabilities through the Outlook Form Designer. (Forms are an interesting and useful feature in Outlook. In Outlook, ask the Assistant for more information using the words "form designer." If no pertinent information appears, then you must install additional Visual Basic Help files from the Microsoft Office ValuPack, which is also described in online Help.)

Each Microsoft Office application provides a starting point for programming a Visual Basic solution, so where do you begin? You can choose from a number of factors when deciding which Microsoft Office application to use as your main platform. These factors will be examined closely in Part 3. In the remaining lessons of Part 1, you will be introduced to the concepts of Visual Basic using several Microsoft Office applications. Keep in mind that what you learn in one application can easily be applied to the other Microsoft Office applications.

Examining the Visual Basic Editor

The Visual Basic Editor provides a number of advanced programming and development tools that were once found only in development programs like Microsoft Visual C++.

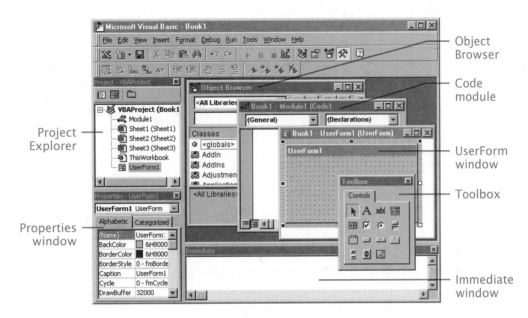

Project Explorer   This window displays a hierarchical list of the projects and all of the items contained in and referenced by each of the projects. When you open a document in Word, for example, a Visual Basic for Applications project is associated with it in the Project Explorer. The items in a Visual Basic for Applications project can be any number of code modules or UserForms.

Properties window   Displayed here is an alphabetical or categorized property list of an ActiveX control in a UserForm, a UserForm itself, or a code module. The list of properties for an item is listed on the left side of the window and the corresponding values on the right side.

Object Browser   Think of this as a map for navigating through the objects, methods, properties, and events provided by an ActiveX control or an application such as Word, Excel, PowerPoint, Access, or Outlook. You'll learn in Lesson 2 that the Object Browser will be an invaluable tool for determining how you can program a specific object provided by Microsoft Office.

Code module   This is where you write all of your Visual Basic code. (You see the code in a code module through the Code window.) There are three types of code modules: standard, class, and form; each type serves a specific purpose. Code modules allow you to group code with common functionality together.

UserForm window   This window contains a UserForm that allows you to create custom dialog boxes for use in your Visual Basic for Applications programs. With a UserForm (and the ActiveX controls in the Toolbox), you can re-create any dialog box you've interacted with in Microsoft Office and add your own customizations; or you can create your own dialog boxes to suit the needs of your Visual Basic for Applications program.

Toolbox Listed here you'll find a set of ActiveX controls. Like the Control Toolbox in the Word, Excel, and PowerPoint windows, controls in the Visual Basic Toolbox can be dragged and dropped. However, in the Visual Basic Editor, you can drag and drop controls only onto a UserForm.

To debug means to find and correct errors in your code.

Immediate window Here you can enter and execute one line of Visual Basic code and immediately see the results of that code. The Immediate window is commonly used while debugging Visual Basic code.

What Visual Basic for Applications Can Do for You

Microsoft Office offers a lot of tools and functionality to help you create, edit, and organize content and information to serve a wide range of audiences and customers. Visual Basic for Applications brings you a set of tools that allow other programs to interact with the same tools provided by Office and with the content you create. If you find a situation where Microsoft Office does not provide the exact tool to improve your productivity, you can use Visual Basic to build what you need.

Most users will use Visual Basic for Applications to develop the following common types of solutions: macros, add-ins, and wizards. You will develop each type of Visual Basic solution for Office depending on the specific scenario you need to satisfy.

Recording Macros

A macro is a Visual Basic for Applications program that automates a series of actions you perform. These can range from a simple procedure you conduct with your document content and application tools, to complex solutions that manipulate your document content and interact with other Microsoft Office functionality. A macro resides within the Visual Basic project of a Word document, Excel workbook, PowerPoint presentation, or Access database. Macros are usually actions grouped together, so you can accomplish a series of common, often repetitive, tasks automatically in a single command. Simple macros are often created to make editing and formatting tasks readily available via a dialog box.

Word, Excel, and PowerPoint each offer an easy way to create a simple macro: with the macro recorder. Microsoft Access does not provide a macro recorder (or, remember, the Visual Basic Editor). The contents of a recorded macro can be seen in the Visual Basic Editor, where you can easily modify the macro. Recording a macro is analogous to recording music or video. When you play back a recorded macro, it automatically repeats recorded actions.

Each macro you record is stored in a Visual Basic code module that's attached to the open document, workbook, presentation, or template. Using the Visual Basic Editor, you can edit macros or move macros from one code module to another in any open Visual Basic project.

Record a macro that sets the same formatting to multiple shapes

If, for instance, you want to manually change the color of a shape on a PowerPoint slide, you must select the shape, choose AutoShape from the Format menu, and then select a color from the Fill Color drop-down list (in the Color And Lines tab in the Format AutoShape dialog box). To determine the equivalent functionality in Visual Basic syntax is not necessarily a straightforward task for a beginner or even an experienced Visual Basic programmer. Fortunately, macro recording provides what you need without much effort.

1   Start Microsoft PowerPoint. In the opening PowerPoint dialog box, select Blank Presentation and click OK.

2   In the New Slide dialog box, select the second slide AutoLayout (Bulleted List) and click OK.

3   On the Tools menu, point to Macro, and then click Record New Macro.

The Record Macro dialog box is displayed. Notice the default macro name in the Macro Name box and the presentation name in which the recorded macro will be stored.

4   Click OK to accept the default names.

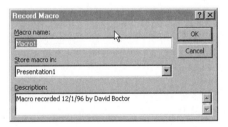

Macro recording has started. The Stop Recording toolbar is displayed on your screen.

Until macro recording is stopped, the equivalent Visual Basic code of most of the actions you conduct is recorded in a code module in the Visual Basic Editor.

Rectangle

5 On the Drawing toolbar, which is the same for Microsoft Word, Excel, and PowerPoint, click the Rectangle button.

6 Drag a rectangle anywhere on the slide.

7 On the Format menu, click AutoShape to display the Format AutoShape dialog box.

8 In the Colors And Lines tab, click the Color drop-down list and select a color from the color grid. Click OK.

Stop Recording

9 Stop macro recording by clicking the Stop Recording button on the Stop Recording toolbar.

10 Start the Visual Basic Editor by pressing ALT+F11 and, in the Project Explorer window, open Presentation1 by clicking the plus sign next to it.

This is the presentation that you selected to store the recorded macro.

11 If necessary, open the Modules folder by clicking the plus sign next to it.

12 Double-click Module1.

This displays the Code window. The following code was recorded:

```
Sub Macro1()
'
' Macro recorded 12/1/96 by David Boctor
'
    ActiveWindow.Selection.SlideRange.Shapes _
        .AddShape(msoShapeRectangle, 246, _
        288, 138, 132).Select
    With ActiveWindow.Selection.ShapeRange
        .Fill.Visible = msoTrue
        .Fill.Solid
        .Fill.ForeColor.RGB = RGB(128, 0, 0)
    End With
End Sub
```

Your recorded code may be slightly different. This macro is currently stored in the Visual Basic project of the active presentation.

Run the recorded macro to create a shape on another slide

View Microsoft PowerPoint

1 Switch to PowerPoint by clicking the View Microsoft PowerPoint button on the Standard toolbar in the Editor.

2 On the Insert menu, click New Slide.

3 Select the second slide AutoLayout (Bulleted List) and click OK.

4 On the Tools menu, point to Macro, and then click Macros.

5 In the Macro dialog box, select Macro1 from the list, and then click Run.

On the new slide, Visual Basic automatically re-creates the same shape in the same color that you previously created manually.

Loading Add-In Programs

An add-in is a supplemental program that adds custom commands and specialized features to extend the capabilities of an application such as Word, Excel, or Access. For example, you can write an add-in program that numbers bullet points on Microsoft PowerPoint slides.

You can obtain add-ins from independent software vendors, or you can write your own custom add-in programs using the Visual Basic Editor. To use an add-in, you must install the add-in program on your computer and then load it into Word, Excel, PowerPoint, or Access. A Visual Basic add-in in Word has the filename extension *.dot* or *.wiz*; in Excel it has *.xla*; in PowerPoint it has *.ppa* or *.pwz*; and in Access it has *.mda* or *.mdz*. Add-ins with extension .wiz, .pwz, or .mdz are referred to as Wizard add-ins because these extensions allow them to be displayed in the New dialog box of Word, PowerPoint, or Access, respectively. They also have a common Wizard icon associated with them when displayed in the Windows Explorer. For example, the Letters & Faxes tab of the New dialog box in Word (displayed by clicking New on the File menu) lists several wizards, each a Visual Basic add-in for Word.

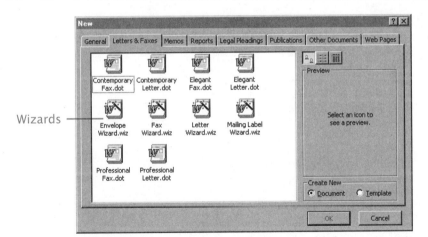

Wizards

After they are installed, you can load and unload add-ins whenever you require their functionality. When you do not use an add-in very often, you should unload it in order to conserve memory and increase the speed of the specific Microsoft Office application. When you unload an add-in, its features and commands are removed from the Microsoft Office application, but the program itself remains on your computer for easy reloading when you need it.

Number your points

Many presenters are inclined to number their points so that they can easily reference them during a presentation or in notes. Microsoft PowerPoint, however, has no automatic way of numbering the bullet points entered in a frame on a slide. A user can easily place the cursor at the beginning of each bullet point and click the Bullet item on the Format menu, but this can become a very monotonous task—especially because this must be done each time a new bullet point is added between two previously numbered points. Using the Visual Basic Editor, accessed through Microsoft PowerPoint, a Number Bullets toolbar was created and provided in the Lesson 1 practice folder to allow a user to easily number or renumber the bullets within a selected frame or frames.

1   In PowerPoint, on the File menu, click New. In the New Presentation dialog box, select Blank Presentation and click OK.

2   In the New Slide dialog box, select the second slide AutoLayout (Bulleted List) and click OK.

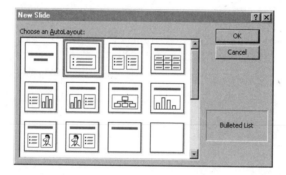

3   Add a list of numbers from 1 through 7 in the body text frame.

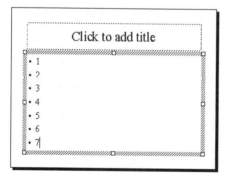

4 On the Tools menu, click Add-Ins.

This displays the Add-Ins dialog box.

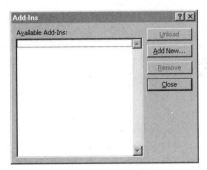

5 Click the Add New button, select the file NumBlts.ppa from the Lesson 1 practice folder, and click OK.

 NOTE If Macro Virus Protection is selected in the General tab of the Options dialog box (click Options on the Tools menu), the Warning dialog box for viruses is displayed when you install a new add-in to PowerPoint. When this dialog box is displayed, click Enable Macros so that you can use the add-in. However, if you receive an add-in from an unknown or distrusted source, click Do Not Open. It is important to protect your documents from viruses. In Microsoft Word, Excel, or PowerPoint, ask the Assistant for information using the words "virus protection."

When you click the Add New button, an "x" is automatically placed before the Number Bullets add-in name in the Available Add-ins list in the Add-Ins dialog box. The Number Bullets add-in, and hence, toolbar, will be loaded each time Microsoft PowerPoint is loaded. If you select the Number Bullets item in the list and click the Unload button, the add-in is unloaded and is not loaded automatically when Microsoft PowerPoint is restarted after you quit the current session.

Different applications use different indicators in the Add-Ins dialog box. In Microsoft Word and Excel, a check mark before the name of the add-in in the Add-Ins dialog box indicates that the add-in is currently loaded and is automatically loaded into memory each time that the application starts. In Microsoft PowerPoint and Microsoft Access, an "x" replaces the check mark. A variation of the Add-Ins dialog box is provided by each Microsoft Office application to help manage the state and number of add-ins loaded at any given time. The Add-Ins dialog box indicates the add-ins currently available to the user.

6 With the NumBlts add-in loaded, click Close to close the Add-Ins dialog box.

7 Select the bulleted list on the slide and click the first button on the Number Bullets toolbar. (The button name in the ToolTip is also Number Bullets.)

The bullets within the selected shape are now numbered sequentially. With the frame selected, select a different font from the Font drop-down list on the Number Bullets toolbar. Experiment with the other items on the toolbar as well. If you want to reset the bulleted list back to its default state, just click the Remove Number Bullets button, which is the second button from the left on the toolbar.

8 Exit PowerPoint. You may save the presentations if you want.

The Visual Basic code for this toolbar was saved as a Microsoft PowerPoint add-in and can now serve as a functionality extension to anyone's personal copy of Microsoft PowerPoint. You can use this extension for any presentation in which you want to easily number bullet points.

Add-Ins Dialog Box

Using the Add-Ins dialog box is the most common method of quickly integrating a Visual Basic add-in with a Microsoft Office application. This dialog box was displayed in step 4 above. In Lessons 9 and 10, the intricacies of the Add-Ins dialog box will be closely examined, as well as different methods for a user to begin using your Visual Basic add-in.

Loading Wizards

Wizards present the user with a number of steps that save time in creating many common types of documents, workbooks, presentations, and databases. For example, you can use the Memo Wizard in Microsoft Word to easily create professional-looking memos, or the Web Page Wizard to get a head start on authoring Web pages.

A wizard is really just an add-in program, but with a specific file extension and an icon in the Windows Explorer. A Word wizard has the filename extension *.wiz*; Excel does not have a specific wizard file extension (but wizards can still be in the form of an .xla file); PowerPoint has *.pwz*; and Access has *.mdz*. Many Microsoft Office wizards are installed by default when you install Office on your machine, and are located in subfolders within the Templates folder of your Microsoft Office installation.

For example, in the Letters & Faxes subfolder, you see the Word wizards listed: Envelope Wizard.wiz, Fax Wizard.wiz, Letter Wizard.wiz, and Mailing Label Wizard.wiz. In the Presentations subfolder, you see one PowerPoint wizard listed: AutoContent Wizard.pwz. All of these wizards were created using Visual Basic for Applications. Wizards specific to each Office application are located in a subfolder of the Templates folder and can also be listed in the New dialog box of the application. In Lesson 11, "Developing Office Wizards," you will learn how to create wizards that are similar in style and look to the Fax Wizard in Word or the AutoContent Wizard in PowerPoint.

Accessing Macros, Add-Ins, and Wizards from Menus and Toolbars

After you assign a macro to a toolbar, menu, or shortcut keys, running the macro is as simple as clicking the toolbar button or menu item, or pressing the shortcut keys. You can also point to Macro on the Tools menu, click Macros, and then click the name of the macro you want to run. In Part 2, the most common methods of creating menu items and toolbar buttons will be described so that you can easily run macros, load add-ins, or display wizards.

Lesson Summary

To	Do this
Open the Visual Basic Editor	On the Tools menu, point to Macro, and then click Visual Basic Editor; or double-click an ActiveX control if one exists; or press ALT+F11.
Add a command button to an Excel worksheet	Display the Control Toolbox, click the Command Button control, and then click the worksheet.
Select an ActiveX control, such as a command button, without running its Click event handler	Click the Design Mode button on the Control Toolbox toolbar, and then select the control.
Assign Visual Basic code to an ActiveX control, such as a command button, that should run when the control is clicked	In design mode, double-click the control. When the Editor opens, type the code within the click event procedure.
Change a property, such as the caption, of an ActiveX control	In design mode, right-click the control, click Properties on the shortcut menu, and then type the property value in the right column of the Properties window.

Lesson Summary, *continued*

To	Do this
Record a macro	On the Tools menu, point to Macro, click Record New Macro, type a name for the macro, click OK, and perform the actions you want to record.
Stop recording a macro	On the Stop Recording toolbar, click the Stop Recording button.
Run a macro	On the Tools menu, point to Macro, click Macros, select the macro name, and click the Run button; or, in run mode, click an ActiveX control if one exists.
Install a new add-in in PowerPoint	On the Tools menu, click Add-Ins, click the Add New button, and locate and select the add-in filename.
Load or unload an installed add-in in PowerPoint	On the Tools menu, click Add-Ins, select the add-in, and click the Load or Unload button. (An "x" or a check mark next to the add-in's name indicates that it is loaded.)

To retrieve the correct informa-tion, make sure the Visual Basic Editor is the active application.

For online information about	Ask the Assistant for help, using the words
Creating command buttons	"Command buttons"
ActiveX controls	"ActiveX"
Recording or running macros	"Recording or running macros"
Loading or unloading add-ins	"Add-Ins"

Preview of the Next Lesson

In the next lesson, you will learn how, through Visual Basic, Office exposes the tools and functionality you can manipulate in the graphical user interface.

Microsoft Office Objects

In this lesson you will learn how to:

■ Represent an object model in code.

■ Count the number of objects in a collection.

■ Work with properties, methods, and events.

■ Examine macro code recorded for objects.

■ Use the Object Browser and Auto List Members tool to list the members for an object.

Estimated time
45 min.

Look around and you'll see that you're surrounded by material things you perceive by vision or touch. You distinguish things by the properties they possess, how they are related to other objects, and how they are affected by an action. Most objects provide some sort of functional or aesthetic purpose and many are actually collections of objects grouped together. An obvious example would be your computer. It consists of a monitor, keyboard, speakers, processor, disk drives, and mouse, and possibly other components. Each computer component is further composed of objects until you finally reach a fundamental element.

Software provides a similar paradigm of objects. You cannot, of course, place them on your mantel, but you can distinguish them by the properties they possess and the relationships they have with one another. In Microsoft Office, almost all functionality you work with and all content you create that is viewable on your screen is represented by an equivalent object in Visual Basic for

Applications. These objects are programmable, so you can develop a Visual Basic program that manipulates properties an object exposes. The collections of Microsoft Office objects are categorized by either Word, Excel, PowerPoint, Access, Outlook, or Office, and they allow you to navigate down to the smallest detail of information in any of your documents.

Introducing the Object Model

Most objects are described in relation to another. For example, a key on your keyboard does not stand on its own; it's a functioning part of the whole keyboard, which in turn is part of your computer. It is the relationship of objects that forms the basis of an object model in Microsoft Office; the model is the hierarchy of objects in relation to each other.

Microsoft Office applications all have the same, general hierarchy model of objects, with the Application object residing at the top of the hierarchy. Each *object* represents an element of an application such as a shape on a slide, a cell in a worksheet, a word in a document, or a table in a database. Navigating up and down the object model hierarchy is very similar to using a road map, which displays the routes you might take to reach certain destinations.

The Application object represents the starting point. From the Application object, you traverse down a branched highway, selecting different objects to pass through until you reach the object you want to access. If you want to change the color of a shape in a Microsoft PowerPoint slide, you start with the Application object (PowerPoint), indicate which presentation the slide belongs to, and then which slide contains the shape. Finally, you reach your destination by selecting the shape on the slide with which you want to work. You navigate down the object model tree to manipulate the basic elements.

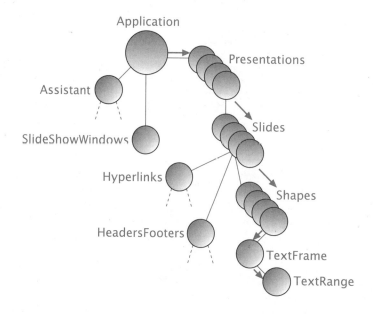

Represent the object model in code

To manipulate a property of an object, such as the text of the first shape on the first slide in a PowerPoint presentation, you have to traverse down the branches of the PowerPoint object model hierarchy tree. In Visual Basic programming, each branch in the object model diagram is represented by the dot operator (.), which is accessed by the period key on your keyboard.

 TIP The verbal translation of Visual Basic code uses "dot" instead of "period." It is used in the same way as when you hear "dot" used to distinguish the extension of a filename in the Windows operating system. For example, for a file named MyFile.xls, you'll usually hear "MyFile dot X-L-S."

1   Start Microsoft PowerPoint. In the opening PowerPoint dialog box, select Blank Presentation and click OK.

2   In the New Slide dialog box, select the second slide layout (Bulleted List) and click OK.

3   On the Tools menu, point to Macro, and then click Visual Basic Editor on the submenu.

4   In the Editor, on the Insert menu, click Module.

5   In the inserted module, type **Sub ChangingText** and press ENTER.

6   Insert the following line of code just after the line Sub ChangingText() and before End Sub:

```
Application.Presentations(1).Slides(1).Shapes(1) _
        .TextFrame.TextRange = "Some text."
```

In the above line of code, you do not need to type "Application" and the subsequent period. The Application object, which in this case represents the PowerPoint application, is implied when you are writing Visual Basic code in the PowerPoint Visual Basic Editor window. Likewise, if you are writing Visual Basic code in Excel, when you access a Workbook object, you do not need to specify the Excel application object (though it never hurts to be explicit about which application you are using). However, if you want to access a PowerPoint object while writing code in Excel, you need to make an explicit reference to the PowerPoint application object. In Lesson 5, "Communicating Across Microsoft Office," you will see how to drive other applications from one specific application.

25

Pressing F5 runs the procedure you're currently working on.

7 Place the cursor within the Sub ChangingText procedure and press F5. Switch to PowerPoint and notice the new text on the slide.

With this procedure, you added text to the first shape of the first slide in the first presentation in Microsoft PowerPoint.

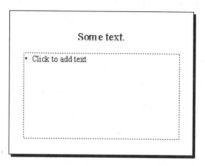

 IMPORTANT The text in the line of Visual Basic code in step 6 of this step-by-step example parallels the objects being manipulated. However, as you'll see in the "Object Browser" section of this lesson, in a number of cases, what you type in code does not map directly to the object name in the hierarchy tree.

8 Exit PowerPoint without saving changes.

Collections and Objects

In Microsoft Office, you'll find that a number of objects are of the same type but that each is distinguished by a unique name or index value. Together, these objects form a *collection*. Think back to the computer metaphor. Your computer keyboard has a set of keys that represent a collection of keys. Each key is uniquely distinguished by an index value in the collection of keys, but many keys are used for the same purpose (entering text) and thus are of the same object type. Collections are always plural, such as Sections in Word, Worksheets in Excel, and Shapes in PowerPoint.

In Microsoft PowerPoint, the Presentations collection object represents a collection of all presentations currently open in PowerPoint. The objects within the Presentations collection are Presentation objects, with each Presentation object in the collection containing a collection of Slide objects. To access a singular object item in a collection in Visual Basic, you can choose from two ways of referring to the item. The first is to type the collection name followed by a period (.), and then type **Item**(*<index>*), where *<index>* represents either the name of the specific item in the collection or its index value (position) in the collection. Using this method, the code sample used in step 6 in the preceding step-by-step example would then look like this:

```
Application.Presentations.Item(1).Slides.Item(1) _
    .Shapes.Item(1).TextFrame.TextRange = "Some text."
```

Or, as shown in step 6, you can remove the keyword Item and the preceding period, and just type in the collection name followed immediately by the index value. Either syntax works, but the abbreviated version results in less typing and sometimes more readable code.

In Excel, the equivalent to the Presentations collection in PowerPoint is the Workbooks collection. The Workbooks collection object represents all workbooks currently open in Excel. Within each Workbook object, there is a collection of Worksheet objects. In Word, the equivalent to the Presentations or Workbooks collection is the Documents collection, which represents all documents currently open in Word. Within each Document object in the collection, a Sections collection represents all sections in the document.

Count the number of objects in a collection

All collections in Microsoft Office allow you to access each item in the collection as well as the number of objects in the collection.

1   Start Microsoft Excel. On the Tools menu, point to Macro, and then click Visual Basic Editor on the submenu.

2   In the Visual Basic Editor, on the Insert menu, click Module.

3   In the inserted module, type **Sub NumberOfShapes** and press ENTER.

4   Insert the following line of code just after the line `Sub NumberOfShapes()` and before `End Sub`:

```
MsgBox ActiveSheet.Shapes.Count
```

ActiveSheet refers to the worksheet currently displayed in the Excel application window. In each worksheet, there is a collection of Shape objects. A *shape* in Excel is any object in the worksheet that floats above the cells. The Count property in the line of code you just inserted returns the number of shapes in the current, active worksheet.

5   Place the cursor in the line `SubNumberOfShapes()` and press F5.

A message box should be displayed showing the value 0 (zero). Currently, there are no shapes in the Shapes collection of the active worksheet object.

6   Click OK to close the message box, and then switch to Excel.

7   If the Drawing toolbar is not displayed, then on the View menu, point to Toolbars, and then click Drawing on the submenu.

8 On the Drawing toolbar, click any of the shape buttons (oval, rectangle, and so on), and add any AutoShape to the worksheet.

9 On the Tools menu, point to Macro, and then click Macros on the submenu. Select NumberOfShapes and click Run.

10 Click OK to close the message box.

11 Repeat steps 8 through 10 several times.

Notice that each time you add shapes to the active worksheet, the value displayed in the message box is incremented by the number of shapes you added. Try deleting shapes from the active worksheet as well, and when you run the macro, you'll see the number of shapes in the Shapes collection decrease by an equivalent amount.

12 Exit Excel without saving changes.

Understanding Properties, Methods, and Events

Each object that makes up a computer contains components with specific characteristics. For example, the keyboard is made up of a collection of keys, each with properties that distinguish it from the others. Each key has a different label, such as "A," "ESC," or "F1," and is uniquely positioned on the keyboard. The SPACEBAR is usually much bigger than the other keys, and it doesn't have a label. The label and position are *properties* of a key. In addition, the keys provide a method of entering data into the computer by allowing the user to perform the action of pressing them. Thus, a *method* of a key is "press."

When a key such as the "A" key is pressed, an *event* is triggered. The Microsoft Windows operating system working with another program *handles* the event in a number of different ways, depending on certain conditions. If the computer is off, nothing happens. If the computer is on and the current, active application is a word processor such as Microsoft Word, the letter "a" is displayed on the screen at the position of the cursor.

Each Microsoft Office object contains one of three types of members: a property, a method, or an event.

Object Member Type	Description
Property	A characteristic attribute, such as size, position, or shape, that defines or describes an object. (Adjective)
Method	An action, such as save, close, or delete, that you can perform on or with an object. (Verb)
Event	Something that takes place, such as a click, a press, or a change, that causes an object to react. (Noun)

Properties

In most cases, you can get the value of the property or you can set the property to a specific value; the range or type is defined by the property. However, you'll find a number of instances where a property is read-only. This means you can get the property value but you cannot set it.

Set a property value

To set a property, you equate a value to the property with an equal sign. To get a property value, you just specify the property and, in most cases, assign it to a temporary variable.

1 Start Microsoft PowerPoint. In the opening PowerPoint dialog box, select Blank Presentation and click OK.

2 In the New Slide dialog box, select the second slide layout (Bulleted List) and click OK.

3 If the PowerPoint window is maximized or minimized, restore the window so that it can be moved or resized.

To insert a new code module, click Module on the Insert menu in the Visual Basic Editor.

4 Open the Visual Basic Editor and insert a new code module. In the module, type **Sub MoveWindow** and press ENTER to create a new procedure.

5 Add the following code:

```
MsgBox Application.Left
Application.Left = 50
MsgBox Application.Left
```

6 Place the cursor in the MoveWindow procedure and press F5. Click OK to close the message boxes.

29

The PowerPoint application window is moved to approximately position 50 (near the left side of your screen). The first line of code within the procedure sets the Left property value of the application window and displays the property value in a message box. The second line sets the property value to 50, and the third displays the resulting value.

Enumerations

An integer is a positive or negative whole number or the number zero.

Throughout a Microsoft Office object model, whether Word, Excel, PowerPoint, or Access, you often set object properties to an integer value within a range specified by the specific application. However, setting a property value to a valid integer requires that you know the valid range of integers and understand what each value represents. The enumeration value is a label that represents an integer, but you do not necessarily have to know what the integer is. In order to provide a convenient way to select a value from a known number of choices—and to make your code more readable and understandable—each object model provides a list of enumeration values. An *enumeration* represents a finite list of unique integers, each of which has a specific name and special meaning in the context in which it is used.

NOTE   Each application in Microsoft Office provides a set of enumeration values. Each enumeration value in a specific application has a name that is prefixed with two letters. In Word, Excel, PowerPoint, Access, and Outlook, enumeration names are prefixed with *wd*, *xl*, *pp*, *ac*, and *ol*, respectively.

Use enumeration values to select a slide layout

In PowerPoint, when you create a new slide, you can select a slide layout from the list provided in the New Slide dialog box. Each layout is different and displays a title, text, chart, clip art, or a few other placeholders in some unique combination and position on a slide. Layout is a property of a Slide object, and through Visual Basic, you can set what layout you want the slide to have or determine the current slide layout.

1   In the Visual Basic Editor of PowerPoint, move the cursor beneath the procedure you created earlier (MoveWindow) and create a new procedure called EnumList.

2 Add the following line of code:

```
ActivePresentation.Slides(1).Layout=
```

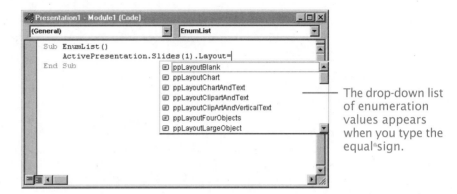

The drop-down list of enumeration values appears when you type the equal sign.

When you type the equal sign, a drop-down list is displayed listing all the possible values to which the Layout property can be equated. As you'll see later in the "Object Browser" section of this lesson, these are enumeration values, and they are really integers.

 NOTE If you do not see the drop-down list of enumeration values, the Auto List Members feature is not currently selected. To see the drop-down list, on the Tools menu in the Visual Basic Editor window, click Options. In the Editor tab, select the Auto List Members check box in the Code Settings group and click OK.

3 Select an item from the drop-down list and press the TAB key.

4 Place the cursor in the EnumList procedure and press F5 to run it.

In the PowerPoint application window, the layout of the first slide in the active presentation is set to the value you selected in step 3.

5 Go back to step 2, remove the enumeration value and the equal sign, and then retype the equal sign and set the Layout property to a different enumeration value in the drop-down list.

6 Run the procedure again, and then switch to the PowerPoint application window to see the new layout of the slide.

Notice how the name of the enumeration value describes the actual property setting. For example, ppLayoutBlank represents a slide with a blank layout.

TIP Each application in Microsoft Office provides a set of enumerations that represent predefined integer values. For example, ppLayoutBlank, referred to in the preceding step-by-step example, represents the number 12. You should use the enumeration instead of the integer value because it makes your code more understandable when other developers are reading it or when you come back to read it later.

Methods

Unlike properties, you do not use an equal sign when you work with an object's methods. With some methods, you just type the method name. However, in a number of cases, you can send information, or pass *arguments*, to a method.

Pass arguments to the SaveAs method in PowerPoint

1. In the Visual Basic Editor, place the cursor below the last line of code in the Code window. Type **Sub SavePres** and press ENTER.

2. Add the following line of code just after the line Sub SavePres():

   `ActivePresentation.SaveAs`

3. Press the SPACEBAR just after the word SaveAs, and a list of arguments you can pass to the SaveAs method is displayed. The list of arguments is displayed in the Auto Quick Info window.

The list of arguments appears in the Auto Quick Info window when you press the SPACEBAR after SaveAs.

NOTE If the Auto Quick Info window is not displayed, click Options on the Tools menu in the Visual Basic Editor. In the Editor tab of the Options dialog box, select Auto Quick Info and click OK.

For now, you just need to pass the first argument to the SaveAs method. This argument is the filename with which you want the presentation to be saved. The other arguments in the list are optional.

As you'll see later in this lesson, in the section "Learning the Members of the Object Model," Auto Quick Info and Auto List Members are features the Visual Basic Editor provides so that you don't have to memorize the syntax of every member in an object model.

4 Type "**MyPresentation**" (including the quotation marks) and press ENTER.

5 Press F5.

Notice that the title bar changes, showing that you saved the presentation with a new name. The title appears in both PowerPoint and the Visual Basic Editor.

The title bar changes when you save the presentation with a new name.

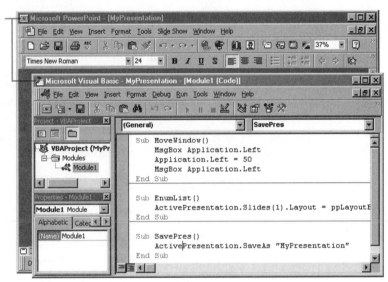

6 Exit PowerPoint. Your changes are already saved.

Events

In the context of Visual Basic programming, when an event that you are concerned about occurs, code (procedures) should be ready to respond to it. These procedures have specific names and are referred to as *event procedures*. An event procedure contains code you write that performs some action to handle the event when the event is triggered. Event procedures have a syntax like that shown in the following table.

Application	Event Procedure Example
Excel	Sub Workbook_Open() Sub Workbook_NewSheet (ByVal Sh As Object)
Word	Sub Document_Open Sub Document_Close

In some cases, an argument is passed to the event procedure by the application. In one of the preceding cases, when you open a new worksheet in Microsoft Excel, Excel passes the newly created sheet to the NewSheet event procedure so that you can start working instantly with the new worksheet.

 NOTE   Microsoft PowerPoint and Outlook do not provide an equivalent set of events. In Microsoft Access, all events are related to ActiveX controls and UserForms, which is the topic of Lesson 4.

Work with properties, methods, and events in Word

A Microsoft Word Document object exposes properties, methods, and events. The Document object represents an open document in Word and allows you to access every word, table, shape, or other element in the document.

1   Start Microsoft Word. On the Tools menu, point to Macro, and then click Visual Basic Editor on the submenu.

2   In the Editor, if the Project Explorer window is not open, then on the View menu, click Project Explorer. Double-click the ThisDocument item.

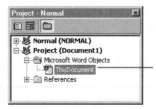

The ThisDocument project item is the code module for the Document object.

The ThisDocument project item is often referred to as the code module "behind" the Document object. When you insert ActiveX controls in a document, the controls are listed in the code module belonging to the document in which they reside. In Excel, controls reside on a worksheet and are listed in the code module for the Worksheet object. In PowerPoint, controls on a slide are listed in the code module for the Slide object.

 NOTE   By default, Microsoft PowerPoint does not display the code module for each Slide object in the Project Explorer. When the first ActiveX control is inserted into a slide, the code module for the Slide object is then listed in the Project Explorer. In Excel, code modules for each Worksheet object are listed by default.

3 In the ThisDocument module, type **Sub WordDoc** and press ENTER.

4 In the WordDoc procedure, add the following line of code:

```
MsgBox ActiveDocument.Name
```

This line displays the name of the active document. Name is a read-only property of the Document object, and it returns a string value representing the document's filename. If the document has not been saved yet, the Name property represents the default name given to the document when it was created. (The default name for the document is displayed in the title bar of the Word application window.) The Name property for the Workbook object in Excel and the Presentation object in PowerPoint both behave the same way.

5 Now, add the following two lines:

```
ActiveDocument.SaveAs "C:\Temp\MyDoc.doc"
MsgBox ActiveDocument.Name
```

The Document object supports a SaveAs method that represents the act of saving the document with a specified filename. The complete procedure looks like this:

```
Sub WordDoc()
    MsgBox ActiveDocument.Name
    ActiveDocument.SaveAs "C:\Temp\MyDoc.doc"
    MsgBox ActiveDocument.Name
End Sub
```

 IMPORTANT Make sure that the folder "C:\Temp" is a valid folder on your machine. If it is not, either create C:\Temp or change the line above to reflect a valid folder where the document can be saved. Once the document is saved, the line above displays a message box with the text: "MyDoc.doc." The Name property of the Document object now represents the filename, without the path.

6 Place the cursor in the WordDoc procedure and press F5.

A message box is displayed showing the default name of the active document (Document1). The document is then saved, and the filename, without the path, is displayed in another message box.

7 Click OK twice to close the two message boxes.

8 In the Object drop-down list of the ThisDocument code module, select Document.

9 In the Procedure drop-down list of the ThisDocument code module, select Close.

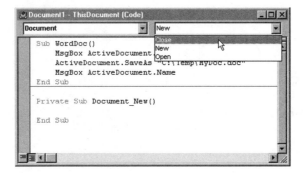

The items in the Procedure drop-down list represent the list of exposed events the Document object can react to. The Document object provides three separate event procedures: Document_Close, Document_New, and Document_Open. If a placeholder was created for the New event procedure, you can ignore it.

10 In the Document_Close event handler, type the following line:

```
MsgBox "This document is now CLOSING."
```

When the document closes, it is an event. When this event occurs, if code exists in the event handler for the Close event of the document, the event handler runs. In this case, a message box displaying the text "This document is now CLOSING." is displayed just before the document is closed and removed from memory.

11   In the Procedure drop-down list of the ThisDocument code module, select Open and add the following line in the Document_Open event handler:

```
MsgBox "This document is now OPEN!"
```

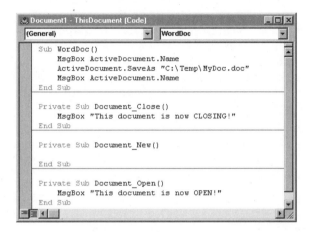

When the document opens, it is an event. When this event occurs, if code exists in the event handler, the event handler runs. In this case, a message box displaying the text "This document is now OPEN!" is displayed just after the document is opened and loaded into memory.

12   Switch to Word and then, on the File menu, click Close.

13   Click OK to close the message box, and then click Yes to save changes.

14   On the File menu, click 1 C:\Temp\MyDoc.doc (the recently opened file list) to open the document again.

You can open and close the document several times. Each time you open and close the document, the Open and Close events are triggered, and the code you wrote in the event procedures runs each time one of these events occurs.

15   Click OK and then exit Word.

Learning the Members of the Object Model

Just as an application is rich in features and functionality, the equivalent object model is filled with members that represent the same features and functionality. On average, each object model in Microsoft Office contains hundreds of members. This includes all collections, objects, properties, methods, and events. Learning all of the members of a model often may involve frequent switching between the corresponding Visual Basic Help file and the Visual Basic Editor window.

Visual Basic for Applications provides four tools you can use to simplify the search for the list of properties, methods, or events that an object supports. This set of tools consists of the Macro Recorder, the Object Browser, Auto List Members, and Auto Quick Info.

Macro Recorder

Microsoft Word, Excel, and PowerPoint provide a macro recorder that helps you quickly learn the object model of the respective application. (Microsoft Access and Outlook do not provide a macro recorder.) Macro recording provides the equivalent Visual Basic code of an action you conduct through an application's graphical interface.

For example, to change the color of a shape on a PowerPoint slide, you select the shape, click AutoShape on the Format menu, and then select a fill color from the Color drop-down list (in the Color And Lines tab). The equivalent macro-recorded code is as follows:

```
Sub Macro1()
'
' Macro recorded 12/1/96 by David Boctor
'
    ActiveWindow.Selection.SlideRange.Shapes _
        .AddShape(msoShapeRectangle, 246, _
        288, 138, 132).Select
    With ActiveWindow.Selection.ShapeRange
        .Fill.Visible = msoTrue
        .Fill.Solid
        .Fill.ForeColor.RGB = RGB(128, 0, 0)
    End With
End Sub
```

 NOTE Macro Recording is selection-based. This means that the Macro Recorder will record actions on selected objects in an active window.

The macro-recorded code gives you a good start on what you might want to do or create with Visual Basic code. Look at the first working line of code in the macro above and you will see how to add a shape to a slide. If you wanted to add a shape to a specific slide (for example, the second one) rather than the slide in the active window, you can replace the code in the Macro1 procedure with the following code:

```
Sub Macro1()
    Dim NewShape As Shape
    Set NewShape = ActivePresentation.Slides(2). _
        Shapes.AddShape(msoShapeRectangle, 246, _
        288, 138, 132)
End Sub
```

If you have two slides in your presentation, the code above adds a rectangle to the second slide. This line closely resembles the first line of the recorded macro. You just replaced ActiveWindow.Selection.SlideRange with ActivePresentation.Slides(2) so that your code works on a specific slide; it does not require that the slide be displayed in the active window. This macro also demonstrates declaring a variable (NewShape) that represents the new shape that is added to the slide. You will learn more about declaring variables and working with shapes and other objects later in this book.

Most macro-recorded code does not provide the exact code you need for your solution. It does, however, provide the exact syntax to manipulate many objects within Word, Excel, and PowerPoint, and helps you write Visual Basic code without constantly searching through the Help file.

Object Browser

On many road maps, an index is provided that lists all destinations for quick reference and easy navigation. To give the Visual Basic programmer the same convenience for navigating through an object model, the Visual Basic Editor provides a tool window called the Object Browser. By learning to effectively use the Object Browser, you will reap many time and efficiency benefits.

Look at the Object Browser

1 Start PowerPoint. In the opening PowerPoint dialog box, click Blank Presentation and click OK.

2 In the New Slide dialog box, select any slide layout and click OK.

3 On the Tools menu, point to Macro, and then click Visual Basic Editor on the submenu.

4 In the Editor, on the View menu, click Object Browser. (You can also
press F2.)

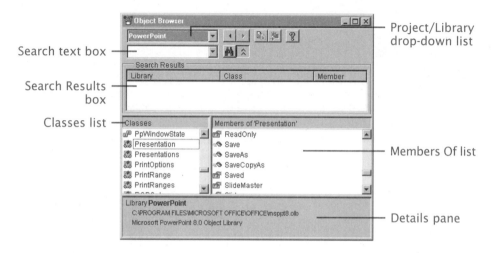

The Object Browser contains five main elements in its window: Project/Library
drop-down list, Search text box with Search Results box, Classes list, Members
Of list, and the Details pane.

Project/Library drop-down list The list displays the currently referenced
libraries for the active Visual Basic project. By default, <All Libraries> is selected
in the text box, which allows all of the libraries to be displayed in the Object
Browser at one time.

The object model definition for each application in Microsoft Office and for any
other application that supports an object model is contained in a file referred
to as an *object library*. The filename of an object library usually contains the
extension .olb. However, sometimes an object library may be contained within
a dynamic-link library (.dll) file. The object library file, in general terms, is just
an information file for whatever objects, properties, methods, events, and enumerations an application exposes. By providing an object library, Visual Basic
can search for the objects an application exposes without having to load the
entire application itself and then ask it for a list of exposed objects.

In Part 2, you'll see that referencing an object library is important when programming Microsoft Office using objects and functionality from multiple applications because it can be done from within one Visual Basic Editor window.

Search text box with Search Results box The Search Results box
displays a list of libraries, classes, or members matching the criteria you specify
in the Search text box. These boxes are examined in more detail in the next
step-by-step example.

Classes list This list displays all of the objects exposed in a given object
library. When <All Libraries> is selected in the Project/Library drop-down list,

all objects in all libraries are listed. However, if you select a specific library in the Project/Library drop-down list, only the objects in the specified library are listed.

For example, you can start PowerPoint, display its Visual Basic Editor, and press F2 for the Object Browser. In the Project/Library drop-down list, select PowerPoint. In the Classes list, you'll see only the objects Microsoft PowerPoint exposes. There are a number of objects in the list, including familiar objects such as Presentation, Slide, and Shape.

Members Of list   All the properties, methods, and events that are supported by a selected item in the Classes list are displayed here.

If you select PowerPoint from the Project/Library drop-down list and then select Presentation from the Classes list, then in the Members Of 'Presentation' list you'll see the methods and properties that you might be familiar with through the PowerPoint menus and toolbars. Familiar methods include Close, Save, SaveAs, and PrintOut, while common properties include Name, Path, and FullName.

Details pane   When you select an item in the Members Of list, the contents of the Details pane reveal detailed information about the selected member.

If you select Presentation from the Classes list and then PageSetup in the Members Of list, the Details pane displays the following information:

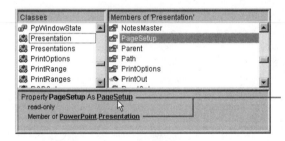

Words that are underlined and green are links to other items in the Object Browser.

Note that the last word in the first line in the Details pane, "PageSetup," is underlined and green. This indicates two things: (1) the PageSetup property returns an object called PageSetup, and (2) you can navigate to the PageSetup object by clicking the link.

Search for information about an object

The Search Results box provides a quick method for determining which members in an object library support certain properties, methods, or events. It lists members that match the criteria specified in the Search text box after searching through the specified object library or libraries. If <All Libraries> is selected in the Project/Library box, the search is conducted in all libraries in the Project/Library list; if a specific library is selected, the search scans only the specified library.

1   In the Object Browser, in the Project/Library box, select PowerPoint.

2   Right-click anywhere in the Object Browser window. This displays the shortcut menu for the Object Browser.

3   Select Find Whole Word Only.

4   In the Search text box, type **name**.

5   Click the Search button next to the Search text box.

Search

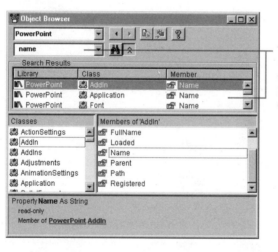

The Search Results list reveals all instances of the property Name in the Microsoft PowerPoint 8.0 object library.

The first column in the Search Results list is the Library; the second column is the Class, or object; and the third is the Member property. Selecting any row in the Search Results list refreshes the contents of the Classes list and the Members Of list, so you can navigate to the exact location of the search result item in the object library.

Auto List Members

One of the newest and most exciting additions to the Visual Basic Editor is the Auto List Members drop-down list, which you saw briefly in a previous step-by-step example. Never again do you have to memorize the methods or properties of an object. All you need to do is start typing, and once you type in a period (.) after a valid object name, Auto List Members automatically displays a drop-down list of all properties and methods supported by the object. You can scroll down the list with the mouse, or you can continue typing the method or property name. If you continue typing, an item in the list is selected that matches your typing.

Enter properties the hard way

A simple example illustrates this benefit. Imagine that you want to define a name of an object within one of your procedures.

1   In the Visual Basic Editor, insert a code module, type **Sub WithoutDeclaration**, and press ENTER.

2   Between the lines `Sub WithoutDeclaration` and `End Sub`, add the following line of code:

```
MsgBox sldSlide.Name
```

When you start to use a term or variable that the Editor doesn't recognize, you have to do all of the work yourself. In this case, you must already know that sldSlide is the name of a slide and that a Name property applies to slides.

Take advantage of Auto List Members to enter properties the easy way

When you declare an object variable, you also take advantage of the Auto List Members tool. The Auto List Members drop-down list displays information that would logically complete the statement at the current insertion point.

1   Add the following declaration and Set statements above the line of code you've already typed:

```
Dim sldSlide As Slide
Set sldSlide = ActivePresentation.Slides(1)
```

43

You have now declared the sldSlide variable as representing a PowerPoint Slide object; the Visual Basic Editor now knows what type of object this variable references. Your procedure should look like this:

```
Sub WithoutDeclaration()
    Dim sldSlide As Slide
    Set sldSlide = ActivePresentation.Slides(1)
    MsgBox sldSlide.Name
End Sub
```

2   Now delete the line you previously typed, MsgBox sldSlide.Name, and then type it again. (Yes, this is the same line that you typed before, but something different should happen.)

```
MsgBox sldSlide.Name
```

When you start typing the line above and get to the point where you type a period (.) after sldSlide, the Auto List Members drop-down list appears.

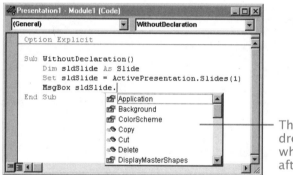

The Auto List Members drop-down list appears when you type a period after sldSlide.

At this point, you can scroll down the list and select the property or method item, or you can continue to type the name of the property or method if you know it. As you continue to type, the list automatically scrolls down to find a match for the text you started to type. If the property or method name is long and the item is selected in the Auto List Members drop-down list, you can press TAB in order to insert the item in your line of code.

3   Select Name in the list and press TAB.

4   Press F5 to run the macro.

5   Exit PowerPoint without saving changes.

Auto Quick Info

As you write your code, there are a number of ways to determine the exact syntax of the object, methods, and properties you use. One of the easiest ways is by displaying the Auto Quick Info window, which shows function information and parameters as you type. The Auto Quick Info window is similar to the ToolTip displayed when the cursor is over a toolbar button.

In the section "Pass arguments to the SaveAs method in PowerPoint" earlier in this lesson, when you pressed the SPACEBAR after typing the SaveAs method name, the Auto Quick Info window appeared as follows:

```
Sub SavePres()
    ActivePresentation.SaveAs "MyPres",|
End Sub
```

You can see in the Auto Quick Info window that the SaveAs method of the Presentation object in PowerPoint takes three arguments. Each argument in the Auto Quick Info window is separated by a comma (,); as you type a comma, the next argument in the window becomes bold. Some arguments are encased in square brackets, which indicates that specifying the argument is optional. In the SaveAs method above, the first argument is required and the second and third are optional. If the argument is optional, the application defines a default value for the argument.

In the SaveAs method, the second argument, *FileFormat*, defaults to the current version of a PowerPoint presentation. You can also see in the case of the second argument that when you type a comma, both the Auto Quick Info window and the Auto List Members drop-down list are displayed. The Auto List Members drop-down list is displayed because the FileFormat argument is one of the enumeration values (PpSaveAsFileType) in the list.

 TIP You can toggle between the Auto Quick Info window and the Auto List Members drop-down list when both are displayed by clicking either one to bring it in front of the other.

Lesson Summary

To	Do this

Traverse the branches of an object hierarchy tree	Use a period (.). For example:
	`Application.Presentations(1).Slides(1). _`
	`Shapes(1).TextFrame.TextRange = "Some Text"`

Count the number of objects (such as shapes) within another type of object (such as a worksheet)	Use the Count property. For example: `ActiveSheet.Shapes.Count`
Specify a particular object in a collection	Use the object's index or name. For example: `Sheets(2) or Sheets("Sales")`
Turn on the Auto List Members feature	In the Visual Basic Editor, on the Tools menu, click Options, click the Editor tab, and select the Auto List Members check box.
Display an Auto List Members list of enumeration values	Type an equal sign (=) immediately after a property name (or type a comma after a method) to which a list applies.
Set the value of a property	Type an equal sign after the property name followed by the value you want to assign.
Run a method	Type the object name followed by a period, the name of the method, and any required or optional arguments. For example: `ActivePresentation.SaveAs "MyPresentation"`
Run an event handler procedure when an event happens to an object	Double-click an appropriate project item in the Project Explorer window, select an object from the Object drop-down list (at the top of the Code window), select an event procedure from the Procedure drop-down list, and then type code in the procedure.
Display the Object Browser	In the Visual Basic Editor, on the View menu, click Object Browser; or press F2.
Search for information about an object in the Object Browser	Select a library in the Project/Library drop-down list, type a name (such as a class or member) in the Search text box, and click the Search button.
Declare an object variable	Type **Dim** followed by the object name, **As**, and the object type. For example: `Dim sldSlide As Slide`

For online information about	Ask the Assistant for help, using the words
Object, properties, methods, and events in general	"Understanding objects"
Displaying information in a message box	"MsgBox"
Saving documents in code	"SaveAs"
Using the Project Explorer	"Project Explorer"
Using the Object Browser	"Object Browser"
Declaring variables in advance	"Declaring variables"

Preview of the Next Lesson

In the next lesson, you will learn how to create a procedure in which you write Visual Basic code, declare variables and constants, process string and numerical data from user input, control program flow using Visual Basic decision-making statements, and repeat a series of steps with looping structures.

The Fundamentals of Writing Visual Basic Code

In this lesson you will learn how to:

Estimated time
50 min.

- Create a procedure in which you write Visual Basic code.
- Declare variables and constants.
- Control program flow using Visual Basic decision-making statements.
- Repeat a series of steps with looping structures.
- Debug the values of variables and constants.

A language, whether spoken, written in text, or programmed in computer code, contains certain fundamental elements: a set of symbols and rules organized in combinations and patterns for the purpose of communication. For example, when writing a report you use the rules and symbols of your spoken language to tie words, sentences, and paragraphs together to form a written document. The report is organized into components such as sections or chapters, each conceived to present a specific point, but ultimately tied together to support the main communication goal of the report.

This lesson will introduce you to the fundamentals of the Visual Basic programming language so that you can fully exploit its features when writing Visual Basic programs for Microsoft Office. Although the Visual Basic programming language is based on the same principles as most other programming languages, Visual Basic is much easier to learn than most. This allows for the quick and easy design and development of programs.

Beginning to Write Code

In Visual Basic for Applications, the Visual Basic Editor is your development environment and your written code lies within a code module. You can insert as many code modules as you need to organize your code into manageable pieces that can be easily used in other programs or by other users.

Get ready to program a code module

One of the first steps in writing Visual Basic code is opening a blank module.

1   Start Microsoft PowerPoint. In the opening PowerPoint dialog box, select Blank Presentation and click OK.

2   In the New Slide dialog box, select the second slide layout (Bulleted List) and click OK. (The particular slide layout selected has no effect on the process of opening a blank module.)

3   On the Tools menu, point to Macro, and then click Visual Basic Editor on the submenu. (Or, press ALT+F11 as a shortcut to display the Visual Basic Editor.)

4   In the Editor, on the Insert menu, click Module.

Create a procedure

Many of the things you use every day are built from components, and each component performs one or more related tasks. A car, for example, is constructed along an assembly line from a number of functional components that ultimately come together to provide mobility for its driver.

In Visual Basic programs, components are represented by procedures you create to organize your code into logical tasks, each serving a specific function. There are two common types of procedures you can create in Visual Basic: Sub and Function. A *Sub* procedure performs actions and does not return a value, whereas a *Function* procedure returns a value. A third type, the *Property* procedure, is often used to create and manipulate custom properties. The Property procedure, however, is beyond the scope of this book.

Sub procedures start with the keyword Sub followed by the name of the procedure and end with the keywords End Sub. To create a procedure, give it a unique name or header.

1   In the Code window of the module you just opened, type **Sub MyNewProcedure** and press ENTER.

Visual Basic will automatically insert the keywords End Sub two lines below. End Sub indicates where the procedure ends, just as a paragraph ends with a "return" in a word processor. Generally, procedures within a code module have specific things in common.

2   Add the following lines between the line `Sub MyNewProcedure` and `End Sub`:

```
MsgBox "This text is displayed in a " & _
    "message box"
```

Visual Basic treats the two separate lines as one. The space and under-score (_) at the end of the first line indicate that you want to continue a line of code onto the next line. The textual analogy would be adding a hyphen where you want to continue a word from one line to the next. The ampersand (&) is used here to concatenate (join sequentially) two pieces of text. You complete each line of code by pressing ENTER at the end of the line.

3   Make sure that the cursor is placed within the MyNewProcedure proce-dure and press F5 to run the procedure.

 NOTE   When you press the F5 key, Visual Basic runs the code starting from the first line of the procedure in which the cursor is placed. Pressing F5 is equivalent to clicking Run Sub/ UserForm on the Run menu in the Visual Basic Editor.

A message box is displayed.

4   Click OK to close the message box.

By creating individual procedures, you break your code into distinct elements so that if your program does not function as it should, you can track down problems systematically. In addition, if you encap-sulate a specific programming task in a procedure, you can more readily copy the procedure and paste it into another program with little or no changes. As you will see in Chapter 6, "Creating Custom Menus and Toolbars," procedures that you create to add or remove menus and toolbars can easily be used in any Visual Basic program for Microsoft Office.

Add comments to code

When you write Visual Basic code, you may want to include comments to remind yourself or tell others why you structured your code the way you did or to flag work items that are still outstanding. In a word processor like Microsoft Word, you usually add a comment by clicking Comment on the

Insert menu. In Visual Basic, you add comments to your code by adding a single quotation mark (') at the beginning of the comment. Visual Basic does not read nor run anything in this line.

1   In the same procedure you just created, move to the end of the first line Sub MyNewProcedure and press ENTER.

2   On the new blank line, press TAB and add the following text:

    ' The line below will display a message box

    Once you type this line and press ENTER, Visual Basic colors this line of code green for easier readability. You can also add comments at the end of a line of code just by adding a single quotation mark. Green text in a code module indicates comments unless you specify another color.

3   Click the end of the line "message box" and then add the following text:

    ' This line is continued

    The procedure should look like the following:

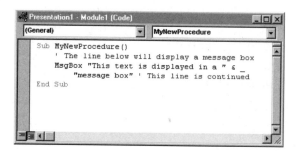

4   Finally, press F5.

    Observe once again that a message box is displayed. Visual Basic ignored the comment line above the message box code and the comment attached to the end of the line of code.

5   Click OK to close the message box.

   TIP   It is common practice in Visual Basic programming to indent code by inserting a tab at the beginning of each line of code, between the lines Sub <Procedure> and End Sub, as shown in the preceding illustration. This greatly improves readability. To insert a tab, just press the TAB key on your keyboard.

Categorizing Data in Visual Basic

Every day you work with many types of data, ranging from textual information to numerical values. When you work on your computer, you decide where to store information depending on the type it represents. Probably, if it's text, you'll store it in a Microsoft Word document; if it's numerical values or mathematical formulas, you'll store it in a Microsoft Excel workbook or Access database; and if it's graphics, you'll store it in a PowerPoint presentation. By storing information in a file of a Microsoft Office application, you are telling a recipient of that file what type of data it contains.

Variables and Constants

In Visual Basic, as in most other programming languages, a variable or constant is used to represent and temporarily store data that you use in your program. A *variable*, on the one hand, represents data that changes; thus, its value varies within a program. A *constant*, on the other hand, represents data that remains the same throughout your program. The syntax for defining variables and constants has two parts that are joined by an equal sign: a name and a corresponding value. The name of the variable or constant is stated on the left side of the equal sign, and the value is stated on the right. In the section "Specifying Declaration Statements" later in this lesson, you will see how variables and constants are used in code.

Determining the Data Type

When you assign a value to a variable or constant, it is of a specific type. In Visual Basic, you can explicitly categorize your data, or information, type. For example, if you are working with text, the equivalent Visual Basic data type category is String. If you are working with whole numbers less than 32,767, the data type is Integer. The table below lists more details on other numerical data types, as well as listing the Boolean, String, and Object data types.

Data type	Range
Integer	–32,768 to 32,767
Long (long integer)	–2,147,483,648 to 2,147,483,647
Single (single-precision floating-point)	–3.402823E38 to –1.401298E-45 for negative values; 1.401298E-45 to 3.402823E38 for positive values
Double (double-precision floating-point)	–1.79769313486232E308 to –4.94065645841247E-324 for negative values; 4.94065645841247E-324 to 1.79769313486232E308 for positive values

Data type	Range
Boolean	True or False
Object	(set to an object member of an object model)
String	1 to approximately 65,400

 NOTE The preceding table is not comprehensive; there are many other data types. For more information, in the Visual Basic Editor, ask the Assistant for help using the words "data type summary."

Examine user input

1. In the Code window, move the cursor beneath the End Sub line of the procedure you created earlier (MyNewProcedure) and create a new procedure by typing **Sub InputType** and pressing ENTER.

2. Between the lines Sub InputType and End Sub, add the following line:

```
sInput = InputBox("Enter text or a number.")
```

InputBox is a function built into the Visual Basic programming language. This function displays a dialog box containing a text box in which you can type. If you enter text and click the OK button in the dialog box, the function returns the value you entered. In this case, the returned value is stored in the variable sInput.

3. After the line containing the InputBox function, enter the following If...Then...Else statement:

```
If IsNumeric(sInput) Then
    sType = "number"
Else
    sType = "string"
End If
```

In this code segment, the built-in Visual Basic function IsNumeric is used to determine whether the value the user enters, which is stored in the variable sInput, is numeric. If it is numeric, the string value "number" is stored in the variable sType. If the input value is not numeric, the string value "string" is stored in the variable sType.

4 Finally, add the following message box statement as the last line (above End Sub) in the InputType procedure:

```
MsgBox "The data you entered was a " & sType
```

If Visual Basic displays a "Variable not defined" error, remove the Option Explicit statement at the top of the module.

5 Place the cursor anywhere within the InputType procedure and press F5.

The dialog box is displayed, prompting you to enter text or a number. You can also enter a combination of text and numbers, although this combination is always considered a String data type in Visual Basic.

6 Click OK to close the dialog box.

 TIP Visual Basic provides a convenient function called TypeName that returns a string indicating the type of information within a variable you specify. For more information, ask the Assistant for help, using the word "typename."

Specifying Declaration Statements

As you just learned, when you work with data, it often is of a specific type. For example, the whole number 12 is an Integer data type, and the text "Hello there" is a String data type. When you assign data to a variable, you'll want to tell Visual Basic what type of data you are using. To formally indicate this, you need to use a declaration statement.

Declaration statements for variables usually start with the keyword Dim, followed by the variable name and the type of data the variable should hold. The common syntax appears as:

```
Dim VariableName As DataType
```

The variable name must begin with a letter, cannot be more than 255 characters long or contain any periods or mathematical operators, and must not be the name of a Visual Basic keyword. The data type can be any of the types discussed in the section "Determining the Data Type" or any others provided by Visual Basic.

In a declaration statement, you can specify more than one declaration at a time, but you must specify the exact type for each variable. Visual Basic does not assume that the second variable is declared the same type as the first or any other declaration on the same line. By default, Visual Basic assigns the declaration without a specified type to the data type Variant. The following illustration shows variable declarations of several types.

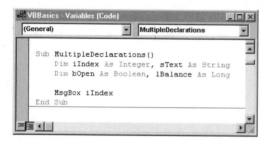

Declaration statements for constants start with the keyword Const, followed by the constant name, the type of data the constant should hold, and the value assigned to the constant. The common syntax appears as:

```
Const ConstantName As DataType = Value
```

The naming convention for a constant follows that of a variable name, specified above. The data type can also be any of the types specified by Visual Basic. The value set to the constant must be a valid value within the range of the data type. The following simple procedure reveals how the Dim and Const statements are used in your code.

```
Sub VariablesAndConstants()
    Dim iMyVariable As Integer
    Const iMyConstant As Integer = 10
    iMyVariable = 4
    MsgBox iMyVariable & ", " & iMyConstant
End Sub
```

TIP It is a common practice in programming to prefix the name of each variable and constant with a letter that indicates the data type. This helps you and others reduce the amount of time spent reading and debugging code because you can easily distinguish what type of data a variable or constant should contain. For Visual Basic data types, a common syntax is to prefix each variable or constant as shown: *s* or *str* for String data type, *i* for Integer, *bln* or *b* for Boolean, *lng* or *l* for Long, *sng* or *sg* for Single, and *vnt* or *v* for Variant.

Declaring variables and constants helps you reduce coding errors such as assigning an incorrect value or misspelling a name. As a good programming practice, you should place the keywords Option Explicit at the top of your code module. If you do, when Visual Basic runs your code, it ensures that you explicitly declared and set a valid type of value to any variables and constants in your code. To have Visual Basic automatically add the keywords Option Explicit to every new code module you insert, in the Visual Basic Editor, click Options on the Tools menu, click the Editor tab, and then select the Require Variable Declaration check box.

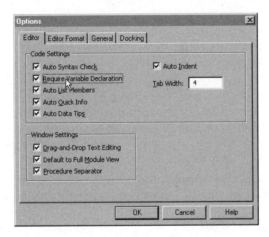

Do I Need to Declare My Variables and Constants?

Declaring variables is one of the most common programming practices and, by most programming standards, is a necessity. It allows for more readable code and lets Visual Basic know with what type of data you are working. If you do not declare a variable or constant as a specific type, Visual Basic, by default, declares the variable as a Variant data type.

The Variant data type allows you to set any type of data to a variable. For example, if MyVariable is declared as a Variant data type, you can set it to equal a String, an Integer, a Boolean, or any other data type. The ability to assign any data type to a variable is useful in cases where you are not sure what type of data the user will enter, or what type of data has been entered in a database.

When Visual Basic runs a line of code that uses a variable or constant declared as a Variant data type, however, it must determine what the variable type is, possibly slowing the execution of your program. A variable or constant declared as a Variant data type also uses more memory.

Declare the scope of variables and constants

When you declare variables and constants, you also must think about the scope in which they will be available. *Scope* refers to the availability of a variable, constant, or procedure for use by another procedure. You can declare variables and constants at three levels: procedure-level, module-level, and public.

Procedure-level   As the name suggests, these variables and constants are available only within the procedure in which they are declared. They are declared at the beginning of a Visual Basic procedure.

Module-level   The top of a code module is referred to as the Declarations section. Module-level variables and constants cannot be declared anywhere else in a code module other than in the Declarations section. They are available to all procedures within the code module in which the declaration is contained. If declarations are made between procedures or at the end of a code module, an error is displayed when Visual Basic tries to run the code.

Public   These variables and constants are also declared at the top of a code module, in the Declarations section. However, the declaration statement is prefixed with the keyword Public, indicating that the variable or constant is available to all procedures in all code modules in your program.

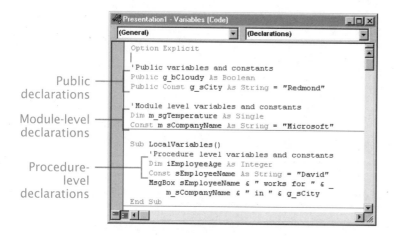

Public declarations

Module-level declarations

Procedure-level declarations

 TIP   In addition to prefixing variables and constants with letters that indicate the data type, it is a good idea to include letters that indicate scope. This also helps you and others reduce the amount of time spent reading and debugging code because you can easily find where the variable or constant is declared. A common syntax is to prefix each variable or constant with *m_* if it is module-level or *g_* if it is public (the "g" stands for "global"). If the variable or constant is procedure-level, an additional prefix is not used.

Making Decisions with Condition Blocks

In any production process, whether you're producing a report, software, or a car, you need to decide what materials you need and how to control the flow of those materials through your different departments, individuals, and technologies. At each point in the process, you may gather input from certain sources such as quality control or computer sensors, until the final output is achieved. In Visual Basic, you decide what data you need to work with, create a program flow in order to work with the data, gather any required input from users or data sources on your system or network, and finally produce a result.

In many situations, you find yourself directed in a path depending on conditions, just like on a drive from city to city (to make another analogy). On such a drive, you'll decide which roads to take depending on weather conditions, traffic congestion, scenery, and time constraints. Your Visual Basic program is no different. Once you decide what conditions determine the flow, a program will follow a logical path to the final output. Visual Basic provides a number of different syntax choices to allow you to evaluate information and run appropriate code, depending on criteria and conditions that you specify.

Pick an option with If...Then...Else statements

The most often used and simplest condition statements in Visual Basic are *If...Then* and *If...Then...Else*. These statements allow you to evaluate a condition or set of conditions in order to run a particular block of statements. (You already used this structure in the procedure you wrote to determine a data type.)

1   In the Code window, create a new procedure by typing **Sub IfThenCondition** and pressing ENTER.

2   Between the lines `Sub IfThenCondition` and `End Sub`, add the following line of code:

```
sInput = InputBox("Enter a number greater than 10.")
```

As discussed earlier, the built-in Visual Basic InputBox function prompts the user to enter a value in a text box and returns a string representing the value entered by the user. In this case, you prompt the user to input a number greater than 10.

3   After the line containing the InputBox function, enter the following If...Then condition block:

```
If sInput > 10 Then
    MsgBox "You entered a number greater than 10."
End If
```

Within this If...Then condition block, if the value entered by the user is greater than 10, the message box is displayed. Otherwise, nothing else happens.

4 Place the cursor anywhere in the IfThenCondition procedure and press F5.

The InputBox is displayed, prompting you to enter a number greater than 10. If the condition is evaluated to True (that is, the input value is a number greater than 10), the confirmation message is displayed. If the number is less than or equal to 10, no message is displayed.

5 Enter a number greater than 10 and click OK.

6 Click OK to close the message box.

7 Within the If...Then condition block you just created, add the following two lines between the line containing the MsgBox function and End If:

```
Else
    MsgBox "You entered a number less than 10."
```

The If...Then...Else condition block goes one step further. It provides an alternative if the condition is not met. Now, if you enter a number less than 10, a different message box is displayed.

8 Press F5.

9 Enter a number less than 10 and then click OK.

10 Click OK to close the message box.

11 Within the If...Then...Else condition block you created above, add the following two lines just above the line Else:

```
ElseIf sInput = 10 Then
    MsgBox "You entered the number 10."
```

Finally, the If...Then...ElseIf condition block goes yet another step and adds more flexibility than the If...Then...Else condition block. With the If...Then...ElseIf condition block, you can evaluate more than one condition within the same block. Now, a different message box is displayed for all three cases for the input value. This value can either be greater than, equal to, or less than 10.

The completed If…Then…ElseIf condition block should look like the following:

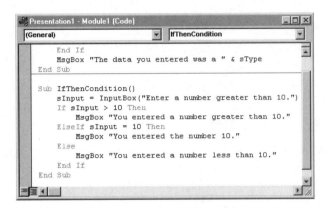

12 Press F5.

13 Enter the number 10 and then click OK.

14 Click OK to close the message box.

Select among options with Select Case

The Select Case condition block is very similar to the If…Then…ElseIf condition block. Select Case evaluates the test expression in the first line and compares it to the value in each case thereafter.

1 In the procedure you created above, delete the If…Then…ElseIf condition block and replace it with a Select Case statement. The revised procedure looks like this:

```
Sub IfThenCondition()
    sInput = InputBox("Enter a number greater than 10.")
    Select Case sInput
    Case Is > 10
        MsgBox "You entered a number greater than 10."
    Case Is = 10
        MsgBox "You entered the number 10."
    Case Is < 10
        MsgBox "You entered a number less than 10."
    End Select
End Sub
```

Note particularly the similarities between the overall structure of the Select Case condition with the If...Then...ElseIf condition block. In the Select Case condition block, the variable sInput is the test expression and it is entered at the beginning of the condition block. Then, a number of Case statements follow to handle the possible conditions of the test expression.

2　Run the procedure and enter numbers as you did before.

The procedure responds the same way.

Repeating Actions with Loops

You'll find many occasions where you'll want to continually increment a value and run some code repeatedly with the incremented value. At other times you'll want to delay running code until the value of a variable meets certain conditions. Looping structures in Visual Basic come in a variety of options to suit each case.

Count with For...Next

The For...Next loop runs a block of code repeatedly and also increments a variable you specify. The incremental changes in value to the variable can be in steps with positive or negative integers. By default, the incremental step value is +1.

1　Create a new procedure called ForNext.

2　Within the procedure, declare the two integers i and iTotal by adding the following two lines of code:

```
Dim iTotal As Integer
Dim i As Integer
```

3　Add the following For...Next loop:

```
For i = 1 To 5
    iTotal = iTotal + i ^ 2
Next i
```

The For...Next loop increments the integer variable i by a value of 1. The loop has a range from 1 to 5. Thus, i is initially assigned a value of 1 the first time the loop runs, and then in the following loop, i has a value of 2, and so on. The variable iTotal is used to sum the square of each of the values from 1 to 5 (the range of the For...Next loop).

4　Add a message box after the For...Next loop to display the final value of the variable iTotal by adding the following line of code:

```
MsgBox iTotal
```

The complete procedure should look like this:

```
Sub ForNext()
    Dim iTotal As Integer
    Dim i As Integer

    For i = 1 To 5
        iTotal = iTotal + i ^ 2
    Next i
    MsgBox iTotal
End Sub
```

5   Press F5.

The final value of iTotal is 55. The line within the loop, `iTotal = iTotal + i ^ 2`, adds the square of the numbers between 1 and 5 (that is, 1 + 4 + 9 + 16 + 25).

NOTE   You could also step backward, by setting the range from 5 to 1 and adding the keyword Step and –1 just after the range. The resulting code would look like this:

```
For i = 5 To 1 Step -1
```

The variable i is initially assigned a value of 5, then 4, then 3, and so on. In this case, stepping through backward would produce the same result as the procedure you wrote.

Step out early

If you want to exit the loop when the value of iTotal is greater than 5, you can add an If...Then condition within the loop. If the condition is met, Visual Basic will exit the For...Next loop.

1   In the procedure you just created, add the following If...Then condition block within the For...Next loop, just after the line `iTotal = iTotal + i ^ 2`:

```
If iTotal > 5 Then
    MsgBox i
    Exit For
End If
```

The code `Exit For` tells Visual Basic to exit the For...Next loop that is currently running. The message box just before the Exit For statement shows the value of iCount just before exiting the loop.

2   Press F5.

Two message boxes are displayed now. The first shows the value of the counter i used in the For...Next loop, which is 3. The second displays the value of iTotal, which is 14. Once you jump from a loop, you usually continue with an action right after the loop and use the values altered in the loop in the following actions.

Going Around and Around with Do...Loop

The Do...Loop structure continues to run code within the loop structure until a certain condition is met. You must specify a condition for exiting or stopping a Do...Loop structure or else it loops continuously without stopping. You can specify a condition in three ways: repeat until something changes, continue while things are the same, and leave a loop early.

Repeat until something changes

The first way to exit a loop structure is to add the keyword Until after the word Loop and then specify the condition.

1   Create a procedure called DoLoopUntil.

2   Declare the variable iCount as an integer and create a Do...Loop structure by adding the following lines of code:

```
Dim iCount As Integer
Do
    iCount = iCount + 2
Loop Until iCount > 100
```

In the Do...Loop structure, the variable iCount is incremented by a value of 2 each time through the loop. When the value of iCount is greater than 100, the loop exits.

3   Just after the line iCount = iCount + 2 in the Do...Loop structure, add the following:

```
Debug.Print iCount
```

During each successive loop, Debug.Print prints the value of iCount in the Immediate window so that you can see iCount being incremented.

4   If the Immediate window is not displayed, then in the Visual Basic Editor, on the View menu, click Immediate Window; or press CTRL+G as a shortcut.

5   Add a message box after the Do...Loop structure indicating that the loop has finished:

```
MsgBox "The loop has finished."
```

The complete procedure should look like this:

```
Sub DoLoopUntil()
    Dim iCount As Integer
    Do
        iCount = iCount + 2
        Debug.Print iCount
    Loop Until iCount > 100
    MsgBox "The loop has finished."
End Sub
```

6 Press F5 to run the procedure.

Continue while things are the same

The second way to exit a Do...Loop structure is to add the keyword While after the word Loop and then specify the condition.

1 In the Do...Loop structure you just created, delete the line `Loop Until iCount > 100` and replace it with:

`Loop While iCount <= 100`

2 Press F5.

The procedure performs the same way as in the preceding step-by-step example.

If you closely compare the logic of the Until condition and the While condition, you'll see that they specify the same condition and they produce the same result.

IMPORTANT In both cases above, the keywords Until and While plus the condition following them can be placed after the word Do instead of Loop. You can type **Until** or **While** after the word Do or Loop, but not after both. The difference this has on your code is that if Until and While are placed after the word Loop, the statements are evaluated at least once before reaching the Until or While condition. If placed after the word Do, the condition following the keyword Until or While is evaluated immediately, before any lines within the Do...Loop structure run. For more information, in the Visual Basic Editor, ask the Assistant for help, using the words "Using Do...Loop Statements."

Leave a loop early

The third way to exit a Do...Loop structure is to use only a condition statement in the lines of code within the Do...Loop structure.

1   In the Do...Loop structure, delete the line `Loop While Count <= 100` and replace it with the following If...Then condition and Loop statements:

```
        If iCount > 100 Then Exit Do
Loop
```

The complete procedure looks like this:

```
Sub DoLoopUntil()
    Dim iCount As Integer
    Do
        iCount = iCount + 2
        Debug.Print iCount
        If iCount > 100 Then Exit Do
    Loop
    MsgBox "The loop has finished."
End Sub
```

2   Press F5.

The procedure performs the same way as the two preceding examples.

3   Exit PowerPoint. You may save changes if you want, but you do not need these procedures in other lessons.

Parsing Filenames with For...Next

In many scenarios, you may find that your program handles files and filenames. For example, your program may prompt the user to specify a filename under which information will be saved. In order to verify that the specified pathname of the filename is valid, you need to parse the filename string for the pathname. To *parse* means to separate into more easily processed components (groups of characters, in this case) and then to analyze them.

Parse filenames

Once you develop a function to extract the pathname from a filename string, you use the debugging tools of the Visual Basic Editor to step through each line of code to see the different values assigned to variables.

1   Start Microsoft Word, Excel, or PowerPoint, and open the Visual Basic Editor. The following code and steps work identically in each application.

2   Insert a new code module. In the Code window, type **Sub ParseFileName** and press ENTER to create a new procedure.

3 Add the following line of code to the procedure:

```
MsgBox GetPath("C:\Temp\Test.txt")
```

The string value you specified as the first argument of the MsgBox statement is the value returned from the function GetPath. (GetPath is a Function procedure that you will create in the steps below. Recall that a Function procedure is like a Sub procedure except that it returns a value.) GetPath takes one string argument, representing the filename. In this case, the value you pass to the GetPath function is "C:\Temp\Test.txt", which does not necessarily exist on your system, but is used as a test to verify that the GetPath function works correctly.

4 Below the `End Sub` statement of the ParseFileName procedure, add a blank line by pressing ENTER. Create a new function by typing **Function GetPath(sFileName As String) As String** and pressing ENTER.

The function GetPath accepts an argument, *sFileName*, which is declared as a String data type. The GetPath function is itself declared as a String data type, which indicates that you assign a string to GetPath. By default, the value of GetPath is initially an empty string, or "".

5 Within the GetPath function, add the following declaration statements:

```
Dim sChar As String, i As Integer
```

6 After the declarations in the GetPath function, add the following For...Next loop:

```
For i = Len(sFileName) To 1 Step -1
Next i
```

Because you specify the Step keyword and a step value at the end of the For statement, the loop iterates from the value representing the length of the string sFileName to 1. The Visual Basic function Len is built into the Visual Basic language. The Len function returns the number of characters in the string you specify. In this case, the variable sFileName, or "C:\Temp\Test.txt", is the string value, and its length is 16.

7 Within the For...Next loop, add the following line:

```
sChar = Mid$(sFileName, i, 1)
```

The variable sChar is assigned to the value returned by the Visual Basic built-in Mid$ function. The Mid$ function accepts three arguments: *string*, *start*, and *length*, which are used to return a specified number of characters from the string. The *string* argument represents the string from which you want to extract a subset of characters. The *start* argument specifies the character position in the string at which to start extracting characters. The *length* argument indicates the number of characters to extract.

In the preceding Mid$ function, Visual Basic extracts from the string value represented by sFileName, or "C:\Temp\Test.txt", one character, starting from the position i. The value of i is set by the For...Next loop.

8 After the Mid$ function, add the following If...Then condition block:

```
If sChar = "\" Then
End If
```

The If...Then condition block indicates that if the string sChar equals a backslash, the statements within the block run.

9 Within the If...Then condition block, add the following two lines:

```
GetPath = Left$(sFileName, i - 1)
Exit For
```

The Visual Basic function Left$ is similar to the Mid$ function, except that it accepts only two arguments: *string* and *length*. The Left$ function extracts the number of characters specified by the length argument, starting at the left end of the string.

When the If...Then condition block is entered, you assign to the GetPath function the pathname (the pathname is a subset of the filename previously passed to the GetPath function), and then the For...Next loop exits.

10 Place the cursor in the ParseFileName procedure and press F5.

A message box with the string value "C:\Temp" is displayed. The GetPath function iterates through the specified filename string, evaluating each character in the filename string, starting from the right-most character and working backward. When it finds a character equal to a backslash, it extracts the characters to the left of the backslash in the filename string, which indicates the pathname. The pathname is assigned to GetPath, and the result of GetPath is then displayed in a message box.

 TIP If you want to extract only the portion of the filename without the path in the string "C:\Temp\Test.txt", you can change the line with the Left$ function to the following: `GetPath = Right$(sFileName, Len(sFileName) - i)`. The Right$ function is similar to the Left$ function, but extracts the number of characters specified by the length argument, starting at the right end of the string. Notice also that functions can be nested inside other functions. In this case, the result of Len is an argument to the Right$ function.

Debugging Your Code

Debugging is a common task that all developers must learn. When you are debugging, a number of tools can be used to help track down problems within the logic of the written code. The Visual Basic Editor provides developers with a number of debugging tools normally found only in advanced development environments such as Microsoft Visual C++.

Breakpoints

When Visual Basic runs the code you have written, you can break execution at a specific line of code so that you can evaluate the current state of variables. When you press F5 to run your code, or select a menu item or toolbar button that calls a specific macro, Visual Basic is in run mode because it is running code. If you add a breakpoint at a specific line of code, Visual Basic changes to break mode. While in break mode, you can do one of three things: stop execution, continue execution, or step through your code line by line. Stepping through code allows you to evaluate variables used in your code and see the exact path of code execution that Visual Basic is following.

Set breakpoints in code

1   In the ParseFileName procedure, place the cursor in the line `MsgBox GetPath("C:\Temp\Test.txt")` and press F9.

The F9 key is a keyboard shortcut to clicking Toggle Breakpoint on the Debug menu in the Visual Basic Editor. The line is now highlighted in dark red and indicates that when Visual Basic runs this line of code, break mode will be entered. You remove this breakpoint by placing the cursor within the line of code and pressing F9 again, or by clicking the dot in the left margin next to the line of code.

Click the dot to toggle the breakpoint.

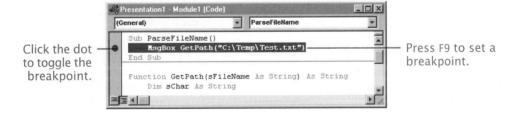

Press F9 to set a breakpoint.

2   With a breakpoint set for the MsgBox statement, and with the cursor placed in the ParseFileName procedure, press F5.

69

Visual Basic will start code execution by entering the ParseFileName procedure and break at the first line within the procedure. In break mode, the line that Visual Basic will run next is highlighted.

The text in the title bar of the Visual Basic Editor indicates that the Visual Basic code execution for the specified project is in break mode.

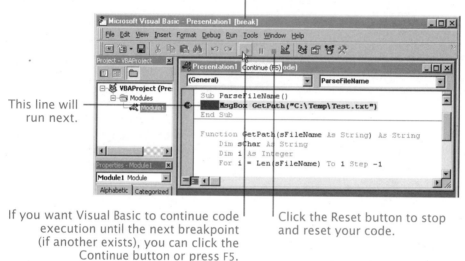

This line will run next.

If you want Visual Basic to continue code execution until the next breakpoint (if another exists), you can click the Continue button or press F5.

Click the Reset button to stop and reset your code.

3   Press F8 several times to step through the code.

The F8 key is a shortcut to clicking Step Into on the Debug menu. As you'll see below, stepping through code by pressing F8 will allow you to examine the values of variables and see the exact path Visual Basic code execution will take. You can press F5 anytime to continue code execution until the next breakpoint, if another exists. If you want to stop code execution while in break mode, click the Reset button (two buttons to the right of Continue) or click Reset on the Run menu in the Visual Basic Editor.

 TIP   If you do not add a breakpoint anywhere in your code, you can start code execution in break mode by placing the cursor in the procedure you want to run and pressing F8. Visual Basic automatically highlights the first line of the procedure containing the cursor and is in break mode.

4   Press F5 to finish running the macro. Click OK to close the message box.

Data Tips Window

As you step through your code, there are a number of ways you can track the value of a variable. However, the easiest way is to place the cursor over the variable in question when Visual Basic is in break mode. When you place the cursor over a variable in break mode, the Visual Basic Editor will display a tip window with the current value of the variable, object property, or function. The Data Tips window is similar to the ToolTip displayed when the cursor is over a toolbar button.

Display Data Tips

1   With the same breakpoint set, place the cursor in the ParseFileName procedure and press F5 to start running the code.

2   Step through the code by pressing F8 until code execution reaches the If...Then condition block.

3   Place the cursor over the variable sChar in the line If sChar = "\" Then.

The Data Tips window is displayed showing the current value of sChar, which is the letter "t". The letter "t" is the last character in the string "C:\Temp\Test.txt" and is the first character to which sChar is assigned.

If the Data Tips window is not displayed, click Options on the Tools menu in the Visual Basic Editor. In the Editor tab in the Options dialog box, select the Auto Data Tips check box and click OK.

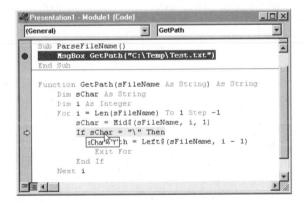

4   Continue pressing F8 to step through the code, and each time the For...Next loop reaches the If...Then condition block, display the Data Tips window by placing the cursor over the variable sChar.

5   Press F5 to finish running the macro. Click OK to close the message box.

The Visual Basic Editor also provides three other windows in which you can display the current value of variables. They are the Watch, Locals, and Immediate windows.

Watch Window

You can select a variable in a code module and drag it to the Watch window, where its contents are automatically updated each time the value changes during code execution.

Add Watch variables

1   If the Watch window is not visible, click Watch Window on the View menu in the Visual Basic Editor.

2   Double-click the variable sChar in the code module. (You can select any of the three occurrences of sChar.)

3   Drag the selected variable name to the Watch window.

You can also add variables to the Watch window by selecting the variable in code, clicking Add Watch on the Debug menu, and clicking OK.

4   Select the variable i in the code module and drag it to the Watch window.

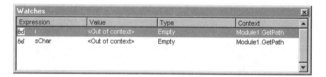

The "out of context" message in the Value column in the Watch window indicates that the corresponding variable has not yet been used within the currently running module. Once a variable has been referenced within the currently running module, the Value column displays the current value assigned to that variable. With a variable that has not yet been declared (either by assigning a value to it or by explicitly creating it with the Dim statement), the third column, Type, displays the notation "Empty." When Visual Basic encounters a statement that declares the variable, the appropriate data type (such as Integer, String, Single, or Long) is displayed.

The fourth column in the Watch window indicates context, which defines the scope of the variables. The variables sChar and i are declared at the procedure level, within the GetPath function. The context of each variable in the Watch window is listed as Module1.GetPath. Module1 represents the name of the code module containing the function GetPath.

5   Step through your code by placing the cursor within the ParseFileName procedure and pressing F8 several times.

As you step through your code, the values of the variables sChar and i are updated in the Watch window. The Watch window allows you to monitor the values of as many variables as you choose. The value of i will be set in the first line of the For…Next loop, and sChar will be set in the next line.

6   Press F5 to finish running the macro. Click OK to close the message box.

Locals Window

The Locals window is very similar to the Watch window. However, you do not need to add the variables to be watched. By default, the Locals window automatically displays the values of all declared variables in the current procedure.

Observe the values of local variables

1   If the Locals window is not visible, then on the View menu in the Visual Basic Editor, click Locals Window.

2   Place the cursor in the ParseFileName procedure.

3   Press F8 several times to step through your code again, until you reach the end of the first iteration through the For…Next loop in the GetPath function.

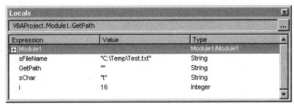

If the Locals window or any of the Editor windows isn't large enough to display needed information, move or resize it as you would any other window.

The values of all variables used in the GetPath function are displayed in the Locals window, including sFileName, which was passed to the GetPath function, and the value of GetPath itself. If any module-level variables existed, you could click the plus sign (+) beside the Module1 item in the Expression list to display the value of any module-level variables.

4   Press F5 to finish running the macro. Click OK to close the message box.

Immediate Window

The third window provided by the Visual Basic Editor as a tool for debugging is the Immediate window. The Immediate window is more versatile than the Data Tips, Watch, or Locals window. You can either explicitly "print" a value of a variable to the Immediate window, or you can type or paste a line of code into the window, press ENTER to run the code, and observe the results.

Print to the Immediate window

1 If the Immediate window is not visible, then on the View menu in the Visual Basic Editor, click Immediate Window.

2 In the Code window, in the GetPath function, add the following line below the line that sets the value of the variable sChar (sChar = Mid$(sFileName, i, 1)):

```
Debug.Print sChar
```

The Debug.Print method accepts one argument, which is the variable or value you want to print to the Immediate window. In this case, you will print the value of sChar to the Immediate window.

3 Place the cursor in the ParseFileName procedure and press F8 several times until the procedure ends.

The value of the variable sChar is printed to the Immediate window during each iteration through the For...Next loop.

Execute a line of code in the Immediate window

1 Step through your code, starting within the ParseFileName procedure, until you reach the line setting the value of sChar in the GetPath function.

2 Click in the bottom of the Immediate window, type **Print i**, and press ENTER.

The value of i will be printed below the line you typed. You can also determine the value of any property of any object defined within the current scope of code execution.

3 Exit your application. You may save changes if you want, but you do not need these procedures in other lessons.

 TIP In the Print statement in the preceding step-by-step example, you can replace the word "Print" with a question mark (?) so the line appears as ?i. The question mark is a shortcut to the word "Print" in the Immediate window.

Lesson Summary

To	Do this
Open a new module in which you can type Visual Basic code	In the Visual Basic Editor, on the Insert menu, click Module. This opens the Code window.
Create a Visual Basic procedure	In the Code window, type **Sub** followed by the procedure name and press ENTER.
Add comments to code	Type a single quotation mark (') followed by the comment, either on a line by itself or at the end of a line of Visual Basic code.
Declare a variable to contain a specific type of data	At the beginning of a procedure or module, type **Dim**, the variable name, **As**, and the data type. For example: `Dim iCount As Integer`
Have your Visual Basic application run certain code based on a condition	Use an If...Then...Else or Select Case statement.
Declare the scope of a variable	For procedure-level variables, declare the variable within the procedure. For module-level variables, declare the variable at the top of the module. For public variables, declare the variable at the top of the module using the keyword Public.
Repeat the same block of code several times	Use a For...Next, Do...Loop, or similar loop structure.
Determine the length of a string variable	Use the Len function.
Retrieve characters from a string variable	Use the Mid$, Left$, or Right$ function.
Have your code pause at a particular place	Set a breakpoint by placing the cursor in the line of code and pressing F9; or click Toggle Breakpoint on the Debug menu.
Determine the value of a variable while in break mode	Place the cursor over the variable name in the Code window (displays the Data Tips window); or drag the variable name to the Watch window; or display the Locals window; or in the Immediate window, type **Print**, the variable name, and press ENTER.
Run a line of code immediately	Type the code in the Immediate window and press ENTER.

For online information about	Ask the Assistant for help, using the words
Modules	"Modules"
Working in the Code window	"Code window"
Commenting your code	"Comments" or "Rem statement" (You didn't use the Rem statement in this lesson; however, you may find the information helpful.)
Declaring variables or constants	"Declaring"
A complete list of data types	"Data type summary"
The scope of a variable or procedure	"Scope"
Making decisions or looping through code	"If then else"
Data Tips, Watch, Locals, or Immediate window	"Data Tips window," "Watch window," "Locals window," or "Immediate window"
Stepping through your code	"Trace code execution"

Preview of the Next Lesson

In the next lesson, you will learn how to create custom dialog boxes, use ActiveX controls in your dialog boxes and Microsoft Office documents, and customize the Visual Basic Toolbox.

ActiveX Controls and UserForms

Estimated time
50 min.

In this lesson you will learn how to:

- Create custom dialog boxes.
- Use ActiveX controls in your dialog boxes and Microsoft Office documents.
- Work with list and tabbed dialog boxes.

Whether you're building a house, a car, a desk, or a computer, construction generally involves the combination of a number of components to form a functional product. Some components may need to be custom built if nothing currently exists that suits the specific project. Builders, however, commonly use available components that they acquire from vendors and incorporate into their own product, because it is generally more efficient to apply the efforts of others in their areas of expertise and to focus on the task at hand.

In today's Visual Basic application development environment for Microsoft Windows, ActiveX controls represent building blocks for you to use and from which to derive benefits. ActiveX controls come in a variety of sizes and functionality, but they all are easily integrated into your own programs. In the end, you'll find that ActiveX controls allow for a more interactive and gratifying user experience with an application or document.

You'll find ActiveX controls applied in two places in Microsoft Office. The first is on a custom form, or dialog box, that you can create in the Visual Basic Editor, in Microsoft Access, or in Microsoft Outlook. In the Visual Basic Editor, a custom form is called a *UserForm*, and that is what you will learn about in this lesson. The second place you use ActiveX controls is directly in your Microsoft Office documents, such as a Word document, Excel worksheet, or PowerPoint slide.

Constructing Custom UserForms

UserForms are the "drawing pad" upon which you design custom dialog boxes. In most cases throughout Microsoft Office, built-in dialog boxes are reproducible using Visual Basic UserForms. The elements within a UserForm are ActiveX controls. By adding ActiveX controls to a UserForm, you can ask for user input or display information.

Create a UserForm

1   Start Microsoft Excel. On the Tools menu, point to Macro, and then click Visual Basic Editor on the submenu.

2   In the Editor, on the Insert menu, click UserForm.

A UserForm is a "drawing pad" upon which you design a custom dialog box.

The components of your custom dialog box come from the Visual Basic Toolbox.

The Toolbox contains a graphical list of ActiveX controls that you can add to a UserForm. Move the cursor over each control to learn its name. When you create a UserForm, a default set of ActiveX controls is listed. You can easily add more ActiveX controls to the list, which you will learn to do later in this lesson.

CommandButton control

3 In the Toolbox, click the CommandButton control.

4 On the UserForm, drag the control to the size you want, and then drag it to the position you want. Use the following illustration as a guide:

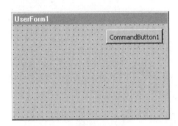

TextBox control

5 In the Toolbox, click the TextBox control.

6 On the UserForm, drag the control to the size you want, and then drag it to the position you want. Use the following illustration as a guide:

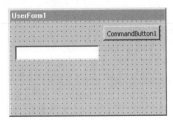

Label control

7 Add one more CommandButton control and a Label control to the UserForm. Again, you can use the following illustration as a guide:

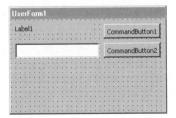

If you have to add several controls to a UserForm, using one of the shortcut methods may help you work faster. The shortcut methods create controls in a default size, but you can use the size handles to resize them later. In Excel, you can use any of the following methods to add controls from the Toolbox to a UserForm:

■ Click a control in the Toolbox, and then click in the UserForm. The control appears where you click.

■ Drag a control from the Toolbox to the UserForm. The control appears where the mouse pointer is when you release the mouse button.

■ Double-click a control in the Toolbox, and then click in the UserForm once for each control you want to create. Each control appears where you click.

Set the properties of controls

Before you can display your controls in a dialog box and put them to use, you must set their properties. Properties determine the captions of controls, the values they can accept or display, when they are available, and so on.

1   On the View menu, click Properties Window; or press F4 as a shortcut.

    In the Properties Window, the properties of the selected control are listed in the left column and the corresponding property values are listed in the right column.

When the Properties window is open, you can also display the properties of a control by clicking the control.

2   Near the top of the Properties window, select CommandButton1 from the Object drop-down list.

3   Click the Alphabetic tab.

4   In the left column of the Properties window, select the Name property (shown in parentheses).

5   Type **cmdOK** and press ENTER.

6   Repeat steps 2 through 5 for CommandButton2. But this time, select CommandButton2 from the Object drop-down list and type **cmdCancel** as the value of the Name property.

7   Continue setting the other properties for all the controls using the values shown in the following table.

    The Object drop-down list in the Properties window will show the new names for CommandButton1 and CommandButton2 (cmdOK and cmdCancel, respectively).

Control	Property	Value
CommandButton1	Name	cmdOK
CommandButton2	Name	cmdCancel
CommandButton1	Caption	OK
CommandButton2	Caption	Cancel
CommandButton2	Cancel	True
Label1	Name	lblMyLabel
Label1	Caption	(Enter text and click OK.)
TextBox1	Name	txtInput

 NOTE When you add controls to a UserForm, Visual Basic automatically assigns a unique name to the control. The default name for a given control is the type of control it is, such as a label or command button, followed by a number; the number is incremented each time you add a new control of the same type. For example, after you add the first command button, the default name of the next command button is CommandButton2. If you delete or add more controls than the step-by-step examples in this lesson tell you to do, the names of your controls will be different. Make sure that you set the properties of the correct control.

8 Click any blank area on the UserForm so that the UserForm's properties are listed in the Properties window. Then in the Properties window, type the value **Text Input** for the Caption property.

9 Resize and move the controls on the UserForm just as you would a drawing shape on a document, worksheet, or slide. The following illustration shows you what the completed dialog box will look like when displayed in Excel. Use it as a guide to moving and resizing the controls on your UserForm.

You just added four controls to your UserForm: two CommandButton controls, a TextBox control, and a Label control. You'll use these controls to gather user input and place text in a cell on a Microsoft Excel worksheet.

Gather user input

*If your
UserForm is
behind the Code
window, display
it by clicking
UserForm1
(UserForm) on
the Window
menu.*

1   Double-click the cmdOK command button. When the Code window opens, type the following program statements between the `Private Sub cmdOK_Click` and `End Sub` statements:

```
If txtInput.TextLength > 0 Then
    ActiveSheet.Cells(1, 1).Value = txtInput.Text
    Unload UserForm1
Else
    MsgBox "Please enter some text.", vbCritical
End If
```

The TextLength property of the TextBox control returns the number of characters of the text string in the TextBox control. If text was entered (indicated by a TextLength greater than 0), the text that was entered in the TextBox control is inserted into cell A1 in the active worksheet. Thereafter, the UserForm is closed, or unloaded, by calling the Unload function and passing to it the name of the UserForm (UserForm1 in this case) as the argument. If the value of TextLength is 0, no text was entered and a message box is displayed asking the user to enter some text.

2   Double-click the cmdCancel command button and type the following program statement in the Code window between the `Private Sub cmdCancel_Click` and `End Sub` statements:

```
Unload Me
```

When this button is activated (by being clicked), the UserForm is unloaded. To unload the UserForm, the Unload statement is called and the name of the UserForm, in this case the keyword Me (which represents the UserForm where the code and control exist), is passed as the argument. It is a common Microsoft Windows design not to run any actions other than closing the dialog box when a Cancel command button is pressed.

3   In the Editor, if the Project Explorer window is not open, on the View menu, click Project Explorer.

4   In the Project Explorer window, double-click UserForm1 to activate the window containing the UserForm.

5   On the Standard toolbar in the Visual Basic Editor, click the Run Sub/UserForm button.

*Run Sub/
UserForm*

The Text Input program runs in Microsoft Excel.

6 Without entering text in the text box, click OK.

A message box is displayed asking you to enter some text.

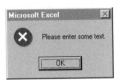

7 Click OK to close the message box.

8 To end the program, click Cancel, or enter text in the text box and click OK.

The code behind the Cancel button in the cmdCancel_Click event procedure has the code `Unload Me`, which was added in step 2. Thus, clicking the cmdCancel control unloads the UserForm and ends your program. You can also end the program by pressing ESC. By setting the Cancel property of the cmdCancel control to True, as you did earlier in the "Set the properties of controls" procedure, pressing ESC when the UserForm is active has the same effect as clicking the cmdCancel control. This is the common Windows behavior.

Save

9 Click the Save button and save the workbook as MyLesson4 in the Lesson 4 subfolder of the Office VBA Practice folder.

This was a simple example of using ActiveX controls on your UserForm. In the next few procedures, we will create a number of UserForms that use many of the ActiveX controls displayed in the Toolbox. These examples also interact more with Excel to retrieve data and display it in a dialog box.

Using the Controls in the Toolbox

Microsoft Office provides a set of ActiveX controls in the Visual Basic Editor Toolbox. However, chances are you'll have other ActiveX controls registered on your system that you also may want to use in a Visual Basic UserForm.

Add a control to the Toolbox

These steps work with Word and PowerPoint in exactly the same way.

1 In the Editor, click Insert, and then click UserForm to insert a new UserForm.

2   On the Tools menu, click Additional Controls.

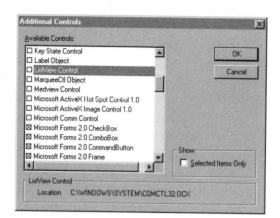

The Additional Controls dialog box displays a list of the registered ActiveX controls available on your system. (Your list may be different.)

3   Just to observe the process, select any item on the list and click OK.

An icon representing the ActiveX control you selected appears in the Toolbox.

4   Click the newly added ActiveX control in the Toolbox and drag the control to the UserForm.

5   While the control is selected, press F1 to get more information about the control. (Help is not available for all controls.) You can also right-click the control and then click Properties on the shortcut menu. Scroll through the properties to learn about the control.

6   You may want to remove the control from the Toolbox. To remove it, right-click the control and then click Delete <control name> on the shortcut menu.

Hundreds of ActiveX controls are currently available through third-party vendors and on the Internet. If you require functionality in your program that you cannot access from the current list of controls available on your machine, you can search for and purchase ActiveX controls from other developers.

NOTE   The Toolbox in the Visual Basic Editor adjusts to accommodate the number of controls in it. When you add controls to the Toolbox, you can resize the dialog box to display all available controls.

Creating List Dialog Boxes

When you start creating Visual Basic projects and features for Microsoft Office, you'll often come across scenarios in which you'll want to position your ActiveX controls on your UserForm to closely resemble existing dialog boxes in Word, Excel, PowerPoint, Access, or Outlook. You'll also find many dialog boxes in Word, Excel, and PowerPoint that share a set of controls and layout, although the tasks of the various dialog boxes may be very different.

Move items between two list boxes

A common dialog box layout is to have two ListBox controls with Add, Remove, and Remove All command button controls in between. You see this layout when you are asked to select items from one full list in order to create a subset of items. The Define Custom Show dialog box in Microsoft PowerPoint is an example of this layout, which you'll create below in Microsoft Excel.

1   Without exiting Excel, start PowerPoint. In the opening PowerPoint dialog box, select Blank Presentation and click OK. In the New Slide dialog box, select any AutoLayout and click OK.

2   On the Slide Show menu, click Custom Shows, and then click the New button.

You're going to create a dialog box in Excel that is similar to the Define Custom Show dialog box.

3   Click Cancel, click Close, and then exit PowerPoint without saving changes.

4   In the Visual Basic Editor of Excel, on the Insert menu, click UserForm.

5   In the Toolbox, click the ListBox control and drag the control to the left side of the UserForm.

6   Click the ListBox control again and drag the control to the right side of the UserForm.

7   Move and size the controls using the following illustration as a guide:

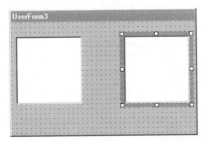

8   Add two CommandButton controls, placing the first control between the two list boxes and the second one just below the first.

85

9 Add two more CommandButton controls, placing them below the second list box, ListBox2. (The fourth command button is to the right of the third.) Use the following illustration as a guide:

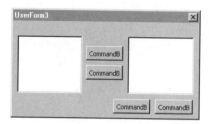

To enter property values more efficiently, click the control on the UserForm before typing its values in the Properties window.

10 In the Properties window, set the following values. You may need to resize the window to see the complete control names.

Control	Property	Value
CommandButton1	Name	cmdAdd
CommandButton1	Caption	Add
CommandButton2	Name	cmdRemove
CommandButton2	Caption	Remove
CommandButton3	Name	cmdOK
CommandButton3	Caption	OK
CommandButton4	Name	cmdCancel
CommandButton4	Cancel	True
CommandButton4	Caption	Cancel
ListBox1	Name	lstEmployees
ListBox2	Name	lstAttendees

 TIP It is common practice when working with controls in Visual Basic code to add a three-letter prefix to the name given to ActiveX controls. The prefix provides an indication of what type of control is being referenced in code. For the controls listed in the Toolbox of the Visual Basic Editor, the following prefixes should be used: *chk* for check box, *cbo* for combo box, *cmd* for command button, *img* for image, *lbl* for label, *lst* for list box, *mpg* for multipage, *opt* for option button, *scb* for scroll bar, *spn* for spin button, *txt* for textbox, and *tgl* for toggle button.

11 Double-click the cmdAdd command button and type the following statements in the Code window between the `Private Sub cmdAdd_Click` and `End Sub` statements:

```
Dim i As Integer
For i = 0 To lstEmployees.ListCount - 1
    If lstEmployees.Selected(i) = True Then
        lstAttendees.AddItem _
            lstEmployees.List(i)
        lstEmployees.RemoveItem i
        lstEmployees.Selected(i) = False
    End If
Next i
```

The For...Next loop, discussed in Lesson 3, iterates through each item in the lstEmployees list box and checks to see whether the item is selected. If the item is selected, it is added to the lstAttendees list box and removed from the lstEmployees list box. The Selected property of the lstEmployees list box control returns a Boolean value indicating whether the item is selected.

If your UserForm is behind the Code window, display it by clicking UserForm3 (UserForm) on the Window menu.

12 Double-click the cmdRemove command button and type the following program statements in the Code window between the `Private Sub cmdRemove_Click` and `End Sub` statements:

```
Dim i As Integer
For i = 0 To lstAttendees.ListCount - 1
    If lstAttendees.Selected(i) = True Then
        lstEmployees.AddItem lstAttendees.List(i)
        lstAttendees.RemoveItem i
    End If
Next i
```

The structure and sequence of this code segment is exactly the same as the code assigned to the cmdAdd command button, but it moves items in the opposite direction (that is, from the lstAttendees list box to the lstEmployees list box).

13 Double-click any blank area on the UserForm, select Initialize from the Procedure drop-down list in the Code window (the list on the right), and type the following program statements in the Code window between the `Private Sub UserForm_Initialize` and `End Sub` statements:

```
With lstEmployees
    .AddItem "Dave"
    .AddItem "Rob"
    .AddItem "Greg"
    .AddItem "Christina"
    .AddItem "Mark"
End With
```

87

When you add the Employees list box to the UserForm, it does not contain any items in the list. The With...End block adds five items to fill the list box when the UserForm is first initialized, just before it is displayed on the screen. In an actual program, the data would probably be loaded from a file stored on disk.

14 Double-click the cmdOK and cmdCancel command buttons and type **Unload Me** between the Sub and End Sub statements.

Now you are ready to go.

15 Run the dialog box by pressing F5, and click each button to reveal its functionality.

When you click the Add button, selected items in the left list box are removed and added to the right list box. The opposite happens when you click the Remove button.

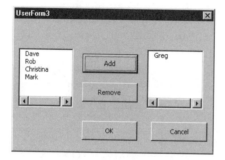

16 Click the Save button to save your work.

Save

Fill multiple-column list boxes

Instead of adding items to a list box through code, programmers commonly provide a data source to automatically fill the items in list boxes on a UserForm. Microsoft Excel is closely integrated with the ListBox control for providing data used to fill the list box items. In the next example, you will take a named cell range on a Microsoft Excel worksheet and use it to fill a multiple-column list box.

1 In the Visual Basic Editor, on the Insert menu, click UserForm.

2 In the Toolbox, click the ListBox control and drag the control to the UserForm, placing it in the upper-left corner of the form.

3 Add two CommandButton controls, placing them on the lower-right side of the UserForm.

4 In the Properties window, set the following values:

Control	Property	Value
CommandButton1	Name	cmdOK
CommandButton1	Caption	OK
CommandButton2	Name	cmdCancel
CommandButton2	Cancel	True
CommandButton2	Caption	Cancel
UserForm4 (or the name of the current UserForm)	Name	frmMyForm
UserForm4	Caption	Employee List

5 Double-click the cmdOK and cmdCancel command buttons and type **Unload Me** between the Sub and End Sub statements.

If your UserForm is behind the Code window, display it by clicking frmMyForm (UserForm) on the Window menu.

6 Double-click any blank area on the UserForm. From the Procedure drop-down list in the Code window, select Initialize, and then type the following program statements in the Code window between the Sub and End Sub statements:

```
With ListBox1
    .RowSource = "a2:c7"
    .ColumnHeads = True
    .ColumnCount = 3
    .BoundColumn = 1
End With
```

RowSource identifies the source cells from which your list box gets its data. The other lines specify headings, the number of columns, and the column from which to use data in your code (if you were going to use it).

7 In the Microsoft Excel application window, on any worksheet, type the following entries in cells A1 to C7:

	A	B	C	D
1	Email	First Name	Area	
2	DaveB	Dave	Engineering	
3	Robert	Rob	Computers	
4	Gregory	Greg	Entertainment	
5	Brian	Brian	Engineering	
6	Angelo	Angelo	Health & Safety	
7	Mark	Mark	Engineering	

Note that the entries in cells A1, B1, and C1 are headers for each column.

8 Switch to the Visual Basic Editor.

9   Run the UserForm by pressing F5.

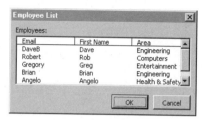

The cell entries from each row of the worksheet are now used to fill the list box. These types of list boxes are useful when you want to fill each row in a list box with items that contain different types of information. You may need to move or resize your controls so that they match the illustration.

Save

10   Click OK to close the form, move or resize controls as necessary, and then click the Save button to save your changes.

Creating Tabbed Dialog Boxes

Tabbed dialog boxes are now very common in Microsoft Windows, and their use has spread throughout Microsoft Office. The Toolbox in the Visual Basic Editor contains a tool with which you can easily create tabbed dialog boxes: the MultiPage control.

Add tabs to a UserForm

1   In the Visual Basic Editor, insert a new UserForm.

2   In the Toolbox, click the MultiPage control and drag the control to the UserForm.

MultiPage
control

3   Add two CommandButton controls to the UserForm so that the UserForm looks like the following illustration:

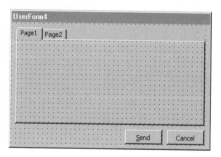

4 Set the properties of the command buttons so that they have appropriate names and captions to match the preceding illustration.

On the first page of the MultiPage control, you'll copy the controls from the UserForm you created in the step-by-step example "Move items between two list boxes" earlier in this lesson. (That form was named UserForm3 if you followed the steps sequentially.)

5 In the Project window, double-click UserForm3.

6 Select all of the controls except the cmdOK and cmdCancel command button controls by holding down the CTRL key and clicking the two list boxes and the Add and Remove buttons.

7 In the Editor, on the Edit menu, click Copy to copy the selected controls to the Clipboard.

8 In the Project Explorer window, double-click the name of the UserForm to which you added the MultiPage control.

If you followed all steps in this lesson sequentially, the name of the UserForm is UserForm4.

9 Select the MultiPage control and click in the center of the first page (Page1).

This selects the first page.

10 In the Editor, on the Edit menu, click Paste to paste the controls to the first page. Move and size the controls as shown in the illustration.

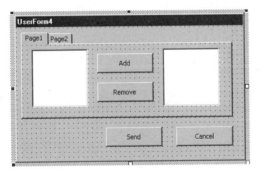

11 In the Project Explorer window, double-click UserForm3 and then double-click a blank area on the form.

12 On the Edit menu, click Select All to select all of the code.

13 On the Edit menu, click Copy.

14 In the Project Explorer window, double-click UserForm4, and then double-click a blank area on the form. If there is any code in the Code window, select it, and press DELETE.

15 On the Edit menu, click Paste.

16 Press F5 to run the dialog box.

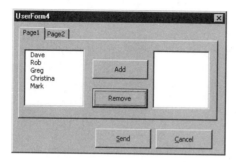

17 Click Cancel to close the box, and then save your changes and close the workbook.

You may also want to experiment by clicking the second tab (Page2) of the MultiPage control and adding any controls you want from the Toolbox.

Examine the fully functional dialog box

In the Lesson4.xls file in the Lesson 4 practice folder, you can examine a fully functional dialog box. For example, the second tab of the MultiPage control contains a number of common controls such as spinners and option buttons. Fully functional code is also provided for each control. In particular, you can look through the code behind UserForm6 in the Lesson 4 practice file. This should give you a good start in creating your own UserForms.

Open

1 In Excel, click the Open button and then change to the Lesson 4 practice folder.

2 Select the Lesson4 workbook, and then click the Open button.

3 Switch to the Visual Basic Editor.

4 Run the dialog box and examine the code that makes it work.

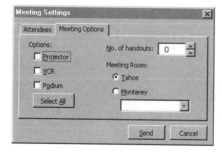

The controls and code for this dialog box are contained in the UserForm6 UserForm.

5 Exit Excel without saving changes.

Incorporating ActiveX Controls into Your Documents

Like a drawing shape in a Microsoft Word document, Excel worksheet, or PowerPoint slide, you simply drag and drop an ActiveX control into your document and modify properties of the control. However, most ActiveX controls provide more functionality than a simple graphic. ActiveX controls are programmable components running inside your document. They may be passive controls that merely display text, like a Label control, or they may be active, like the ActiveMovie control that runs a specified movie file. They also may be interactive, allowing users to enter or extract information from the control, like a TextBox control.

Display the Control Toolbox for an Office application

More Controls

➤ To display the Control Toolbox toolbar in Word, Excel, or PowerPoint, right-click any toolbar and select Control Toolbox on the shortcut menu.

Microsoft Office provides the set of ActiveX controls most commonly found in UserForms. This list includes Check Box, Text Box, Command Button, Option Button, List Box, Combo Box, Toggle Button, Spin Button, and Scroll Bar. However, it is possible to add other ActiveX controls. The More Controls button in the Control Toolbox provides a drop-down list of registered controls on your computer.

IMPORTANT Hundreds of ActiveX controls are now available through the Internet, magazines, computer stores, and mail order. Most ActiveX controls developed recently, specifically with the Internet and fast download times in mind, do not provide the specific functionality that Microsoft Office requires. You can add these controls to a UserForm in the Visual Basic Editor. But if you try to add many commercially available ActiveX controls directly to a Word document, Excel worksheet, or PowerPoint slide, you'll get an error message.

Switching Between Design Mode and Run Mode

The distinction between design mode and run mode is very important. In design mode, your document or application is in the building state because you can add ActiveX controls and manipulate their properties.

> **NOTE**   You will often see the word *time* instead of *mode*; that is, *design time* and *run time*. The words *time* and *mode* both refer to the same concept.

When your document or application is in run mode, you cannot add ActiveX controls and you cannot change control properties; you only can interact with the ActiveX controls. In this mode, all ActiveX controls in the document are in their "running state." Thus, you'll see command buttons animate (appear as if they are being pressed), list boxes scroll, and check boxes selected or cleared when they are clicked.

In Word and Excel, design mode and run mode are both in the same view; when you click the Design Mode button, the view type does not change. (For example, in Excel, the active worksheet remains in view whether you are in run mode or design mode.) In PowerPoint, however, run mode is called Slide Show and design mode is called Slide View. Slide View is the only view in PowerPoint where ActiveX controls can be added.

When you create a UserForm in the Visual Basic Editor, the UserForm is in design mode. When you press F5 or click Run Macro or Run Sub/UserForm on the Run menu in the Editor, the UserForm is in run mode. In Microsoft Access, the same distinction is made between run mode and design mode as in the Visual Basic Editor.

Switch between design mode and run mode

1   Start Microsoft Word.

2   If the Control Toolbox toolbar is not displayed, right-click any toolbar and then click Control Toolbox on the shortcut menu.

3   Click the Command Button control.

In Word, unlike PowerPoint and Excel, when you click an ActiveX control in the Control Toolbox, the control is automatically added to the document. When you add a control, the Word document automatically shifts into design mode, and the Design Mode button on the Control Toolbox appears pressed. Once pressed, the button becomes the Exit Design Mode button.

4   In the Control Toolbox, click the Exit Design Mode button so that it is not pressed.

Exit Design Mode

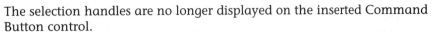

The selection handles are no longer displayed on the inserted Command Button control.

5 You can now click the button, causing it to look pressed, or animated.

6 Exit Word without saving changes.

 NOTE There is no Design Mode or Exit Design Mode button on the Control Toolbox in Microsoft PowerPoint. To set your presentation in run mode, click View Show on the Slide Show menu.

Lesson Summary

To	Do this
Create a UserForm	In the Visual Basic Editor, on the Insert menu, click UserForm.
Add a control from the Toolbox to a UserForm	In the Toolbox, click the control, and then on the UserForm drag the control to the size you want.
Set the value of a property for a control on a UserForm	In the Properties window, select the control from the Object drop-down list, click the property name in the left column, and type or select a value in the right column.
Create code for an event procedure of a control on a UserForm	Double-click the control, and then in the Code window, select a procedure from the Procedure drop-down list, and type the code between the Sub and End Sub statements.
Add controls to the Toolbox	In the Editor, on the Tools menu, click Additional Controls, select the controls you want to add from the Available Controls list, and click OK.
Add tabs to a UserForm	In the Toolbox, click the MultiPage control and drag it to the UserForm.
Display the Control Toolbox in Word, Excel, or PowerPoint	Right-click any toolbar, and then click Control Toolbox on the shortcut menu.
Add an ActiveX control to a document, worksheet, or slide	In the Control Toolbox, click the control, and then click in the document, worksheet, or slide. (In Word, clicking the control inserts it into the document automatically.)

Lesson Summary, *continued*

To	Do this
Switching between design mode and run mode in Word and Excel	Click the Design Mode or Exit Design Mode button.
Switching to run mode in PowerPoint	On the Slide Show menu, click View Show.

For online information about	Ask the Assistant for help, using the words
UserForms	"UserForms"
Using the Toolbox	"Toolbox"
Using the Properties window	"Properties window"
Adding additional controls to the Toolbox	"Additional controls"
Adding pages to the Toolbox	"Toolbox pages"
Tabbed dialog boxes	"MultiPage"
Using ActiveX controls on documents, worksheets, and slides	"ActiveX" (with the Word, Excel, or PowerPoint application window active)

Preview of the Next Lesson

In the next lesson, you will learn how to create a new instance of an application, load an object library, access an application with the GetObject function, and create a link between applications.

Microsoft Office Solutions

Communicating Across Microsoft Office

In this lesson you will learn how to:

- Use Visual Basic code to start an application.
- Load an application's object library.
- Create and return a reference to an application.
- Access an existing application or file.
- Exchange information between applications.

Today many business and educational situations involve interactions between two or more Microsoft Office applications, combining differing forms (such as text, charts, tables, and slides) of the same content to serve a wider range of audiences. The results from a company's sales figures, for example, may be stored in a Microsoft Access database, presented in a detailed report written in Microsoft Word, analyzed with a worksheet in Microsoft Excel, and summarized in a Microsoft PowerPoint presentation. To take advantage of the same content using different Microsoft Office applications, you first need to establish communication between them.

For a person in one city to communicate with a person in another, some sort of connection must first be established. People usually do so through a telephone connection, either using a telephone handset or computer with a modem. In Visual Basic for Applications, the connection made between two applications is commonly established by using the Visual Basic functions CreateObject or GetObject, or by using the keyword New in a declaration statement. The two functions or the keyword New establishes a communication link between any two Office applications, allowing you to use the tools to manipulate and share document content from one application from within another.

In order to work with an application other than the one that contains your Visual Basic code, you must first set an object variable so that it represents the application you want to use. To do this, you can either create the new application from scratch (if the object does not currently exist) or access an existing object (one that is currently running).

Starting Fresh with CreateObject

All applications in Microsoft Office provide at least one type of object you can create using the CreateObject function: the Application object. However, both Word and Excel provide other object types you can create using the CreateObject function. The accompanying table lists the Microsoft Office objects types that you can create.

Application	Object type	Class
Access	Application	Access.Application
Excel	Application	Excel.Application
Excel	Worksheet	Excel.Sheet
Excel	Chart	Excel.Chart
Outlook	Application	Outlook.Application
PowerPoint	Application	PowerPoint.Application
Word	Application	Word.Application
Word	Document	Word.Document

When you create an Excel worksheet or chart, you also implicitly create a new instance of the Excel application. The same holds true when you create a Word document, in which case a new instance of the Word application is created.

CreateObject(*ApplicationName.ObjectType*) is the syntax for the CreateObject function. *ApplicationName* is the name of the application providing the object you want to create, and *ObjectType* is the type or class of object to create.

Create a new instance of an object

To create an object for use with Visual Basic for Applications, you assign the object returned by CreateObject to an object variable.

1   Start Microsoft Excel. On the Tools menu, point to Macro, and then click Visual Basic Editor on the submenu.

2 In the Editor, on the Insert menu, click Module.

3 In the inserted code module, create a new procedure by typing **Sub UsingCreateObject** and pressing ENTER.

4 In the first line of the procedure, add the following line of code:

```
Dim oPPT As Object
```

 TIP As discussed in Lesson 3, a common programming practice is to give variable and constant names a prefix that indicates the object type. The prefix *o* is used generically to denote any type of object variable, but in many cases you will see a prefix that is more specific, such as *app* to denote the Application object.

With this step, you are declaring the variable oPPT as the generic Object type. This lets you use that variable to represent any type of application object that you create (or, in fact, any instance of an even wider range of objects). As you'll see in the next example, you should declare each object variable by using the specific object type whenever possible.

5 After the variable declaration statement, add the following line:

```
Set oPPT = CreateObject("PowerPoint.Application")
```

This assigns to the object variable oPPT the results of the CreateObject function and tells the function what type of object to create (in this case, an instance of the PowerPoint application object). At this point, you can add additional code to create and manipulate the content of a PowerPoint presentation.

6 Add one last line in the procedure:

```
oPPT.Visible = True
```

Each Application object in Microsoft Office provides a Visible property that allows you to display or not display the application window. In many Visual Basic for Applications programming scenarios, you create an Application object first and then, before displaying the application window, manipulate it and any documents you open or create. Once you finish, you then display the application window with the finished document or documents. This technique allows you to make changes without distracting the user of your program.

NOTE When an instance of a Microsoft Word, Excel, PowerPoint, or Outlook application is started using the CreateObject or GetObject function, the application window is not visible; it is not displayed on the screen or on the Windows taskbar. On the other hand, a new instance of Microsoft Access always starts as visible.

7 Place the cursor in the procedure and press F5.

When the code in this procedure runs in Excel, the Microsoft PowerPoint application starts and the application window is displayed on the screen. Once an object is created, it can be referenced in code by using the object variable you declared, and you can use any of the properties and methods within the application's object library.

8 Exit PowerPoint without saving changes.

Visual Basic Syntax Checking

When you press F5 to run your code, Visual Basic first conducts a process called *compiling*, where your program is translated into machine language. During this process, Visual Basic checks to see whether a specific object provides the properties and methods you specified in code. Visual Basic also checks whether you've assigned valid values to variables that are declared as a particular type.

If your code does not contain syntax errors and is successfully compiled, Visual Basic knows what your variables are. If you declare a variable as a specific object type that belongs to an application other than the one in which you are writing your code, you must first make a reference to the other application's object library (demonstrated in the following step-by-step example). Referencing an object library allows Visual Basic to find all the information about an object, its methods, and its properties when Visual Basic compiles your code.

Replacing CreateObject with Strongly Typed Variables and the Keyword New

When you declare variables as type Object, as you did in step 4 of the preceding step-by-step example, Visual Basic does not know what the exact type of object is until the first time it tries to create the object. There are benefits to declaring objects as the generic Object type, but more often you want to declare an object variable as the specific type of object that it represents.

Using Strongly Typed Variables

When you declare an object variable as a specific type, your code runs faster and the Visual Basic Editor can provide assistance to reduce the number of errors in your code. One way the Editor can do this is with the Auto List feature, which displays all of the properties and methods supported by the object so that you can see easily whether the option you are trying to use actually exists. However, you must take an additional step before using the Auto List feature with objects that are not part of the application containing your Visual Basic code: you must make sure that the object library containing the object that you want to reference is loaded into the Editor.

Load the PowerPoint Object Library

1 Switch to the Visual Basic Editor of Microsoft Excel.

2 On the Tools menu, click References.

These four object libraries are always referenced by default.

The References dialog box displays a list of every object library currently registered on your system. In addition to the object library for the application containing your Visual Basic code (in this example, Microsoft Excel), four object libraries are always referenced by default:

- Visual Basic for Applications
- Microsoft Office 8.0 Object Library
- OLE Automation
- Microsoft Forms 2.0 Object Library

The items selected in the list of Available References are saved individually for each Visual Basic for Applications project. This means that setting a reference to a particular object library will not create the same reference in every Visual Basic for Applications project you have open.

It's not enough to select the library name in the list. Make sure that the check box is selected before you click OK.

3 Scroll down the list, select the check box next to the Microsoft PowerPoint 8.0 Object Library, and click OK.

You have set a reference to the PowerPoint 8.0 Object Library for your current Visual Basic project. You now also have access to all of the PowerPoint objects, methods, and properties, and when you work with an object variable that is declared as a PowerPoint object type, the Auto List Members drop-down list appears as you enter your Visual Basic code. Plus, when you add a reference to an object library, it appears in the Libraries drop-down list in the Editor's Object Browser, so you can browse through the object model and conduct member searches if necessary. For more information about the Object Browser, see "Learning the Members of the Object Model" in Lesson 2.

4 Create a new procedure by typing **Sub SetReferences** and pressing ENTER.

5 Add the following line:

```
Dim oPPT As PowerPoint.Application
```

Just after you type the word "As" and a space, the Auto List Members drop-down list appears and PowerPoint is listed (scroll through the list or type **pow** to see it). The Auto List Members drop-down list appears again just after you type the period (.) after the word "PowerPoint". Once entered, this line declares the variable oPPT as an Application object of PowerPoint.

 TIP When the Auto List Members drop-down list appears and you type the first few letters of the member name you need, Visual Basic automatically selects an item in the list matching what you type. You can then press TAB to complete your statement with the selected item and close the drop-down list.

---

6 Add the following two lines:

```
Set oPPT = CreateObject ("PowerPoint.Application")
oPPT.Visible = True
```

Just after you type the period (.) after the variable name oPPT, the Auto List Members drop-down list appears displaying a list of the properties and methods belonging to PowerPoint. Thus, when you declare a variable as a specific type, Visual Basic provides you with a list of property and method members belonging to the object. You don't have to remember what properties and methods the object supports because the Auto List Members list always displays all of them.

NOTE The Auto List Members drop-down list also appears when you type the equal sign (=) to set the value of a property. In this case, the Auto List Members drop-down list displays the possible values you can assign to the Visible property, including two additional True values, msoCTrue and msoTrue, which are the numeric values 1 and –1, respectively. You do not need to worry about the uses of the values at this time, and any of the True values (including True itself) makes the window visible.

7   Place the cursor in the procedure and press F5.

When you run this procedure, Visual Basic compiles your project and checks the syntax of your code, ensuring that you have valid values assigned to variables. Once Visual Basic compiles your code, it runs slightly faster than in the case where you did not declare your object variables as a specific type.

8   Exit PowerPoint without saving changes.

Multiple application instances

In all Microsoft Office applications other than PowerPoint, you can create more than one instance of an application. In PowerPoint, if the application is not already running, the Application object created using the CreateObject function starts PowerPoint. If PowerPoint is running, CreateObject returns the same Application object that is currently loaded in memory. For all other Microsoft Office applications, each time you use the CreateObject function, a new instance is created.

Using the Keyword New

Dim, Sub, End, and so on are *keywords*, words recognized as part of the Visual Basic programming language. These keywords are key to your programming efforts because they are the ones that control how Visual Basic interprets your instructions. The keyword New provides an alternative way of creating an instance of an object to that of using the CreateObject function.

When you use the CreateObject function, you must first declare an object variable and then use the Set statement to assign the object instance to the object variable. If you use New when declaring an object variable, you don't have to use the Set statement in conjunction with the CreateObject function to assign the object reference. Once an object is declared in a Dim statement that includes the keyword New, a new instance of the object is created on the first reference to it in code.

NOTE The New keyword can be used to declare only object variables and not any other data type such as String, Integer, and Long.

Create a New application object

1   In the Visual Basic Editor of Excel, in the same code module, add and run the following procedure:

```
Sub UsingKeywordNew()
    Dim oPPT As New PowerPoint.Application
    MsgBox oPPT.Path
End Sub
```

A new instance of the PowerPoint Application object is created using this syntax, but it is not visible. The message box line where you display the path of the PowerPoint application is the first reference to the PowerPoint Application object you declared in the second line.

After the Dim statement, you do not need the statement Set oPPT = CreateObject ("PowerPoint.Application"). The use of the New keyword in the Dim statement indicates that a new instance of the PowerPoint Application object is available but will not load until the first reference is made to it or to one of its members.

2   Click OK to close the message box.

Referencing an Existing Object with GetObject

Two common scenarios occur where you might choose to use the GetObject function. The first is when you want to access an instance of an object that's already loaded, such as an Excel Application object, and the second is when you want to start an application and load an existing file in a single step. If neither one of these two scenarios is applicable, you would instead use the CreateObject function or the New keyword in a declaration statement.

The function GetObject has the syntax GetObject(*pathname, class*). The *pathname* argument specifies the pathname and filename of a file located on your computer or a drive on your network. If the pathname is not included in the file-name, Visual Basic looks in the current folder of the application containing the code that is running the GetObject function. If *pathname* is omitted, the *class* argument is required.

The *class* argument has the same syntax as the CreateObject function: *ApplicationName.ObjectType. ApplicationName* is the name of the application providing the object you want to create, and *ObjectType* is the type or class of object to create. If you don't specify the class but do specify the filename, Visual Basic determines which application to start and which object to activate based on the filename you provide.

Access an existing application

The GetObject function is useful when you want to determine whether an application is already loaded so that you can avoid loading a separate instance and perhaps confusing the user with multiple instances of an application.

1   In Excel, save the default workbook as Book1 in the Lesson 5 subfolder of the Office VBA Practice folder.

    Later, you will load the workbook in Excel by using the GetObject function.

2   Exit Excel and then start PowerPoint.

3   In the opening PowerPoint dialog box, select Blank Presentationand click OK. In the New Slide dialog box, choose any AutoLayout and click OK.

4   On the Tools menu, point to Macro and then click Visual Basic Editor on the submenu.

5   On the Tools menu, click References, select the Microsoft Word 8.0 Object Library from the list, and click OK.

6   On the Insert menu, click Module. In the inserted module, create a new procedure by typing **Sub GetExistingApp** and pressing ENTER.

7   Add the following procedure-level variable declaration to the GetExistingApp procedure:

```
Dim oApp As Word.Application
```

8   After the procedure-level variable declaration, add the following lines within the procedure:

```
On Error Resume Next
Set oApp = GetObject(, "Word.Application")
```

The line `On Error Resume Next` is added before the Set statement to indicate to Visual Basic that if an error occurs when it is running a line of code, it should continue to the next line. If the first argument, *pathname*, preceding the comma in the Set statement above is omitted from the GetObject function, as it is here, the function returns a currently active object of the specified class type. In this case, the class is the Word application. If no object of the specified type exists, an error occurs.

9   Add the following If...Then condition block:

```
If oApp Is Nothing Then
    Set oApp = CreateObject("Word.Application")
End If
```

The Visual Basic keyword Nothing is used with object variables and indicates whether an object variable has been assigned to an actual object in memory. When you declare an object variable, Visual Basic sets it to Nothing until you set it to an object by using the Set statement. The declaration of an object variable as a specific type tells Visual Basic to what type of object that variable can be set. In the preceding If...Then condition, if the object variable oApp was not successfully set in the GetObject function, oApp is still not assigned to a valid object and is set to Nothing instead. This means that an existing instance of the Word application was not found and you have to create a new one by using the CreateObject function.

10 Add the following as the last line in the procedure:

```
oApp.Visible = True
```

Setting the Visible property of the Word Application object to True displays the Word application window on the screen.

11 Place the cursor in the procedure and press F5 to run it.

If Microsoft Word is not running, the procedure creates a new instance of the application. However, if Word is running, the GetObject function returns the current instance.

12 Exit PowerPoint without saving changes. Do not exit Word.

Load an Excel workbook

When you use the GetObject function to start an application with a file that's already loaded, it is essentially the same as first using the CreateObject function to create an instance of an application and then using an Open method of the document collection of the specific application to open the file. The GetObject function reduces the number of lines of code needed to do the same thing.

Make sure the new module is inserted into the project for the new document, not into the Normal project (Normal.dot). If you're not sure, open the Project Explorer window and notice the project under which the new module appears.

1 Switch to Word and open a new document. Open the Visual Basic Editor. On the Tools menu, click References, select Microsoft Excel 8.0 Object Library from the list, and click OK.

2 Insert a new code module, and then add the following module-level variable declaration:

```
Dim m_oXLBook As Excel.Workbook
```

By adding a module-level declaration, you ensure that Excel will not automatically close the workbook that will be loaded by the GetObject function once all the lines of code in the procedure created in the next step run.

3 Create a new procedure by typing **Sub UsingGetObject** and pressing ENTER.

4   Type the following line within the procedure:

```
Set m_oXLBook = GetObject("C:\Office VBA Practice\Lesson5\Book1.xls")
```

The Set statement is used to assign the object returned by GetObject, an Excel Workbook object, to the module-level object variable m_oXLBook. The *pathname* argument specified in the GetObject function above assumes you have correctly saved an Excel file named Book1.xls to drive C in the Lesson 5 subfolder of the Office VBA Practice folder. If you saved the Excel file in step 1 of "Access an existing application" on page 107 to a different file location, make sure that the *pathname* argument in the GetObject function reflects the correct location.

 NOTE   If an instance of Excel is already running, the GetObject function used in the code accesses and loads only the specified file in that instance of Excel. If Excel is not running, the GetObject function creates and loads the specified file in a new instance of Excel.

5   Type the following two lines after the Set statement:

```
m_oXLBook.Windows(1).Visible = True
m_oXLBook.Application.Visible = True
```

When GetObject runs, it loads the Excel workbook invisibly. By default, each workbook contains at least one window; to make it visible to the user, you set its Visible property to True.

6   Place the cursor in the procedure and press F5 to run it.

When this code runs, the application associated with the specified pathname (Excel, in this case) starts, and the object in the specified file (Book1.xls) opens.

Disconnecting a Variable from an Object

When you use the CreateObject or GetObject function or the New keyword to assign a variable to an object, the object you have set a reference to resides in your computer system's memory. Depending on the complexity of your program, releasing certain objects from memory may speed up other parts of your program. To disconnect an object variable from an object in memory that you no longer need, set the object variable to the keyword Nothing. Once an object variable is set to Nothing, it no longer references an actual object in memory. If no other object variable refers to that object, it is removed from your system's memory.

109

NOTE If the object variable is declared as a procedure-level variable, it will be set to Nothing automatically by Visual Basic once Visual Basic finishes executing the procedure containing the procedure-level variable. Explicitly setting object variables to Nothing is common for public or module-level object variables.

All Microsoft Office applications provide, as a member of the respective Application object, a Quit method that closes the application, whether or not it is visible. Running the Quit method in Visual Basic is the same as clicking Exit on the File menu in a Microsoft Office application. In some cases, running the Quit method does not release the reference to the actual object until you explicitly set the object variable to Nothing or until the object variable goes out of scope.

Quit Excel using Visual Basic code

1 Exit any running versions of Excel without saving changes.

2 In the UsingGetObject procedure you just created in the Visual Basic Editor of Word, add the following message box statement and With…End block after the last line of the procedure and just before the End Sub statement:

```
MsgBox "Excel will now be closed."
With m_oXLBook.Application
    .DisplayAlerts = False
    .Quit
End With
```

The DisplayAlerts property of the Excel Application object indicates whether Excel displays a dialog box asking whether you want to save changes or any other alert dialog box Excel normally displays. If DisplayAlerts is set to False, no dialog boxes are displayed. Thus, when the Quit method of the Excel Application object is executed by Visual Basic, Excel will not display a dialog box asking whether you want to save changes to the current workbook.

3 Place the cursor in the procedure and press F5 to run it.

When you run the UsingGetObject procedure, Excel starts and the file, Book1.xls, is activated.

4 Switch to Word, but do nothing to Excel.

Once Book1.xls is displayed, Word displays a message box indicating that Excel will now be closed. When you click OK in the Word message box, Excel, along with the Book1 workbook, is closed.

Creating a PowerPoint Presentation from a Word Document

After spending time putting together a report using Microsoft Word, you may find that your report contains a logical breakdown of topics that could easily be integrated into a PowerPoint presentation. Word provides you with the ability to send your active Word document to PowerPoint by pointing to Send To on the File menu, and then clicking Microsoft PowerPoint on the submenu. However, to your dismay, the output may not match the formatting in your Word template. You can easily create your own Send To PowerPoint feature by using Visual Basic for Applications to customize the output to meet your specific needs.

 NOTE The practice files for Lesson 5 already include a Word document with the necessary code to generate a PowerPoint presentation and an Outlook e-mail message to which the presentation will be attached. This file is located in the Lesson 5 subfolder of the Office VBA Practice folder. You can load the practice file, browse through the code in the Visual Basic project of the Word document, and run the code to see the results.

Create source information and define module-level variables

1   Switch to Microsoft Word.

When you install Word, the Normal template that is attached to newly created blank documents contains a short list of predefined text styles: Heading 1 through Heading 9, Normal, and a few others. To see this list of text styles, on the Format menu, click Style, and then select All Styles from the List drop-down list. In the Styles box, you should see a full list of the Word text styles that are defined in the Normal template.

You can also see an abbreviated list by clicking the Style drop-down list on the Format toolbar.

2 In the default document (Document1 or a similar name), add a few one-line paragraphs and format each line as one of these text styles: Heading 1, Heading 2, Heading 3, or Heading 4. Use the following illustration as a guide to your formatting. You can also copy these lines from the CreatePP.doc file.

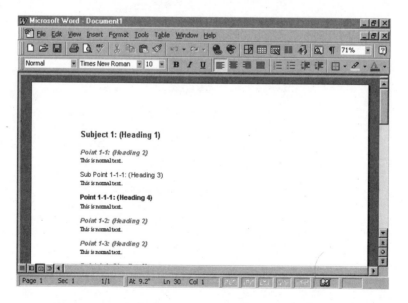

From the document you just created, you will examine the text style of each paragraph and then place the text of the paragraph at a specified position on a PowerPoint slide in a presentation.

3 In the Visual Basic Editor of Word, insert a new code module.

4   On the Tools menu, click References, select the Microsoft PowerPoint 8.0 Object Library from the Available References list, and click OK.

5   In the declarations section (the top) of the code module, add the following module-level variable declarations:

```
Dim m_oSlide As PowerPoint.Slide
Dim m_oWordPara As Paragraph
```

6   Add the following module-level constant declaration:

```
Const m_sPresFile As String = _
"C:\Office VBA Practice\Lesson5\MyPres.ppt"
```

The module-level constant m_sPresFile is set equal to the filename given to the slide presentation that will be created. Save the presentation to your hard disk so that you will be able to use the file as an attachment in an Outlook e-mail message, as you'll do later in this lesson.

Write the code to examine the headings

1   Create a new procedure in the code module by typing **Sub Main** and pressing ENTER, and then add the following declarations and a Set statement within the procedure:

```
Dim oPPT As New PowerPoint.Application
Dim oPres As PowerPoint.Presentation
Dim sStyle As String

Set oPres = oPPT.Presentations.Add(WithWindow:=msoFalse)
```

Note the use of the keyword New in the first object variable declaration. The first time the variable oPPT is used in code, a PowerPoint Application object is created and implicitly set to the object variable oPPT.

The last line represents the first time that oPPT is referenced in code. Thus, the PowerPoint Application object is automatically created. You use the Application object to access the Presentations collection object, which consists of the list of presentations currently open in PowerPoint, whether or not they are visible to the user. The Add method of the Presentations object creates a new presentation.

2   Add the following With…End block containing the For Each…Next loop:

```
With ActiveDocument.Range
    For Each m_oWordPara In .Paragraphs
    Next m_oWordPara
End With
```

113

You will use this loop to iterate through each paragraph in the active Word document.

3 Add the following line as the first line in the For Each...Next loop, just after the line `For Each m_oWordPara In .Paragraphs`:

```
sStyle = m_oWordPara.Style
```

The Style property of the Paragraph object in Word returns a string that represents the name of the text style used in the paragraph. The string is assigned to the variable sStyle.

4 Add the following Select Case block:

The Call keyword is optional. If used, it requires parentheses following the procedure name. For more information, in the Editor, ask the Assistant for help using the word "Call."

```
Select Case sStyle
Case "Heading 1"
    Set m_oSlide = oPres.Slides _
        .Add(oPres.Slides.Count + 1, ppLayoutText)
    Call SetText(ppTitleStyle, 1)
Case "Heading 2"
    Call SetText(ppBodyStyle, 1)
Case "Heading 3"
    Call SetText(ppBodyStyle, 2)
Case "Heading 4"
    Call SetText(ppBodyStyle, 3)
End Select
```

The Select Case block examines the value of the string variable sStyle. If the value of sStyle is Heading 1, a new slide in the PowerPoint presentation is created. The Add method of the Slides collection object accepts two arguments. The first argument is the index position of the newly added slide in the presentation, and the second is the slide layout type. In this case, you always create a slide with Title and Body placeholders and add it to the end of the Slides collection. The text of a paragraph in Word with the text style Heading 1 is used as the slide title in the first newly created slide.

For each case in the above Select Case block, you call the SetText procedure and pass it two arguments: an integer (an enumeration value in the form of a built-in PowerPoint constant) representing the text style, and an integer representing the paragraph indent level in the body-text placeholder of a PowerPoint slide. Heading 1 represents a slide title; Heading 2 represents a first-level paragraph in the body-text placeholder; Heading 3, a second level paragraph in the body-text placeholder; and Heading 4, a third-level paragraph in the body-text placeholder.

Generate a correctly formatted PowerPoint slide from Word text

1   Below the Main procedure, create a new procedure by typing **Sub SetText (iTextStyle As Integer, iIndentLevel As Integer)** and pressing ENTER.

This procedure will place the text from the Word document in the appropriate slide placeholder in the PowerPoint presentation. The code between the parentheses declares the arguments to the procedure. Note that the way you declare arguments is similar to the way you declare variables.

2   Add the following declaration within the procedure:

```
Dim oTitleText As TextRange
```

3   Create the first half of an If...Then...Else statement by adding the following lines of code:

```
If iTextStyle = ppTitleStyle Then
    Set oTitleText = m_oSlide.Shapes.Title _
        .TextFrame.TextRange
    With oTitleText
        .Text = m_oWordPara.Range
        .Text = .TrimText
    End With
```

The If...Then statement determines the value of the Integer variable iTextStyle, which was passed as an argument to the SetText procedure from the Main procedure. The value of iTextStyle is determined by the text style in the Word document. If the text style of the paragraph in the Word document is Heading 1, the equivalent text style is set to the title style of a PowerPoint slide.

The object variable oTitleText is set to the text range of the title shape on the PowerPoint slide. The With...End block following the Set statement sets the actual text in the title shape to the text in the paragraph in the Word document. The TrimText method of the TextRange object in PowerPoint removes any spaces, carriage returns, or linefeeds from the text.

4   Complete the If...Then...Else statement by adding the following lines
of code:

```
Else
    m_oSlide.Shapes.Placeholders(2).TextFrame _
        .TextRange.InsertAfter(m_oWordPara.Range) _
        .IndentLevel = iIndentLevel
End If
```

If the text style of the paragraph in the Word document is not Heading 1, the text from the paragraph is added to the body shape in the
PowerPoint slide. The body shape is represented by the second placeholder for a slide with the Bulleted List layout (specified by the constant
ppLayoutText in Visual Basic code). The paragraph from the Word
document is inserted into the text range of the body shape after the last
paragraph in the body shape.

The IndentLevel property of the TextRange object in PowerPoint determines how many times the bulleted point in the shape is indented. The
value of the Integer variable iIndentLevel was passed as an argument
to the SetText procedure from the Main procedure, and the value is
determined by the text style in the Word document.

5   Finally, add the following With...End block to the end of the Main
procedure:

```
With oPPT
    .Visible = msoTrue
    oPres.SaveAs m_sPresFile
    oPres.NewWindow
    .Activate
End With
```

The first line inside the With...End block sets the PowerPoint application window to visible. The second line saves the presentation to the
location specified by the module-level string constant m_sPresFile.
This constant was previously set to "C:\Office VBA Practice\Lesson5\
MyPres.ppt." The third line adds a new window to the presentation,
making the presentation visible to the user. (When the presentation
was added using the Add method of the Presentations collection object,
it was, by default, created without a visible window.) The final line
activates the PowerPoint application window and brings it to the front
of all windows on the screen.

6 Place the cursor in the Main procedure and press F5 to run it.

After iterating through the Word document and determining the text style of each paragraph in the document, the text is used to create a new PowerPoint presentation. The automatically generated presentation should look like the following:

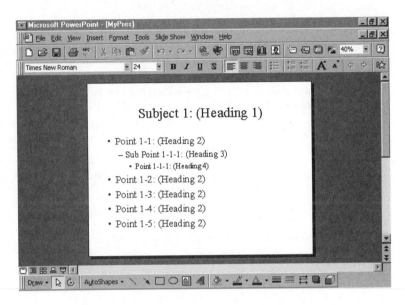

7 Exit PowerPoint. (Changes have already been saved.)

Send your presentation in e-mail

Once you've automatically created your PowerPoint presentation, you might want to send it automatically to a specific audience. Using the Microsoft Outlook object library, you can easily extend your program that generates a PowerPoint presentation from a Word document to create an Outlook e-mail message containing the presentation as an attachment.

NOTE In the following step-by-step example, an e-mail message created using Visual Basic for Applications uses Microsoft Outlook and does not work for any other e-mail client. You also need to be connected to a network or the Internet in order to actually send e-mail. However, as long as you have Outlook installed on your computer, you can still run the code in this example without sending the e-mail message created.

1. In the same Visual Basic for Applications project, in the Visual Basic Editor of Word, on the Tools menu, click References, select the Microsoft Outlook 8.0 Object Library (it may be called the Microsoft Outlook 8.0 Object Model) from the Available References list, and click OK.

2. Below the SetText procedure, create a new procedure by typing **Sub SendMail** and pressing ENTER.

3. In the SendMail procedure, add the following two declarations:

```
Dim oOutlook As Outlook.Application
Dim oMessage As Outlook.MailItem
```

You could use the New keyword in the declaration of the object variable oOutlook just as you did when you created the PowerPoint Application object in an earlier example. When you do not use the New keyword, you have to explicitly set the oOutlook object variable using the CreateObject function.

4. Just below the added declarations, add the following Set statement with the CreateObject function:

```
Set oOutlook = CreateObject("Outlook.Application")
```

You've now created a Microsoft Outlook Application object, with which you are ready to work.

5. Just below the Set statement with the CreateObject function, add the following:

```
Set oMessage = oOutlook.CreateItem(olMailItem)
```

You declared the object variable oMessage as an Outlook MailItem object and, using the Set statement, assigned the MailItem object to a newly created mail item with which you are ready to work. The CreateItem method is a member of the Outlook Application object. CreateItem accepts one of seven possible values, each represented by an enumeration value (in the form of a built-in Outlook constant), which is a predefined name for an Integer or Long value.

6. Add the following With...End block:

```
With oMessage
    .To = "Executive Committee"
    .Subject = "New Sales Report"
    .Body = "The following presentation reflects" & _
        " the final sales figures for Q2." & vbCrLf
End With
```

The With...End block allows you to set properties of the mail item without having to continuously prefix each property of the MailItem object with oMessage. This has two benefits: it improves performance because Visual Basic needs to determine what oMessage is only once, and it improves the readability of your code. The first line in the With...End block sets the To property of the MailItem object to equal the e-mail alias "Executive Committee." (Of course, you should set this to a valid e-mail alias on your e-mail system.) The subject of the e-mail message is set using the Subject property, and the body text of the mail item is set using the Body property. The constant vbCrLf is a Visual Basic constant representing a "carriage return and linefeed" in the text you specify.

7   At the end of the With...End block, add the following line just before the line End With:

```
.Attachments.Add m_sPresFile, , , "Q2 Sales"
```

The MailItem object provides an Attachments collection to which you can add items or iterate through the attachments already contained in the mail item. In this case, you will add the PowerPoint presentation you created in the previous step-by-step example. The third argument in the Add method of the Attachments object, called the *Position* argument, indicates the character position within the body text after which to add the attachment. By default, if nothing is specified, as in the above line, the Add method adds the attachment after the last character in the MailItem.Body text. The fourth argument, *DisplayName*, represents the text used with the icon of the attachment. By default, the filename of the attachment is used. Here, you explicitly set it to "Q2 Sales."

8   Just after the method to add attachments, add the following line before End With:

```
.Display
```

The Display method of the MailItem object displays the mail item you created.

9   Now, add the following line as the last line in the With...End block:

```
.Send
```

The Send method of the MailItem object sends the newly created e-mail message automatically. However, instead of sending the item now, you would probably prefer to temporarily store the mail item in your Outlook Inbox until you are ready to send it manually.

10   If you want to store the e-mail in Outlook, replace .Send with the following line:

```
.Close (olSave)
```

The Close method then closes the mail item, so you no longer see it displayed on the screen. The olSave constant specifed in the argument of the Close method saves the mail item to the Outlook default folder for the item type. In this case, it is saved to the Outlook Inbox.

Now that you've created your e-mail procedure, you need to call the procedure that creates and sends the mail item from the same code that automatically generates the PowerPoint presentation.

11   In the Main procedure, add the following line just before End Sub:

```
Call SendMail
```

12   Place the cursor in the Main procedure, and press F5.

In the Main procedure, once the code finishes creating the PowerPoint presentation based on your Word document, it saves the presentation file to your hard disk and then calls the SendMail procedure, which creates a new mail item in Outlook and adds the generated presentation as an attachment.

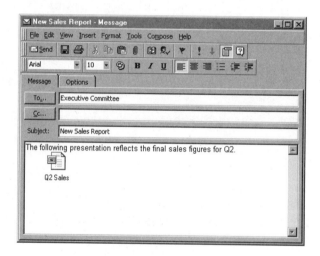

13   Exit all Office applications. If you want, save changes to Word.

Lesson Summary

To	Do this
Assign an object to an object variable	Use the Set statement at the beginning of the assignment statement.

Create a new instance of an object	Return a reference to the object with the CreateObject function, and then assign the reference to a variable with the Set statement. For example:
	`Set oPPT = CreateObject _`
	`    ("PowerPoint.Application")`

Declare a variable as a generic object	Type the variable name between Dim and As Object. for example: `Dim MyObject As Object`
Load application object libraries	In the Visual Basic Editor, on the Tools menu, click References, select the libraries, and click OK.
Declare a variable as a specific object type	With the appropriate object library loaded, type **Dim**, followed by the variable name, **As**, and the object type. For example: `Dim oPPT As PowerPoint.Application`
Declare an object variable and assign an instance of an object to it in one step	Type **Dim**, followed by the variable name, **As New**, and the application object name. For example: `Dim oPPT As New PowerPoint.Application`
Assign an instance of an object that is already loaded to an object variable	Return a reference to the object with the GetObject function and *class* argument, and then assign the reference to the variable with the Set statement. For example: `Set oApp = GetObject(, "Word.Application")`
Start an application, open an existing file, and assign it to an object variable in one step	Return a reference to the object with the GetObject function and *pathname* argument, and then assign the reference to the variable with the Set statement. For example: `Set oXLBook = GetObject("Book1.xls")`
Disconnect a variable from an object	Assign the value Nothing to the variable.

Declare a constant	Type **Const** followed by the constant name, **As** and its type (optional), (=), and the value. For example:
	`Const m_sPresFile As String = _`
	`    "C:\Office VBA Practice\MyPres.ppt"`

Lesson Summary, *continued*

To	Do this
Run (call) a procedure from another procedure	Type **Call** (optional) followed by the procedure name. If Call is used, the procedure's arguments, if any, must be enclosed in parentheses.

For online information about	Ask the Assistant for help, using the words
Establishing a link between applications	"Communicating with applications"
Creating an instance of an object with the CreateObject function	"CreateObject"
Accessing an existing object with the GetObject function	"GetObject"
Creating an instance of an object with the New keyword	"Dim statement"
Disconnecting a variable from an object	"Set statement"
Declaring arguments to procedures	"Sub statement" or "Function statement"
Exiting an application	"Quit method"

Preview of the Next Lesson

In the next lesson, you will learn how to create custom toolbars; add buttons and drop-down lists to toolbars; create custom menu commands; and add and remove menus, toolbars, and custom menu commands.

Creating Custom Menus and Toolbars

Estimated time
45 min.

In this lesson you will learn how to:

- Create custom toolbars.
- Add buttons and drop-down lists to toolbars.
- Create custom menus and menu items.
- Remove buttons, toolbars, menus, and menu items.

To use most of the tools and functionality provided by Microsoft Office, you need to click an item on a menu, click a button, or make selections from a drop-down list on a toolbar. Menus and toolbars are the interface between you and the tools Office provides, just as they will be between your users and the custom Visual Basic for Applications programs you develop. You can easily reuse any code you write that accesses and manipulates menus and toolbars within Microsoft Word, Excel, PowerPoint, Access, or Outlook, because the CommandBars object model resides in the shared Microsoft Office 8.0 Object Library.

Creating Your Own Toolbars

Each Microsoft Office application provides a collection of toolbars, each of which helps you perform a set of common functions. For example, the Formatting toolbar consists of a set of buttons and drop-down lists that help you format text in your document, worksheet, or slide. The list of toolbars available in a particular Office application appears in the Toolbars tab of the Customize dialog box.

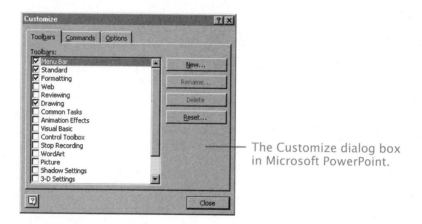

The Customize dialog box in Microsoft PowerPoint.

To access the Customize dialog box, on the Tools menu in Word, Excel, or PowerPoint, click Customize; or, on the View menu in Word, Excel, PowerPoint, or Access, point to Toolbars, and then click Customize on the submenu. You can also right-click any toolbar and then click Customize on the shortcut menu. The Toolbars list displays all available toolbars, and the check box beside each item indicates whether that toolbar is visible.

Creating your own toolbars by using Microsoft Visual Basic allows you to add elements to the user interface that, in turn, allow your customers to access the functionality in your programs. For example, if you develop a wizard that steps a user through the process of creating a specific type of Word document, you will want to add a toolbar button or menu item that, when clicked, displays the custom wizard.

Create a simple toolbar with Visual Basic

The Microsoft Office 8.0 Object Library provides an object model that allows you to manipulate any of the menus or toolbars provided by an Office application, or add custom menus and toolbars. The object model is represented by the CommandBars collection object and the methods and properties it exposes.

> **IMPORTANT** The CommandBar object model represents both menus and toolbars in all Office applications, so, a toolbar or menu may be referred to as a *command bar* within the context of Visual Basic programming.

1   Start Microsoft PowerPoint. In the opening PowerPoint dialog box, select Blank Presentation, click OK, select any AutoLayout, and click OK.

2   Open the Visual Basic Editor and insert a new code module.

3   In the code module, type **Sub AddNewToolbar** and press ENTER.

4   Type the following declaration lines in the procedure:

```
Dim oMyCommandBar As CommandBar
Dim oCmdButton As CommandBarButton
```

You are declaring the object variable oMyCommandBar as the object type CommandBar. Every toolbar and menu bar available to you in an Office application is considered a CommandBar object. Depending on what items you place on the command bar, it may appear as a menu bar, a toolbar, or a hybrid. The second declaration is for a button control you are going to add to the newly created command bar.

5   Add a command bar by typing the following line after the declaration of oMyCommandBar and oCmdButton:

```
Set oMyCommandBar = Application.CommandBars.Add
```

Each Application object in a Microsoft Office application, excluding Outlook, provides access to the CommandBars collection object. The CommandBars collection object allows you to add a command bar to, or access an individual command bar from, the collection. In this case, the Add method of the CommandBars collection object returns a CommandBar object, which you assign to the object variable oMyCommandBar.

6   Below the Set statement in which you added a new CommandBar object to the collection, add the following line to name the newly created command bar:

```
oMyCommandBar.Name = "My CommandBar"
```

Each newly created CommandBar object is given a default name. Before you assign a name to a new command bar, the name appears with the syntax Custom *number,* where *number* represents the next available integer. The name of a floating command bar is the name that appears on its title bar. A floating command bar is not docked to any side of an application window. The name of a command bar also appears in the Toolbars list in the Toolbars tab of the Customize dialog box.

7 To add a button to your custom command bar, add the following With...End block below the name assignment line:

```
With oMyCommandBar.Controls
    Set oCmdButton = .Add(msoControlButton)
End With
```

Each CommandBar object contains a Controls collection object that represents all of the buttons, drop-down lists, pop-up menus, and any other controls available on the command bar. When you create a command bar, no controls exist in the Controls collection. The Set statement above adds a button control to the command bar. The Add method of the Controls collection object accepts five arguments, with the first one representing the type of control to add. You can specify the type of argument as msoControlButton, msoControlEdit, msoControlDropdown, msoControlComboBox, or msoControlPopup.

8 Set the properties of the newly created button by adding the following With...End block just after the Set statement that adds a new button control to the Controls collection object:

```
With oCmdButton
    .Style = msoButtonIconAndCaption
    .Caption = "My Button"
    .FaceId = 59
    .TooltipText = "My ToolTip"
    .Visible = True
End With
```

You can set a number of properties for a button on a command bar, but you have already set five of the main ones. The first is the button style, which allows a button to be represented as a combination of an icon and a caption (to the right of the icon), or as just an icon or caption alone. To change the style of either one of the latter choices, assign to the Style property the value msoButtonIcon or msoButtonCaption, respectively.

Because both an icon and a caption are specified, both the Caption property and the FaceId property are set. More than 1,000 face IDs are built into Office. Most of them are the buttons on the toolbars that you see in the application window (such as New, Save, or Print). The TooltipText property is used to set the text of the ToolTip that appears when the mouse is over the button on the command bar. Finally, the Visible property indicates whether the button is visible on the command bar.

9 Add the following line to the procedure, just before the End Sub line:

```
oMyCommandBar.Visible = True
```

When you add a command bar, it is not visible by default; you have to explicitly set the control to visible. The complete procedure for adding a command bar is as follows:

```
Sub AddNewToolbar
    Dim oMyCommandBar As CommandBar
    Dim oCmdButton As CommandBarButton

    Set oMyCommandBar = Application.CommandBars.Add
    oMyCommandBar.Name = "My CommandBar"
    With oMyCommandBar.Controls
        Set oCmdButton = .Add(msoControlButton)
        With oCmdButton
            .Style = msoButtonIconAndCaption
            .Caption = "My Button"
            .FaceId = 59
            .TooltipText = "My ToolTip"
            .Visible = True
        End With
    End With
    oMyCommandBar.Visible = True
End Sub
```

10   Place the cursor in the procedure and press F5.

The final toolbar should look like the following example, containing just one button displaying an icon and a caption. When you move the cursor over the button, the ToolTip is displayed.

When a Toolbar Is a Menu Bar

In the CommandBars object model, a menu bar and a toolbar are essentially the same—only their appearances are different. The menu bar is a special toolbar at the top of the screen that contains menus such as File, Edit, and View. You can customize menu bars just like any built-in toolbar; for example, you can add and remove buttons and menus.

Add menus

Sometimes your solution may require a set of custom menu commands. Adding a set of custom commands to an existing toolbar may expand the menu until it contains too many items. Introducing a new menu may be a good alternative.

This step-by-step example works the same way in Word and Excel, except where indicated. You may prefer to enter your code there.

The "cascade" in oPopupCascade refers to cascading menus, a term that is occasionally used for submenus.

1   In the Visual Basic Editor of PowerPoint, at the bottom of the code module, type **Sub AddMenu** and press ENTER.

2   Type the following declaration lines in the procedure:

```
Dim oMyCommandBar As CommandBar
Dim oPopup As CommandBarPopup
Dim oPopupCascade As CommandBarPopup
```

You are declaring the two object variables oPopup and oPopupCascade as the object type CommandBarPopup. The pop-up menu that is displayed when you click a menu on the menu bar in any application is of the object type CommandBarPopup.

3   Set the object variable oMyCommandBar to the main menu bar:

```
Set oMyCommandBar = CommandBars("Menu Bar")
```

Word, PowerPoint, and Access have a main menu bar named Menu Bar. If you were running this example in Excel, you would need to change the value between the parentheses in the above Set statement to "Worksheet Menu Bar".

4   To add a menu to the Menu Bar, add the following With...End block and Set statement below the Set statement you just entered:

```
With oMyCommandBar.Controls
    Set oPopup = .Add(msoControlPopup, , , 2)
End With
```

The Menu Bar, which is itself represented by a CommandBar object, contains a Controls collection object that represents all of the pop-up menus, including File, Edit, View, Insert, and so on. The Set statement above adds a new pop-up control to the Menu Bar command bar and assigns the control to the object variable oPopup. The fourth argument in the Add method of the Controls collection object, named *Before,* indicates the index position within the Controls collection where the menu is to be placed. In this case, a value of 2 places the new menu to the right of the File menu.

5   Add the following With...End block just after the Set statement that assigns the object variable oPopup to the newly added menu:

```
With oPopup
    .Caption = "PopupMenu"
    With .Controls.Add(msoControlButton)
        .Caption = "&Menu Item 1"
        .OnAction = "DisplayMessageBox"
    End With
End With
```

The caption that appears on the Menu Bar is set to "PopupMenu". Just after setting the first Caption property, another With...End block simultaneously adds a new CommandBarButton object, sets its Caption property to "Menu Item 1", and then sets its OnAction property to the DisplayMessageBox procedure, which will be created in the section "Add an action" later in this lesson. The ampersand (&) in the text value of the Caption property indicates that the letter following the ampersand is displayed as the accelerator key. Thus, when the menu is displayed, you can press ALT+M and click the first menu item.

6   After the With...End blocks (but still within the With...End block you created in step 4), add the following Set statement:

```
Set oPopupCascade = oPopup.Controls.Add(msoControlPopup)
```

The Set statement adds a second control to the Controls collection object of the newly created menu, represented by the object variable oPopup. The first argument of the Add method of the Controls collection object is specified as *msoControlPopup*. This creates an object of the same type, CommandBarPopup, as the PopupMenu menu itself. By adding this type of control as an item on the menu PopupMenu, you are creating the start of a submenu (also occasionally called a cascading menu). An example of a submenu is the menu of available toolbars you see when you point to Toolbars on the View menu in Word, Excel, PowerPoint, Access, or Outlook.

7   To set the caption and add menu items to the new submenu, add the following With...End block just after the Set statement that assigns the object variable oPopupCascade to the newly added pop-up control:

```
With oPopupCascade
    .Caption = "My &Cascading Menu"
    With .Controls.Add(msoControlButton)
        .Caption = "&Item 1"
        .OnAction = "DisplayMessageBox"
    End With
    With .Controls.Add(msoControlButton)
        .Caption = "I&tem 2"
        .OnAction = "DisplayMessageBox"
    End With
End With
```

The two inner With...End blocks simultaneously add a new CommandBarButton object and set the Caption property to "&Item 1" and "I&tem 2", respectively; they also set the OnAction property for each control to the DisplayMessageBox procedure that will be created in the section "Add an action" later in this lesson.

The complete procedure looks like this:

```
Sub AddMenu()
    Dim oMyCommandBar As CommandBar
    Dim oPopup As CommandBarPopup
    Dim oPopupCascade As CommandBarPopup
    Set oMyCommandBar = CommandBars("Menu Bar")
    With oMyCommandBar.Controls
        Set oPopup = .Add(msoControlPopup, , , 2)
        With oPopup
            .Caption = "PopupMenu"
            With .Controls.Add(msoControlButton)
                .Caption = "&Menu Item 1"
                .OnAction = "DisplayMessageBox"
            End With
        End With
        Set oPopupCascade = oPopup.Controls _
            .Add(msoControlPopup)
        With oPopupCascade
            .Caption = "My &Cascading Menu"
            With .Controls.Add(msoControlButton)
                .Caption = "&Item 1"
                .OnAction = "DisplayMessageBox"
            End With
            With .Controls.Add(msoControlButton)
                .Caption = "I&tem 2"
                .OnAction = "DisplayMessageBox"
            End With
        End With
    End With
End Sub
```

8 Place the cursor in the AddMenu procedure and press F5.

The menu PopupMenu is added as the second menu, next to the File menu in the application window. When you click the PopupMenu menu and point to My Cascading Menu, the submenu with its two items is displayed. Later in this lesson, when you click either of these two menu items, the DisplayMessageBox procedure is called and a message box is displayed.

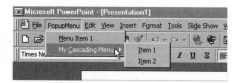

Add a menu item to an existing menu

This step-by-step example works the same way in Word and Excel, except where indicated.

1   In the Visual Basic Editor, at the bottom of the Code window, create a new procedure by typing **Sub AddMenuItem** and pressing ENTER.

2   Declare the object variables oCmdPopup and oCmdButton by typing the following lines in the AddMenuItem procedure:

```
Dim oCmdPopup As CommandBarPopup
Dim oCmdButton As CommandBarButton
```

When you click a menu on the Menu Bar, such as the File or Edit menu in any application, a list of commands is displayed. This list is displayed in a pop-up menu, which is a CommandBarPopup object. Despite its different use, the pop-up menu that is displayed when you click a menu, such as File or Edit, is the same type of CommandBarPopup object that appears when you right-click an element in the user interface, such as a shape on a PowerPoint slide. When you right-click an element, the pop-up menu that appears is called a *shortcut menu*.

The second object variable declared above, oCmdButton, is declared as a CommandBarButton object.

3   To access the PowerPoint File menu, add the following line:

```
Set oCmdPopup = CommandBars("Menu Bar").Controls("File")
```

If you were running this example in Excel, you would need to change the value between the parentheses in the above Set statement to "Worksheet Menu Bar".

4   To add a new menu item, type the following line:

```
Set oCmdButton = oCmdPopup.Controls _
    .Add(Type:=msoControlButton, before:=4)
```

In the Set statement, you set the object variable oCmdButton to a new control of type msoControlButton and added it to the Controls collection object of the oCmdPopup object, which you assigned to the File menu in step 3. The *Before* argument of the Add method indicates the position on the menu where the button control should be added. In this case, you are adding it before the current fourth menu item. Your new menu item is now the fourth item on the menu, and the previous fourth item and all other menu items below it are moved one down on the list.

5   To set the properties of the new menu item, type the following just after the Set statement that assigned the object variable oCmdButton to the newly added menu item:

```
With oCmdButton
    .Caption = "My Menu Item"
    .OnAction = "DisplayMessageBox"
End With
```

131

The caption "My Menu Item" is the text that appears when you click the File menu and the menu items are displayed. The OnAction property is set to the same DisplayMessageBox procedure that you will write in the next step-by-step example.

6 Place the cursor in the AddMenuItem procedure and press F5.

My Menu Item is added as the fourth menu item, just below the item Close, on the File menu in the application window. After you add some code, later in this lesson, when you click the menu item, the DisplayMessageBox procedure is called and a message box is displayed.

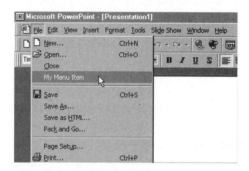

Writing Generic Code for Accessing Controls on the Menu Bar

Excel has two built-in menu bars, the Worksheet Menu Bar and the Chart Menu Bar. These two menu bars are listed in the Toolbars list of the Customize dialog box. Word, PowerPoint, and Access have only one built-in menu bar, called the Menu Bar. To write generic code that can be plugged easily into Word, Excel, or PowerPoint, you can write a Select Case statement block that determines the name of the application in which the code is running and sets the value of a string variable to the correct name of the menu bar. For example, you can add the following Select Case statement block above the line that sets the object variable in step 3 of the preceding step-by-step example.

```
Dim sMenuName As String
Select Case Application.Name
Case "Microsoft Excel"
    sMenuName = "Worksheet Menu Bar"
Case Else
    sMenuName = "Menu Bar"
End Select
```

Writing Generic Code for Accessing Controls on the Menu Bar, *continued*

> The Set statement in step 3 should be replaced by the following Set statement, which uses the sMenuName variable:
>
> ```
> Set oCmdPopup = CommandBars(sMenuName).Controls("File")
> ```
>
> This code would not work in Access because the Access Application object does not provide a Name property member. However, its menu bar is named Menu Bar.

Assigning Actions to Toolbars

Now that you've created the user interface elements, you need to provide a hook that connects the toolbar buttons (or menu items) to your program. When a button or menu item is clicked, Office looks for a procedure name in a Visual Basic for Applications project that is equal to the value you assign to the OnAction property of a command bar control. In the example below, you will add an action to call a simple procedure that displays a message box. In Lesson 7, you add an action that calls a procedure to display a custom UserForm.

Add an action

1 In the AddNewToolbar procedure you created at the beginning of the lesson, add the following line at the end of the With...End block for the oCmdButton object variable, just below `.Visible = True`:

    ```
    .OnAction = "DisplayMessageBox"
    ```

    This line sets the OnAction property. Every control that you can add to a CommandBar object has an OnAction property. The String value of the OnAction property represents the procedure that is called when the control is clicked on a toolbar or menu. If the procedure with the specified name is not found in any of the open Visual Basic projects in an application, nothing happens when the button or menu item is clicked.

2 Create a new procedure by typing **Sub DisplayMessageBox** and pressing ENTER.

3 Add the following message box statement to the DisplayMessageBox procedure:

    ```
    MsgBox "You just clicked a custom item."
    ```

4 Switch to PowerPoint. Right-click any toolbar and then click Customize on the shortcut menu. In the Toolbars list box in the Toolbars tab, select My CommandBar and click Delete.

5 Click OK to close the message box, and then click Close to close the Customize dialog box.

6 In the Visual Basic Editor, place the cursor in the AddNewToolbar procedure and press F5 to create the toolbar again.

7 On the new My CommandBar toolbar in the PowerPoint application window, click the My Button button.

Now, whenever you click the button on the custom toolbar, the message box is displayed. Buttons and menu items can point to the same OnAction procedure, or they can point to different ones, whichever is applicable.

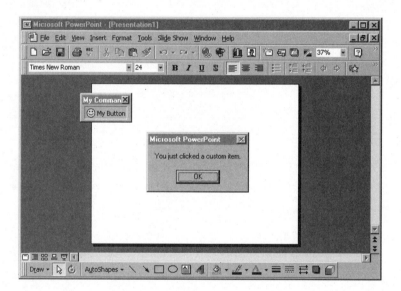

8 Click OK to close the message box.

Work with *drop-down controls*

A number of toolbars contain drop-down controls that provide a list of items from which to choose. The Font and Font Size drop-down list boxes are two such controls that you see on the Formatting toolbar in Word, Excel, and PowerPoint.

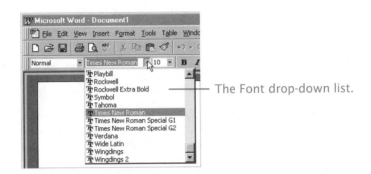

The Font drop-down list.

You can create two types of drop-down lists. The first is the combination, or combo box, which allows the user either to type a value in a text box or to select an existing value from a list box. Font Size on the Formatting toolbar and Zoom on the Standard toolbar in Word, Excel, and PowerPoint are examples of drop-down combo boxes. The second type is the drop-down list box, where the user must select a value from the list and cannot type a value.

1   Now delete the command bar you created, using the Customize dialog box. (In PowerPoint, right-click any toolbar, click Customize on the shortcut menu, select My CommandBar, and click Delete.)

2   At the bottom of the code module, create a new procedure by typing **Sub AddComboToolbar** and pressing ENTER.

3   Declare object variables oMyCommandBar, oComboBox, and oDropDown by typing the following lines within the AddComboToolbar procedure:

```
Dim oMyCommandBar As CommandBar
Dim oComboBox As CommandBarComboBox
Dim oDropDown As CommandBarComboBox
```

The CommandBarComboBox object type represents both a drop-down combo box and a drop-down list box. The main difference is that one allows you to type a value in an edit region and the other does not.

4   Add the following code under the variable declarations:

```
Set oMyCommandBar = Application.CommandBars.Add("My CommandBar")
```

This Set statement adds a new command bar and gives it a name by specifying the first argument of the Add method, called Name, as My CommandBar.

5 Add the following With...End block just after the Set statement that set the object variable oMyCommandBar:

```
With oMyCommandBar.Controls
End With
```

6 Within the With...End block you just added, add the following Set statement:

```
Set oComboBox =.Add(msoControlComboBox)
```

The Add method of the Controls collection object allows you to specify what type of control you want to add as the first argument. In this case, the enumeration value msoControlComboBox represents a drop-down combo box control.

7 After the Set statement assigning the object variable oComboBox to the newly added drop-down combo box control, type the following With...End block to set some properties of the control:

```
With oComboBox
    .AddItem "Item 2"
    .AddItem "Item 1", 1
    .AddItem "Item 3"
    .Caption = "My Combo Box"
    .ListIndex = 1
    .OnAction = "DisplayMessageBox"
End With
```

The first three lines in the With...End block add items to the drop-down combo box using the AddItem method. The first argument of the AddItem method of a CommandBarComboBox object is a String value that you specify, which is listed in the drop-down list. The second argument, *Index,* is optional, so it does not have to be specified. When the second argument is specified, it represents the index position within the current drop-down list where the item is to be placed.

The ListIndex property sets the item in the drop-down list that is to be displayed. When the drop-down list of the combo box is first displayed, "Item 1" is the first item on the list. The OnAction property is set to the same DisplayMessageBox procedure that you added in the previous step-by-step example. The Caption property is used for two purposes. The first is to name the combo box control on the toolbar. The second is to designate a label when the Style property of the combo box control is set to msoComboLabel, as it will be in the following steps.

8 After the With...End block that set the properties for the oComboBox object, add the following Set statement:

```
Set oDropDown = .Add(msoControlDropdown)
```

The Add method of the Controls collection object specifies as the first argument the enumeration value msoControlDropdown, which represents a drop-down list control.

9 After the Set statement assigning the object variable oDropDown to the newly added drop-down list control, type the following With...End block to set some properties of the control:

```
With oDropDown
    .BeginGroup = True
    .AddItem "Item 1"
    .AddItem "Item 2"
    .ListIndex = 1
    .Style = msoComboLabel
    .Caption = "My Label"
    .OnAction = "DisplayMessageBox"
End With
```

The BeginGroup property can be set for any control within the Controls collection of a CommandBar object. This property represents the vertical separator bar displayed between a group of controls on a toolbar, or the horizontal separator bar displayed between two menu items. The Style property allows you to specify whether the drop-down control is displayed with a label to its left. The Style property is applicable to both types of drop-down controls. In this case, you set the property to equal msoComboLabel, indicating that the combo drop-down list is displayed with a label. The label is represented by the String value of the Caption property.

If you make a mistake in your code and have to debug it, you may also have to delete the My CommandBar toolbar again before rerunning the code. To do this, see step 1.

10 Place the cursor in the AddComboToolbar procedure and press F5 to run it.

The procedure adds two new controls to My CommandBar. The first control is a drop-down list box, and the second is a drop-down combo box with a label displayed. The second drop-down box added is also at the beginning of a new group of controls, which is indicated by the vertical separator bar to its left.

11 To see the new toolbar, switch to PowerPoint, right-click any toolbar, and select My CommandBar on the shortcut menu.

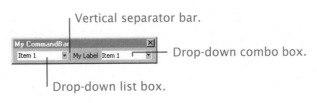

Vertical separator bar.

Drop-down combo box.

Drop-down list box.

Cleaning Up the Interface

The structure for a procedure that removes a menu item from an existing menu is very similar to that of the procedure that removes a toolbar from the toolbar collection. As with a toolbar, if a menu item does not exist, an error results when you try to delete it. To ensure that the menu item is removed if it exists and that no error is raised if it does not, a loop is used to iterate through the items in the menu.

Remove a menu item from an existing menu

1   In the Visual Basic Editor, in the code module, create a new procedure by typing **Sub RemoveMenuItem** and pressing ENTER.

2   In the RemoveMenuItem procedure, add the following object declarations.

```
Dim oCmdPopup As CommandBarPopup
Dim oCmdCtl As CommandBarControl
```

The first object variable, oCmdPopup, is declared as the object type CommandBarPopup, and is used to assign the menu that contains your custom menu item. The second object variable, oCmdCtl, is used in the For Each...Next loop added in step 4.

3   Set the oCmdPopup object variable to the menu that contains your custom menu item by typing the following line just after the object declarations:

```
Set oCmdPopup = CommandBars("Menu Bar").Controls("File")
```

Remember, in the CommandBars object model, built-in menus (File, Edit, and so on), custom menus, and shortcut menus (displayed by right-clicking an item) are all CommandBarPopup objects.

In the section "Add a menu item to an existing menu," you added the custom menu item My Menu Item as the fourth item on the File menu. Thus, you set the oCmdPopup object variable to the File pop-up menu.

If you were running this example in Excel, you would need to change the value between the parentheses in the above Set statement to "Worksheet Menu Bar".

4   Set up a loop to iterate through the CommandBarControls collection of the File pop-up menu by adding the following For Each...Next loop after the Set statement:

```
For Each oCmdCtl In oCmdPopup.Controls
Next oCmdCtl
```

The For Each...Next loop is used to iterate through a collection of objects. Each time For Each...Next loops through the CommandBarControls collection, it implicitly sets the object variable oCmdCtl to the next CommandBarControl object in the collection.

5   Within the For Each...Next loop, add the following If...Then condition block:

```
If oCmdCtl.Caption = "My Menu Item" Then
    oCmdCtl.Delete
    Exit For
End If
```

During each loop of For Each...Next, Visual Basic checks the name of the CommandBarControl object assigned to the object variable oCmdCtl to determine whether it equals the name of the custom menu item My Menu Item. If the condition is found to be true, the custom menu item is deleted and the For Each...Next loop exits using the Exit For statement.

6   Place the cursor in the RemoveMenuItem procedure and press F5 to run it.

Each time you run this procedure, the custom menu item My Menu Item is deleted only if it exists. If it does not exist, nothing happens and Visual Basic continues through the procedure without raising an error. If you previously deleted My Menu Item, run the AddMenuItem procedure created in the section "Add a menu item to an existing menu," and then run the RemoveMenuItem procedure. You should see My Menu Item appear and then disappear on the File menu.

Remove a menu

The steps for removing an entire custom menu are the same as those for removing a menu item from an existing menu. Instead of iterating through the controls of the File menu, however, you iterate through the controls of the Menu Bar command bar.

➤   Add the following RemoveMenu procedure and press F5:

```
Sub RemoveMenu()
    Dim oCmdCtl As CommandBarControl

    For Each oCmdCtl In CommandBars("Menu Bar").Controls
        If oCmdCtl.Caption = "PopupMenu" Then
            oCmdCtl.Delete
            Exit For
        End If
    Next oCmdCtl
End Sub
```

The PopupMenu menu on the Menu Bar menu bar in PowerPoint is removed.

Remove a toolbar item

Removing an item from a toolbar is very similar to removing an item from a menu. You iterate through the controls on the toolbar, just as you would with menu items, until you find the control you want to delete. Once you find it, you delete the item and exit the iteration through the controls on the toolbar.

➤ Add the following RemoveToolbarItem procedure and press F5:

```
Sub RemoveToolbarItem()
    Dim oMyCommandBar As CommandBar
    Dim oCmdCtl As CommandBarControl
    Dim sToolbarItem As String

    sToolbarItem = "My Label"
    Set oMyCommandBar = CommandBars("My CommandBar")
    With oMyCommandBar
        For Each oCmdCtl In .Controls
            If oCmdCtl.Caption = sToolbarItem Then
                oCmdCtl.Delete
                Exit Sub
            End If
        Next oCmdCtl
    End With
End Sub
```

This procedure removes the drop-down combo box along with its label from the toolbar named My CommandBar. The custom toolbar created earlier in the chapter now looks like the one in the following illustration:

Remove a toolbar

Custom additions and changes you make to the menu bar and toolbars are saved in a toolbars settings file in your Windows folder, so every time you exit and restart an Office application, the settings you made are preserved. If you want to delete a custom toolbar, on the View menu, point to Toolbars, and then click Customize on the submenu. On the Toolbars list box in the Toolbars tab, select My CommandBar, and click Delete. You can also do this by using Visual Basic for Applications. In Lesson 9, you will create procedures that automatically add and remove command bar items when your Visual Basic for Applications program is loaded and unloaded.

1 In the Editor, create a new procedure by typing **Sub RemoveToolbar** and pressing ENTER.

NOTE The easiest way to remove your toolbar with Visual Basic code is to add this line of code:
`Application.CommandBars("My CommandBar").Delete`
You then press F5. However, if the toolbar does not exist, an error results when the line above runs. In order to ensure that the toolbar is deleted if it exists and that no error is raised if it does not, a loop is used to iterate through the toolbars in the CommandBars collection.

2 In the RemoveToolbar procedure, add the following object declarations:

```
Dim oMyCmdBar As CommandBar
Dim oCmdBar As CommandBar
```

The first object variable, oMyCmdBar, is declared as a CommandBar object type and is used to assign your custom My CommandBar object to a variable. The second object variable, oCmdBar, is used in the For Each…Next loop added in the next step.

3 Set up a loop to iterate through the CommandBars collection by adding the following For Each…Next loop after the object declarations:

```
For Each oCmdBar In Application.CommandBars
Next oCmdBar
```

The For Each…Next loop is used to iterate through a collection of objects. Each time that For Each…Next loops through the CommandBars collection, it implicitly sets the object variable oCmdBar to the next CommandBar object in the collection.

4 Within the For Each…Next loop, add the following If…Then condition block:

```
If oCmdBar.Name = "My CommandBar" Then
    Set oMyCmdBar = oCmdBar
    Exit For
End If
```

Make sure the spelling of "My CommandBar" is exactly as shown, including the use of upper-case letters.

During each loop of For Each…Next, the name of the CommandBar object assigned to the object variable oCmdBar is checked to determine whether it equals the name of the custom command bar My CommandBar. If the condition is found to be true, the object variable oMyCmdBar is assigned to the My CommandBar toolbar and the For Each…Next loop exits using the Exit For statement.

5 Just after the For Each…Next loop, add the following If…Then condition:

```
If Not oMyCmdBar Is Nothing Then oMyCmdBar.Delete
```

When you declare an object variable, Visual Basic implicitly assigns the value of the object variable to the Visual Basic keyword Nothing. An object variable continues to be assigned to Nothing until it is explicitly set using the Set statement or until it is used in a For Each...Next loop. The If...Then condition specifies that if the object variable oMyCmdBar is not set to Nothing (that is, it's been assigned to an actual object), the custom command bar My CommandBar will be deleted. If the object variable oMyCmdBar is still assigned to Nothing, Visual Basic continues on to the next line in the procedure, which happens to be *End Sub* in this procedure.

6   Place the cursor in the RemoveToolbar procedure and press F5 to run it.

When you run this procedure, the custom command bar My CommandBar is deleted only if it exists. If it does not exist, nothing happens and Visual Basic continues through the procedure without raising an error. If you already deleted the custom command bar My CommandBar, run the AddNewToolbar procedure created in the section "Create a simple toolbar with Visual Basic," and then run the RemoveToolbar procedure. You should see the custom command bar My CommandBar appear and then disappear.

7   Exit PowerPoint and save your changes as MyCommand Bars.ppt in the Lesson 6 subfolder of the Office VBA Practice folder.

You will use some of this code in Lesson 7.

Lesson Summary

To	Do this

Create a custom toolbar with Visual Basic	Declare a variable as a CommandBar and assign it to the object returned by the CommandBars.Add method. For example:
	`Set oMyCommandBar = Application _`
	`     .CommandBars.Add("My CommandBar")`

Add a control to the custom toolbar	Declare a variable of the appropriate control type and assign it to the object returned by the Controls.Add method. For example:
	`Set oComboBox = oMyCommandBar _`
	`     .Controls.Add(msoControlComboBox)`

Create a custom menu with Visual Basic	Assign to a variable the command bar to which you want to add the menu. For example:
	`Set oMyCommandBar = _`
	`     CommandBars("Menu Bar")`
	
	Set another variable to the object returned by the Controls.Add method. For example:
	`Set oPopup = oMyCommandBar.Controls _`
	`     .Add(msoControlPopup, , , 2)`

To	Do this
Add a control to the custom menu	Declare a variable of the appropriate control type and set it to the object returned by the Controls.Add method. For example: `Set oPopupCascade = oPopup _` `.Controls.Add(msoControlPopup)`
Specify the code to run if a command bar control is acted upon	Set the OnAction property of the control to the name of the procedure to run. For example: `oCmdButton.OnAction = "DisplayMessageBox"`
Remove a menu, menu item, or toolbar item	After assigning the correct control to a CommandBarControl object variable (often done within a For Each...Next loop), use the Delete method of the control. For example: `oCmdCtl.Delete`
Remove a toolbar	After assigning the correct toolbar to a CommandBar object variable (often done within a For Each...Next loop), use the Delete method of the toolbar. For example: `oMyCmdBar.Delete`

For online information about	Ask the Assistant for help, using the words
Creating or modifying toolbars and menu bars in general	"Using command bars"
Adding menus and menu items	"Adding and managing menus"
The CommandBar object and its properties and methods	"Commandbar"
Creating custom menus and toolbars without using Visual Basic code	"Custom menus and toolbars" (with the appropriate Office application window active)

Preview of the Next Lesson

In Lesson 7, you will learn how to use the objects in the Microsoft Office 8.0 Object Library—objects, such as the Assistant or the FileSearch object, for which you can write code once and then share the code among other Office applications.

143

Working with Shared Office Objects

Estimated time
50 min.

In this lesson you will learn how to:

- Find any file in a specified path.
- Determine the properties of a document, such as its Author and Title.
- Customize the Office Assistant and integrate it into your Visual Basic for Applications solution.

As Microsoft Office moves toward more consistency and more complete integration of components among applications, the Microsoft Office Object Library grows in terms of programmable objects—objects for which you can write code once and that can be shared among all Office applications. The biggest benefit of the Office Object Library is that whatever you use in your solution will work, more often than not, in any Office application.

The Microsoft Office 8.0 Object Library provides four main objects: CommandBars, which allows you to create custom menu items and toolbars, as you did in Lesson 6; FileSearch, which returns a list of files from a search; Assistant, which provides online Help and represents the functionality and appearance of the Office Assistant; and DocumentProperties, which represents the collection of built-in and custom properties of an Office document. Any code you write that accesses any of these objects can be reused in Microsoft Word, Excel, or PowerPoint. Microsoft Access and Outlook provide access only to the CommandBars and Assistant objects.

Building a File Search Tool

The Open dialog box in Word, Excel, PowerPoint, and Access, displayed by clicking Open on the File menu, provides a set of drop-down lists and text boxes that allow you to filter certain files. If you click the Advanced button in the Open dialog box, located below the Cancel button, the Advanced Find dialog box is displayed. With the Advanced Find dialog box, you can search for files by specific file properties; the equivalent functionality is represented in Visual Basic by the FileSearch object model in the Office object library. The FileSearch object is accessed from the Application object in Word, Excel, and PowerPoint. The Application object in Access and Outlook does not support access to the FileSearch object.

Create a dialog box for file search results

This step-by-step example works the same way in Word and PowerPoint with exactly the same results. You may prefer to enter your code there.

1 Start Microsoft Excel.

2 In the Visual Basic Editor, on the Insert menu, click UserForm.

3 If the Toolbox window is not displayed, then in the Visual Basic Editor, on the View menu, click Toolbox.

4 In the Toolbox, click the Label control and then click near the upper-left corner on the UserForm.

5 Add a TextBox control and place it adjacent to Label1.

6 Add two CommandButton controls. Place the first control in the upper-right corner of the UserForm, and place the second just below the first.

UserForm1 should now look like the following illustration:

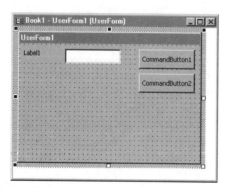

7 Add a second Label control below Label1, and add a ListBox control below Label2.

8   Below ListBox1, add a third Label control, and add a fourth Label control to the right of the third. Use the following illustration as a guide to move and size the controls.

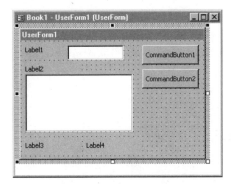

9   If the Properties window is not displayed, then in the Editor, on the View menu, click Properties Window; or, press F4 as a shortcut. In the Properties window, set the following values:

Control	Property	Value
UserForm1	Name	frmSearch
UserForm1	Caption	File Search
Label1	Name	lblFileExt
Label1	Caption	File extension to search:
TextBox1	Name	txtFileExt
CommandButton1	Name	cmdSearch
CommandButton1	Accelerator	S
CommandButton1	Caption	Search
CommandButton2	Name	cmdClose
CommandButton2	Accelerator	C
CommandButton2	Caption	Close
Label2	Name	lblResults
Label2	Caption	Results:
ListBox1	Name	lstResults
Label3	Name	lblTotal
Label3	Caption	Total number of files found:

Control	Property	Value
Label4	Name	lblTotalNumber
Label4	Caption	(Remove the caption string so that there is no text in the label.)

10 Resize and move the controls on the UserForm so that they look like the following:

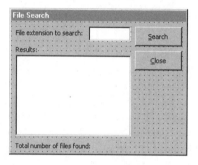

Now you are ready to add code behind the controls of the custom File Search dialog box.

Add file search code

1 In the UserForm frmSearch, which you just created, double-click the cmdSearch control and type the following in the cmdSearch_Click procedure:

```
Call FileSearch
```

You will create a procedure called FileSearch in step 3, and you'll want to keep the file search procedure and functionality separate so that you can easily use, or call, the procedure from another procedure or project.

If the UserForm window is behind the Code window, display it by clicking frmSearch (UserForm) on the Window menu.

2 Double-click the cmdClose control in the frmSearch UserForm, and type the following in the cmdClose_Click procedure:

```
Unload frmSearch
```

The Unload statement removes a UserForm from the screen and from memory. In this case, the argument you specify in the Unload statement is the frmSearch UserForm object. When the Close button is clicked, the Unload statement closes the dialog box and unloads it from memory. Because no other code is run after the Unload statement, your program will end.

TIP   In the Unload statement, you can use the Visual Basic keyword Me in place of the argument frmSearch. In this case, the keyword Me represents the UserForm in which the code is currently executing. The Me keyword behaves like an implicitly declared variable, so Me is set to the object frmSearch.

3   At the bottom of the frmSearch code module, create a new procedure by typing **Sub FileSearch**.

4   In the FileSearch procedure, add the following declaration and two lines to initialize the controls lstResults and lblTotalNumber on the frmSearch UserForm:

```
Dim i As Integer
lstResults.Clear
lblTotalNumber.Caption = ""
```

The Clear method of the ListBox control object, lstResults, removes all items in the list box at once. When the Caption property of the Label control object, lblTotalNumber, is set to an empty string (""), the label is displayed without any text. Each time a new search is conducted, the contents of the list box and the caption of the lblTotalNumber clear first.

5   Add the following With…End block:

```
With Application.FileSearch
End With
```

The FileSearch object is accessed from the Application object in Word, Excel, or PowerPoint.

6   Type the following as the first line in the With…End block created in the previous step:

```
.NewSearch
```

Before a file search can be conducted, the search criteria must be reset to the default settings by using the NewSearch method.

7   Just after the line containing the NewSearch method of the FileSearch object, type the following to set the file search properties:

```
.LookIn = "C:\"
.SearchSubFolders = True
```

The LookIn property of the File Search dialog box allows you to specify a string value that indicates which folder on your hard disk to search for the specified file(s). The SearchSubFolders property indicates whether the search should iterate through the contents of subfolders in the folder specified by the LookIn property.

8 To set two more file search properties, type the following just after the line setting the SearchSubFolders property:

```
.FileName = "*." & txtFileExt.Text
.FileType = msoFileTypeAllFiles
```

The FileName property is set to the name of the file to look for during the file search. You can include two wildcard characters in the filename: * (asterisk) or ? (question mark). When you want to match any single character, use the question mark; when you want to match a number of characters, use the asterisk.

The FileName property is set to type *.<file extension>, where <file extension> represents the text value entered in the txtFileExt TextBox control on the frmSearch UserForm. This syntax finds all files that have the specified extension.

The FileType property is set to the enumeration value msoFileTypeAllFiles, which indicates that the search should include all types of files. Other values that it could be set to are msoFileTypeWordDocuments, msoFileTypeExcelWorkbooks, msoFileTypePowerPointPresentations, msoFileTypeDatabases, msoFileTypeTemplates, msoFileTypeOfficeFiles, and msoFileTypeBinders.

9 To start the search, type the following:

```
.Execute SortBy:=msoSortByFileType, _
    SortOrder:=msoSortOrderAscending
```

The Execute method of the FileSearch object starts the file search using the settings of the specified properties before the method runs. Two arguments the Execute method supports are SortBy and SortOrder, and in this example their values are set to msoSortByFileType and msoSortOrderAscending, respectively.

The SortBy argument can be set to one of the following: msoSortByFileName, msoSortByFileType, msoSortByLastModified, or msoSortBySize. These are the common types of sorts you can perform in the right pane of Windows Explorer. The second argument, SortOrder, can be one of the following: msoSortOrderAscending or msoSortOrderDescending.

Fill a list box with the file search results

Once the Execute method of the FileSearch object finishes searching, the code following the method runs. The list of files that returns can be accessed using the FoundFiles collection object of the FileSearch object, and you can use this list to populate (or fill in) a ListBox control on a UserForm.

1 Just after the Execute method added in the FileSearch procedure, type the following With...End block:

```
With .FoundFiles
End With
```

The complete list of files found is represented by the FoundFiles collection object, which is accessed by the FoundFiles property of the FileSearch object.

2 In the first line of the With...End block, type the following:

```
lblTotalNumber.Caption = .Count
```

Count is a property of the collection object FoundFiles. The Count and Item properties are members of all collection objects across Microsoft Office. The total number of files found is listed in the FoundFiles collection object, and you are setting the Caption property of the lblTotalNumber label control to that total.

3 Type the following For...Next loop just after the line setting the Caption property of the lblTotalNumber label control:

```
For i = 1 To .Count
    lstResults.AddItem .Item(i)
Next i
```

The For...Next loop starts at a value of 1 and increments the value of the Integer i until it reaches the total number of files listed in the FoundFiles collection object; the total number is represented by the value of the Count property. During each loop, each item in the FoundFiles collection object is added to the lstResults list box control using the AddItem method of the ListBox control object. The complete FileSearch procedure can be seen in the following illustration:

```
Book1 - frmSearch (Code)
(General)                              FileSearch

Sub FileSearch()
    Dim i As Integer
    lstResults.Clear
    lblTotalNumber.Caption = ""
    With Application.FileSearch
        .NewSearch
        .LookIn = "C:\"
        .SearchSubFolders = True
        .FileName = "*." & txtFileExt.Text
        .FileType = msoFileTypeAllFiles
        .Execute SortBy:=msoSortByFileType, _
            SortOrder:=msoSortOrderAscending
        With .FoundFiles
            lblTotalNumber.Caption = .Count
            For i = 1 To .Count
                lstResults.AddItem .Item(i)
            Next i
        End With
    End With
End Sub
```

151

4   Press F5 to run the dialog box.

5   In the file extension text box adjacent to the label "File extension to search:", enter the file extension txt and click the Search button.

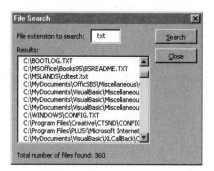

The lstResults ListBox control displays a filename list of all files with the file extension *txt* in the folder C:\ and all of the subfolders. The lblTotalNumber label control displays the total number of files found. Repeat the search by typing different file extensions in the File Search dialog box you created, or change the directory specified by the LookIn property of the FileSearch object.

Save

6   Click the Close button. Then click the Save button and save your workbook as MyFileSearch in the Lesson 7 subfolder of the Office VBA Practice folder.

Connect the custom File Search dialog box to a menu command

You can add a menu item or toolbar button that, when chosen or clicked, displays the custom File Search dialog box. In the following steps, you will add a menu item that displays the custom File Search dialog box, but you can just as easily add a toolbar button to do the same.

1   In the Project Explorer, right-click MyFileSearch project and click Import File on the shortcut menu. In the Import File dialog box, navigate to the Lesson 7 practice folder, select the file modMenu.bas, and click Open.

The file modMenu.bas contains the AddMenuItem procedure that was created in Lesson 6 in the section, "Add a menu item to an existing menu." You will reuse this code with some modifications.

If you are now working with Word or PowerPoint instead of Excel, or if in Lesson 6 you added a Select Case block to the AddMenuItem procedure, you should skip step 2.

2 In the AddMenuItem procedure, replace the first Set statement with the following:

```
Set oCmdPopup = CommandBars("Worksheet Menu Bar") _
    .Controls("File")
```

The main menu bar in Word and PowerPoint (and Access) is named Menu Bar; in Excel, it is named Worksheet Menu Bar.

3 In the AddMenuItem procedure, replace the With...End block with the following With...End block.

```
With oCmdButton
    .BeginGroup = True
    .Caption = "Fi&le Search"
    .OnAction = "ShowDialog"
End With
```

The differences between the two With...End blocks are the property values for Caption and OnAction, and the addition of the BeginGroup property in the With...End block immediately above. The Caption property is set to "File Search," and the accelerator key is specified as the letter "l." When the menu item is chosen, the ShowDialog procedure is called and runs. You will add this procedure in the following step. The BeginGroup property adds a separator between the File Search menu item and the preceding menu item.

4 Place the cursor beneath the AddMenuItem procedure and create a new procedure by typing **Sub ShowDialog**.

5 Add the following statement to the ShowDialog procedure:

```
frmSearch.Show
```

The Show method of the frmSearch UserForm object loads the custom UserForm and displays it on the screen.

 NOTE If you performed the steps in Lesson 6 using Excel instead of PowerPoint, make sure that all previous custom command bars have been removed. On the View menu, point to Toolbars, and then click Customize on the submenu. In the Toolbars list box on the Toolbars tab, select "My CommandBar" and then click Delete.

6 Place the cursor in the AddMenuItem procedure that you revised in step 3 above and press F5 to add the File Search menu item to the File menu in the Excel application window.

After the AddMenuItem procedure runs, the File menu appears as follows:

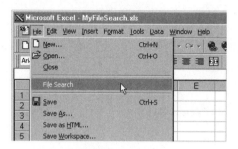

7 On the File menu in the Excel application window, click the custom File Search menu item.

The custom File Search dialog box is displayed each time you click File Search on the File menu. You no longer have to place the cursor in the FileSearch procedure in the Editor window to display the dialog box. Now both you and your users have access to your custom solution through the graphical user interface.

8 Close the File Search dialog box and exit Excel. Make sure that you save the changes to your workbook.

Using Document Properties

Each file created in a Microsoft Office application contains a set of document properties. The set is a combination of built-in document properties that Office defines, including Title, Author, Subject, and Comments, and custom document properties that you can define for the document. The setting and retrieval of built-in and custom document properties in the user interface is conducted through the Properties dialog box. The Properties dialog box is accessed by clicking Properties on the File menu in Word, Excel, or PowerPoint. In Access, click Database Properties on the File menu.

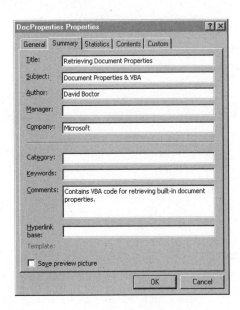

 NOTE The object model associated with the document properties of a file is provided through the Microsoft Office 8.0 Object Library. You access the document properties through the BuiltInDocumentProperties property in Word, Excel, and PowerPoint, as the example below demonstrates. In Microsoft Access, setting and returning document properties of a database is slightly more involved. You can set the built-in and custom properties by using the SummaryInfo and UserDefined Document object in the Documents collection, respectively. For more information, in Access, ask the Assistant for help using the words "database properties."

Retrieve built-in document properties

You might want to build an index of all documents kept on a local file server, cataloged by such document properties as Author, Title, Subject, and Comments. Retrieving these and other built-in document properties is done through the DocumentProperties object, using the BuiltInDocumentProperties property of the Document object in Word, the Workbook object in Excel, or the Presentation object in PowerPoint.

1 Start Microsoft Word. Open the Visual Basic Editor, insert a new module, and create a new procedure by typing **Sub GetDocumentProperties**.

2 Add the following With...End block:

```
With ActiveDocument.BuiltInDocumentProperties
End With
```

NOTE   ActiveDocument should be changed to ActivePresentation if you are running this procedure in PowerPoint or changed to ActiveWorkbook if you are running this procedure in Excel.

3   In the With...End block created in step 2, type the following lines:

```
Debug.Print "Author: " & .Item("Author").Value
Debug.Print "Subject: " & .Item("Subject").Value
Debug.Print "Title: " & .Item("Title").Value
Debug.Print "Comments: " & .Item("Comments").Value
```

These properties are common to Word, Excel, and PowerPoint, and they always return a value. If any one is not set, the value returns an empty string. The Debug.Print statement prints the specified string in the Immediate window, which can be displayed by clicking Immediate Window on the View menu in the Editor. The MsgBox function can serve the same purpose, but it displays the value in a message box that you have to close in order to continue working with the application or the Editor. The Debug.Print statement allows you to continue working without disruption.

4   Just after the built-in properties specified above and before the `End With` statement, add the following lines:

```
Debug.Print "Number of Words: " & _
    .Item("Number of Words").Value
Debug.Print "Number of Pages: " & _
    .Item("Number of Pages").Value
```

Unlike step 3, where the properties you added are common to Word, Excel, and PowerPoint, few built-in document properties are specific to either Word or PowerPoint. These properties are listed in the Statistics tab in the Properties dialog box.

5   If the Immediate Window isn't open, click Immediate Window on the View menu.

6   Place the cursor in the GetDocumentProperties procedure and press F5 to run it.

The specified built-in document properties for Word appear in the Immediate window. The following illustration shows properties for a sample document; your properties will be different.

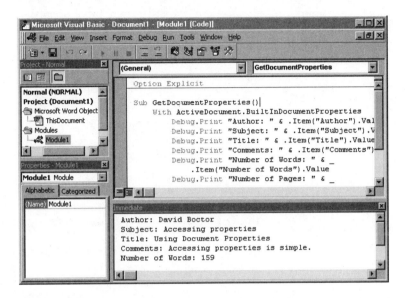

Retrieving Some Document Properties Results in an Error

Some properties, such as Author and Title, can only be returned and cannot be set by the user. These properties are invalid until the first time they are set by the Office application. For example, the Last Save Time built-in document property is not valid until the first time the document, workbook, or presentation is saved. The Last Print Date built-in document property is also invalid until the first time the document, workbook, or presentation is printed.

```
Debug.Print "Last Save Time: " & _
    .Item("Last Save Time").Value
Debug.Print "Last Print Date: " & _
    .Item("Last Print Date").Value
```

If you add the two lines above to the With…End block added in step 2 of the preceding example, an error would occur, and the valid values would not display in the Immediate window.

157

Set document properties

Document properties are usually not the first thing you set in a document, so they are often overlooked. Some companies may have a requirement that every document sent electronically to customers have document properties set. For example, you may want to explicitly set the built-in Company document property to be the same company-wide and set some comments in the built-in Comments document property.

You can perform these steps in Excel or PowerPoint too.

1 If the Project Explorer window is not open, then in the Visual Basic Editor of Word, click Project Explorer on the View menu.

2 In the Project Explorer, double-click ThisDocument on the Visual Basic project of Document1. (You may have to click the plus sign next to the Microsoft Word Objects folder to display ThisDocument.)

> **NOTE** The ThisDocument project item is a module for the Document object. Because the module belongs to an object, the ThisDocument project item is referred to as a *class module*. If a module does not belong to an object, it is referred to as a *code module*. A code module is also called a *standard module* in newer versions of Visual Basic. For more information, ask the Assistant for help using the words "module and class module commands."

3 In the Object drop-down list of the ThisDocument class module, select Document.

4 In the Procedure drop-down list of the ThisDocument class module, select Close.

5 In the Document_Close event handler, add the following lines:

```
With ThisDocument.BuiltInDocumentProperties
    .Item("Company").Value = "My Company"
    .Item("Comments").Value = _
        "Please send mail to Dave@MyCompany.com"
End With
```

The object ThisDocument represents the Document object containing the code that is currently running. This Workbook is the equivalent in Excel. PowerPoint, Access, and Outlook do not have an equivalent. ThisDocument and ThisWorkbook are useful in cases where you want to manipulate the contents or properties of the open document or workbook. In the With…End block above, you are setting the built-in document properties Company and Comments.

6 In Word, on the File menu, click Close.

Each time you close the document, the document Close event is triggered. The code within the event procedure runs, and the built-in document properties Company and Comments are set.

 NOTE Each time the document is closed, the document properties are set in the Close event procedure. This results in a state where the document has been changed, because you are resetting the document properties. Therefore, when you close the document and the document properties are reset, an alert is displayed asking whether you want to save the document.

7 Click Yes and save the document using any name you want.

8 Open the document again, and then on the File menu, click Properties. Notice that the new property information was saved.

9 Exit Word without saving changes.

Creating an Office Assistant for Your Solution

The Microsoft Office Assistant provides a common interface for displaying Help information and tips to users working with any Microsoft Office application. To allow Visual Basic for Applications solutions to use the Office Assistant as well, an associated object model is provided that can be accessed through the Application object of Word, Excel, PowerPoint, Access, and Outlook. By using the Assistant in your custom solution, you can provide Help tips to explain how to use your custom UserForm or to display a set of choices for finding more information.

Create Assistant balloons to display information

If you used Word or PowerPoint to create the File Search dialog box, or if you saved the file with a different name, make sure that you open the correct file.

1 Start Microsoft Excel and open the MyFileSearch workbook you created earlier in this lesson.

2 Open the Visual Basic Editor and insert a new code module.

3 In the Properties window, change the name of the newly added code module to **modAssistant**.

Naming modules helps you remember what the contents of the module may be, especially if you have a Visual Basic project with several code modules.

4 Create a new procedure in the code module modAssistant by typing **Sub DisplayOfficeAssistant**.

5 Type the following declaration as the first line:

```
Dim oBalloon As Office.Balloon
```

When you typed the word Office and then typed a period (.), the Auto List Members drop-down list should have appeared listing the Balloon item. By default, Word, Excel, and PowerPoint automatically reference the Microsoft Office 8.0 Object Library, which contains the Assistant and Balloon objects.

NOTE If the Auto List Members drop-down list did not appear, you may not have the Office Object Library referenced or the Auto List Members feature may not be selected in the Options dialog box. To reference the Office Object Library, on the Tools menu in the Editor, click References, and then select the check box next to the Microsoft Office 8.0 Object Library item in the list. To turn on the Auto List Members feature, on the Tools menu, click Options, and then select Auto List Members on the Editor tab.

6   To assign the object variable oBalloon to a balloon object, type the following Set statement:

```
Set oBalloon = Assistant.NewBalloon
```

The NewBalloon method of the Assistant object returns a Balloon object, which is assigned to the oBalloon object variable.

7   After the Set statement, type the following With...End block:

```
With oBalloon
End With
```

8   Within the With...End block, type the following lines to set the Heading and Text properties of the newly created Assistant Balloon object:

```
.Heading = "File Search"
.Text = "To conduct a file search, " & _
    "follow the steps outlined below."
```

The Heading property is used for text that is displayed at the top of the balloon and is bold. The Text property is assigned text that is displayed just below the heading but is not bold.

9   To set the type of buttons that will appear at the bottom of the balloon, type the following:

```
.Button = msoButtonSetOK
```

The Button property can be set to a wide range of predefined buttons and combinations of buttons that include OK, Cancel, Yes, No, Next, Previous, and more. In this case, the Button property is set to the OK button. The list of enumeration values that you can set to the Button property is extensive. To see the full list of button combinations, scroll down the Auto List Members drop-down list that is displayed after you type the equal sign (=).

10   After setting the Button property, type the following to set the balloon mode:

```
.Mode = msoModeModal
```

The Assistant balloon can be in one of three modes: Modal, which indicates that the balloon must be closed before you can continue working in the application or UserForm; AutoDown, which indicates that the balloon closes once you click anywhere on the screen; and Modeless, which allows you to continue working with the application or UserForm but continues to display the balloon until you close it, either programmatically through Visual Basic or by pressing a button within the balloon. When you specify that the balloon is Modeless (by setting the Mode property to msoModeModeless), you must set a value for the Callback property. The Callback property value is the name of a procedure that is called just after the balloon is closed.

11   To display the balloon on the screen, type the following Show method:

```
.Show
```

12   Place the cursor in the DisplayOfficeAssistant procedure and press F5 to run it.

The Assistant will be displayed as well as a balloon with a heading, text, and button.

Add Label and Checkbox controls to balloons

The Assistant object model provides two types of controls you can display in the Assistant balloon—five Label controls and five Checkbox controls are available. When you specify the text of either a label or a check box, it is displayed in the balloon. You cannot, however, position the controls within the balloon. The set of labels is always displayed before the set of check boxes.

1   Within the With…End block added in the preceding steps, add the following set of lines just before the Show method:

```
.BalloonType = msoBalloonTypeNumbers
.Labels(1).Text = "Specify a file extension in the " & _
    "text box next to the label 'Enter a file extension'."
.Labels(2).Text = "Click the Search button."
.Labels(3).Text = "To display these steps again, " & _
    "click the Assistant button. "
```

The BalloonType property of the Balloon object indicates whether the labels specified by the Label property appear as a numbered list, a bulleted list, or a list with circular buttons. The numbered list is specified using msoBalloonTypeNumbers, the bulleted list with msoBalloonTypeBullets, and the button list with msoBalloonTypeButtons. Because you are listing a set of steps, you want the button type set to a numbered list. Three items will be in the numbered list, because the text of three of the five Label controls was specified.

2   Place the cursor in the DisplayOfficeAssistant procedure and press F5 to run it.

The Assistant is displayed with a numbered list:

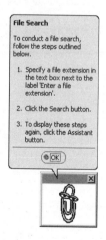

For more information about check boxes within the Assistant balloon, in the Editor, ask the Assistant for help using the word "Checkbox" and select the topic "Checkboxes property."

Add icons and bitmaps to balloons

In the Assistant balloon, you can add bitmaps (.bmp files), Windows metafiles (.wmf files), or one of two built-in icons within the heading or body text. Icons and bitmaps make the information and tips within a balloon more interesting.

1   Within the same With…End block you modified in the preceding steps, add the following line just before the line setting the BalloonType property:

```
.Icon = msoIconTip
```

The Icon property can be set to two built-in icons, Tip and Alert. Tip, specified by msoIconTip, is an image of a lightbulb, and Alert, specified by msoIconAlert, is an image of an exclamation mark (!). The icon appears at the upper-left side of the Assistant balloon, just to the left of the balloon heading. If you do not want to display an icon, set the Icon property to msoIconNone.

2   Switch to the Windows Explorer and navigate to the Lesson 7 practice file. Copy the file Assistnt.bmp to the C:\ folder.

3   Assign a string variable to reference the location of a bitmap by adding the following line above the With…End block:

```
sBitmapFile = "{bmp C:\Assistnt.bmp}"
```

To specify a bitmap, use the syntax {bmp <filename>}, where <filename> represents a valid filename of an existing bitmap file. If you want to specify a Windows metafile instead, change "bmp" to "wmf" in the syntax above, and specify a valid filename to an existing Windows metafile. This picture syntax is represented by a string and can be assigned to a string variable or added directly to a string within the Assistant balloon.

IMPORTANT   When including a bitmap in an Assistant balloon, you must give the bitmap a filename and pathname with no spaces. If the filename or pathname contains spaces, the Assistant balloon may not be displayed.

Also, the filename specified above assumes you have installed the practice files in a particular folder. If you installed them in a different folder, set the filename above to the correct location. Otherwise, you can set the filename to any valid bitmap file on your computer. If the filename is not correct, the Assistant is not displayed when you run the DisplayOfficeAssistant procedure.

4   Declare the string variable sBitmapFile at the beginning of the DisplayOfficeAssistant procedure where the other variables are declared:

```
Dim sBitmapFile As String
```

5 To add the bitmap in the Assistant balloon, concatenate the text of the third label (added in step 1 of the preceding step-by-step example) with the string variable sBitmapFile.

You do this by typing **& sBitmapFile** at the end of the .Labels(3).Text assignment statement. The revised line looks like this:

```
.Labels(3).Text = "To display these steps again, " & _
    "click the Assistant button. " & sBitmapFile
```

6 Place the cursor in the DisplayOfficeAssistant procedure and press F5 to run it.

The Assistant will now be displayed with an icon beside the balloon heading and a bitmap in the third item of the numbered list.

7 In the DisplayOfficeAssistant procedure, change the line setting the Text property to the following and rerun the procedure:

```
.Text = "To conduct a file search, " & sBitmapFile & _
    "follow the steps outlined below."
```

You can add the specified bitmap to any text within the Assistant balloon: simply concatenate any string specified anywhere in the DisplayOfficeAssistant procedure with the string variable sBitmapFile.

8 Place the cursor in the DisplayOfficeAssistant procedure and press F5 to run it again.

NOTE The bitmap file needs to remain in the C:\folder as long as your program contains the line sBitmapFile = "{bmp C:\Assistant.bmp}". If this line was commented out or removed, the program will work correctly and the Assistant balloon will be displayed. Otherwise, if the line above was executed but the bitmap file was removed from the C:\folder, the Assistant balloon will not be displayed.

Hook the Office Assistant to the File Search solution

Once you create code for the Office Assistant, you need to connect the procedure to an element in your custom UserForm so that your users can access the Assistant.

1   In the Project Explorer window, double-click the frmSearch form. (You may have to click the plus sign next to the Forms folder to see the form.)

2   Click the CommandButton control in the Toolbox window and drag the control to the lower-right corner of the UserForm.

3   In the Properties window, set the following values:

Control	Property	Value
CommandButton1	Name	cmdAssistant
CommandButton1	Caption	(Remove the caption string so that there is no text in the label.)
CommandButton1	Picture	Assistnt.bmp*
CommandButton1	PicturePosition	12 – fmPicturePositionCenter

*You cannot type the picture filename in the Properties window. You have to click the button at the right of the Picture property value (the button label has three ellipsis points, a series of three periods) to display the Load Picture dialog box. In the dialog box, change to the Lesson 7 practice folder, select the Assistnt.bmp file, and click OK.

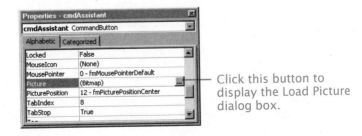

Click this button to display the Load Picture dialog box.

Run Sub/ UserForm

4 Click the UserForm and then click the Run Sub/UserForm button to display the dialog box.

The custom File Search dialog box, frmSearch, should look like the following:

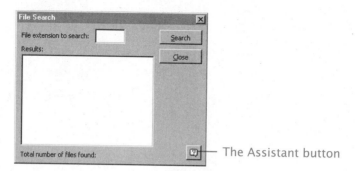

— The Assistant button

5 Click the Close button and then double-click the cmdAssistant control in the UserForm frmSearch you added. Add the following within the cmdAssistant_Click procedure:

```
Call modAssistant.DisplayOfficeAssistant
```

The DisplayOfficeAssistant procedure is located in the code module modAssistant.

TIP In previous uses of the Call statement, only the procedure name was specified. In those cases, the procedure was located in the same code module in which the call was being made. In uses of the Call statement where the procedure is located in a code module other than the one in which the call is being made, it is generally good practice to prefix the procedure name with the name of the code module containing the procedure. Visual Basic allows you to have procedures with the same name, but they must be in different code modules in the project. By prefixing the procedure call with the code module name, you avoid naming conflicts and make sure that the call is to the correct procedure.

6 On the File menu in the Excel application window, click the custom File Search menu item.

The custom File Search dialog box is displayed when you click File Search on the File menu. Click the Assistant button in the dialog box to display the Assistant and its balloon. Now your users can review the steps involved in conducting a file search.

7 Exit Excel and save your changes.

Lesson Summary

To	Do this
Search for files using Visual Basic code	Use the FileSearch object and specify the drive to be searched, and whether to include subfolders, the filename, and file type (LookIn, SearchSubFolders, FileName, and FileType properties).
Retrieve returned information from a file search	Iterate through the FoundFiles collection (a property of the FileSearch object).

Retrieve built-in document properties in Word, Excel, or PowerPoint	Use the BuiltInDocumentProperties property of the Document object in Word, the Workbook object in Excel, or the Presentation object in PowerPoint to specify the property value you want. For example:
	
	`sTheProperty = ActivePresentation. _`
	`    BuiltInDocumentProperties("Author")`

Set document properties using Visual Basic code	Assign the property values to the appropriate property index in the BuiltInDocumentProperties collection. For example:
	
	`ThisDocument _`
	`    .BuiltInDocumentProperties("Company") _`
	`    = "My Company"`

Create a balloon in the Assistant to display Help information	Declare a variable as type Office.Balloon and set it to the returned object of the NewBalloon method. For example: `Set oBalloon = Assistant.NewBalloon`

Add a picture to the Assistant balloon	Set the Icon property of the Balloon object to msoIconTip or msoIconAlert. For example:
	
	`oBalloon.Icon = msoIconTip`
	
	You can also set a string variable to a value with the syntax {bmp <italic>filename</italic>} and concatenate the string variable to text in the Assistant balloon. For example:
	
	`sBitmap = "{bmp c:\temp\Pict.bmp}"`
	`oBalloon.Text = "There is a " & _`
	`    sBitmapFile & " picture here."`

Add a picture to a command button on a UserForm	In the Properties window, set the Picture property of the command button to the picture name and then set the Picture Position property to the value 12 – fmPicturePositionCenter

For online information about	Ask the Assistant for help, using the words
Microsoft Office objects	"Microsoft Office objects" (or the individual object "FileSearch", "Assistant object", or "DocumentProperties")
Ending a program	"End statement"
Loading and unloading a UserForm	"Load UserForm" and "Unload UserForm"
Modifying the Assistant balloon	"Balloon"
Positioning a picture in a command button on a UserForm	"Picture Position"

Preview of the Next Lesson

In Lesson 8, you will learn how to build an Access database and automatically generate a Word document, Excel workbook, PowerPoint presentation, and Outlook message from the database information. The foundation of the database will be used in Lesson 9 through Lesson 11, where you will combine menu customizations and the Office Assistant with your Office solutions.

Part
3

Creating Integrated Office Solutions for Microsoft Office

Developing an Integrated Office Solution

Estimated time

90 min.

In this lesson you will learn how to:

■ Develop an integrated Office solution using an Access database.

■ Complete a report in Word with database information.

■ Create an Excel worksheet and chart from database information.

■ Present an Excel chart in PowerPoint.

■ Send Office documents in Outlook mail.

When you develop Visual Basic for Applications programs for Microsoft Office, you often apply functionality and tools across the Office suite. Building integrated solutions helps you keep the core of your information centralized so that it is easy to manage, while allowing you to communicate that information in ways that best suit your customers' needs.

In this lesson, you will create an integrated Office solution that starts with a Microsoft Access database containing a form with which users interact with your program. The custom form provides options for creating a Microsoft Word report for management and customers, a Microsoft Excel worksheet for data analysis, and a Microsoft PowerPoint presentation for meetings and sales demonstrations, as well as the ability to automatically send the documents your program generates through e-mail using Microsoft Outlook.

You will add the code that drives the automatic generation of all of these documents to the Access database. In Lesson 9, you will learn how to add code to a Word add-in to generate the same Word report you create here, and you will create a workbook and a presentation using Excel and PowerPoint add-ins in Lesson 10.

Creating an Access Database

The integrated Office solution you are about to create involves a fictitious set of data representing an energy usage log for a computer lab in your company. The solution is called "Energy Management," and it tracks the lab's energy use over a one-month stretch so that management can do a cost assessment and determine ways of reducing future energy costs.

The Access database that stores the energy usage data consists of three main elements. The first element is the table containing the data. The second is the user interface, or dialog box, where you select the document items you want to automatically generate. The third is the code, contained in the various code modules, that creates the selected document items. The following steps show you how to create all three elements of the database.

Import data into an Access database table

1 Start Microsoft Access. In the opening Access dialog box, select the Blank Database button and click OK.

2 In the File New Database dialog box, select the Lesson 8 practice folder; in the File Name text box, type **MyEnergy** and click Create.

3 Click the Tables tab, click New, select Import Table from the New Table dialog box, and click OK.

4 In the Import dialog box, select Text Files in the Files Of Type drop-down list. In the Lesson 8 practice folder, select LabEnerg.txt and click Import.

In this fictitious solution, the text file was automatically generated by a digital meter connected to a computer. The hardware and software associated with the meter automatically feed the data to the text file.

5 In the Import Text Wizard dialog box, click Next five times until you reach the final step in the wizard, and then type **LabEnergyUsage** in the Import To Table text box.

Because you are importing a comma-delimited text file containing data that was automatically generated by the tools connected to the circuits, you should accept the default settings in each step of the wizard.

6 In the Import Text Wizard dialog box, click Finish.

7 When the Import Text Wizard displays the message box indicating that Access is finished importing the data file, click OK.

8 Select the LabEnergyUsage table and click Design.

9 In the Field Name column, double-click in the second row, which currently contains the text Field1.

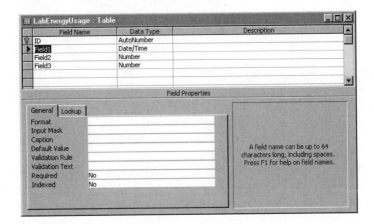

10 In the Field Name column, clear the text and type **Date and Time**.

11 In the Field Name column, double-click in the third row, which currently contains the text Field2. Clear the text and type **Lighting**.

12 In the Field Name column, double-click in the fourth row, which currently contains the text Field3. Clear the text and type **Computer Network**.

Close
Window

13 Close the Table Design View window by clicking the small Close Window button in the upper-right corner of the Table Design View window.

14 When Access asks if you want to save changes to the design of table LabEnergyUsage, click Yes.

The table is now ready for exporting data to Word, Excel, and PowerPoint, and you can start creating the dialog box that will display your document options.

Create a form in Microsoft Access

1 In the MyEnergy: Database window, click the Forms tab of the database and then click New.

173

2   In the New Form dialog box, select Design View and click OK.

The form is now in design view, and you can start adding controls to the form.

Check Box control

3   Click the Check Box control in the Toolbox and then click anywhere on the form to insert a check box control. Repeat these actions three more times to create four check boxes in total.

Command Button control

4   Click the Command Button control in the Toolbox and then click anywhere on the form to insert a command button control. Click Cancel when the Command Button Wizard appears.

Repeat this step once more to create a total of two command buttons.

Label control

5   Click the Label control in the Toolbox and then click anywhere on the form to insert a label control. Type **Generate the following documents:** immediately after inserting the Label control to replace the label's default text. You need to add a caption immediately or else the control will disappear.

6   Click the Image control in the Toolbox and then click anywhere on the form to insert an image control. In the Insert Picture dialog box that is displayed automatically once you insert the Image control, change to the Lesson 8 practice folder, select Logo.wmf, and click OK.

7   Move and resize the controls and the form so that they appear similar to the following illustration:

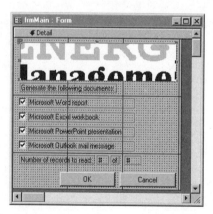

8   If the Properties window is not displayed, on the View menu in Access, click Properties. In the Properties window, click the All tab to see a full list of properties and set the following values for the controls.

NOTE Unlike the Check Box control in the UserForm of the Visual Basic Editor, which has a Caption property, the label associated with a Check Box control in an Access form is listed as a separate control in the Properties window. Select the label of the check box to set its properties.

Control	Property	Value
Check0	Name	chkWord
Label1	Name	lblWord
Label1	Caption	Microsoft Word report
Check2	Name	chkExcel
Label3	Name	lblExcel
Label3	Caption	Microsoft Excel workbook
Check4	Name	chkPowerPoint
Label5	Name	lblPowerPoint
Label5	Caption	Microsoft PowerPoint presentation
Check6	Name	chkOutlook
Label7	Name	lblOutlook
Label7	Caption	Microsoft Outlook mail message
Command8	Name	cmdOK
Command8	Caption	OK
Command9	Name	cmdCancel
Command9	Caption	Cancel
Command9	Cancel	Yes
Label10	Name	lblGenerate
Image11	Name	imgLogo
Image11	Size Mode	Stretch

9 To visually display the progress of your solution when it is running, add four Label controls just above the OK and Cancel buttons. Add the following captions consecutively: **Number of records read:** , **#, of,** **#.** When you insert each Label control, you need to add a caption immediately or else the control disappears.

10 In the Properties window, set the following properties:

Control	Property	Value
Label12	Name	lblProgress
Label13	Name	lblCurrentRecord
Label14	Name	lblOf
Label15	Name	lblTotalRecords

In the Form Design window, click anywhere outside the form design area to display the list of properties for the form. (You may have to scroll down in order to display the area below the form design area.)

11 In the Properties window, set the following values for the form:

Property	Value
Caption	Energy Management
Record Selectors	No
Navigation Buttons	No
Dividing Lines	No
Border Style	Dialog
Shortcut Menu	No

12 Click on the title bar of the form window and Press F5 to display the dialog box.

Try selecting and clearing the check boxes. Notice that the Form Design window creates forms just like UserForms in the Visual Basic Editor of Word, Excel, and PowerPoint.

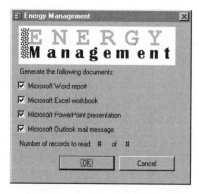

Close Window

13 Click the Close Window button to close the form and, when Access asks if you want to save changes to the design of form Form1, click Yes. In the Save As dialog box, type **frmMain** in the Form Name text box and click OK.

Before adding code, you may want to click the Design button and move or size the controls to resemble the preceding illustration. Press F5 to display the form, click the Close Window button to close the form, and then save your changes.

Add code behind the form

1 In the MyEnergy: Database window, select the item frmMain in the Forms tab of the database and click the Design button.

2 On the View menu, click Code to display the code module behind the form frmMain.

3 In the Object drop-down list of the Code window, select cmdOK.

   By default, the click event procedure is displayed in the Code window.

4 In the event procedure cmdOK_Click, add the following lines of code:

```
Dim bReport As Boolean, bSheet As Boolean
Dim bPres As Boolean, bMail As Boolean

If Me.chkWord.Value = True Then bReport = True
If Me.chkExcel.Value = True Then bSheet = True
If Me.chkPowerPoint.Value = True Then bPres = True
If Me.chkOutlook.Value = True Then bMail = True

Call modMain.Main(bReport, bSheet, bPres, bMail)
End
```

The first two lines contain declarations of the Boolean variables bReport, bSheet, bPres, and bMail. By default, the Boolean variables are set to False when they are declared. The four If…Then condition statements that follow check the value of each check box in the form frmMain and set the appropriate Boolean variable. The Me keyword represents the form in which the code you are writing resides. Once all Boolean variables are set, the Main procedure in the code module modMain, which you will create next, in the section "Add code to the database to create an Office document," is called. The Boolean variables are passed as arguments to the Main procedure.

5 In the Object drop-down list of the Code window, select cmdCancel.

   By default, the click event procedure is displayed in the code window.

6 In the event procedure cmdCancel_Click, add the following lines of code:

```
DoCmd.Close acForm, "frmMain", acSaveNo
End
```

You can specify three arguments in the Close method of the DoCmd object in Access. The first argument is the object type you want to close, the second is the name of the object to be closed, and the third sets whether to save changes to the object when it's closed. In the line of code you just added, you close the Access form frmMain without saving changes to the form in the database.

*Close
Window*

7 Click the Close Window button in the Code window and click the Close Window button in the frmMain: Form window. When asked whether you want to save changes, click Yes.

The dialog box that your users will interact with to generate their required Office documents from the data in the database is complete. You now must add code to create each of the Office documents listed in your custom dialog box.

Add code to the database to create an Office document

1 In the MyEnergy: Database window, in the Modules tab, click New.

2 On the Tools menu, click References to display the References dialog box.

3 Select the following items in the Available References list box and click OK when you finish: Microsoft Word 8.0 Object Library, Microsoft Excel 8.0 Object Library, Microsoft PowerPoint 8.0 Object Library, and Microsoft Outlook 8.0 Object Library (or Model).

You are going to write code that accesses all of these object libraries so that you can create each type of document.

IMPORTANT The procedures in this section assume that you have previously installed Data Access Objects for Visual Basic. If the Microsoft DAO 3.5 Object Library does not appear in your Available References list, run the Office Setup program. In the Office 97 Maintenance list, select Data Access, click Change Option, and select Data Access Objects for Visual Basic.

4 Add the following declarations to the code module:

```
Public g_sgTotalCost As Single
Public g_iTotalHours As Integer
Public Const g_sCircuit As String = "Computer Network"
Public Const g_sFilePath As String = _
    "C:\Office VBA Practice\Lesson8\"
Const m_sgCost As Single = 1.075
Const m_iWattage As Integer = 560
Dim m_dbEnergyUsage As DAO.Database
```

The first two declarations are public variables used to total the data in the database. The public constant g_sCircuit is set to "Computer Network," the circuit that will be analyzed. In the future, you can reset it to "Lighting" so that the lighting data can be analyzed. The public constant g_sFilePath is set to the file folder location containing source files such as the template used to create the Word document. The path also specifies where the generated Office documents are to be saved. The two module-level constants, m_sgCost and m_iWattage, are values used to calculate the energy cost. The module-level variable m_dbEnergyUsage is declared as the database containing the data you imported earlier in the lesson.

5   After the variable declarations, add the following Main procedure:

```
Sub Main( _
     bReport As Boolean, _
     bSheet As Boolean, _
     bPres As Boolean, _
     bMail As Boolean)

     Set m_dbEnergyUsage = DBEngine.Workspaces(0) _
         .OpenDatabase(g_sFilePath & "Energy.mdb")
End Sub
```

The Main procedure will be called by the click event procedure for the cmdOK command button you added to the form frmMain. The four Boolean variables passed into the Main procedure indicate which check boxes were selected in the form frmMain. The Boolean values are set in the click event procedure of cmdOK. The first line within the procedure Main opens the Energy.mdb database and sets the database to the variable m_dbEnergyUsage.

6   After the line calling the OpenEnergyDatabase procedure, add the following If...Then condition blocks:

```
If bReport = True Then
     Call modWord.CreateWordDocument
End If
If bSheet = True Or bPres = True Then
     Call modExcel.CreateExcelSheet
End If
```

If the Boolean variable bReport is passed into the Main procedure with a value of True, the procedure CreateWordDocument, located in the code module modWord, is called. If the Boolean variable bSheet or the Boolean variable bPres is passed into the Main procedure with a value of True, the procedure CreateExcelSheet, located in the code module modExcel, is called. In order to create a presentation with the data in a chart, the chart must first be created in Excel. The procedures modWord and modExcel will be created in the sections "Complete a Word document with Access data" and "Create a chart in Excel," respectively. These two procedures create a document and a worksheet, ready for the database information to be entered.

7   After the two If...Then condition blocks, add the following call to the GetDatabaseInfo procedure:

```
Call GetDatabaseInfo(bReport, bSheet, bPres)
```

The GetDatabaseInfo procedure retrieves the information from the database and sends it to Word and Excel. The Boolean variables bReport, bSheet, and bPres are passed to the procedure so that you can check whether you need to pass the data to Word or Excel.

8   Add the following If...Then condition blocks:

```
If bReport = True Then
    Call modWord.AddTotalRow
End If
If bSheet = True Or bPres = True Then
    Call modExcel.CreateChart
End If
If bPres = True Then
    modPowerPoint.CreatePowerPointPres
End If
If bMail = True Then
    Call modOutlook.SendMail(bReport, bSheet, bPres)
End If
```

If the Boolean variable bReport is True, the row containing the total cost and energy usage is added to the report. If the Boolean variable bSheet or bPres is True, an Excel chart is created. If the Boolean variable bPres is True, a PowerPoint presentation is created that uses the Excel chart created in the procedure CreateChart. If the Boolean variable bMail is True, an Outlook mail message is created.

The Main procedure, which is the heart of the program, is complete. You now need to create the supporting procedures that you have called.

Retrieve data from the database

1   Move the cursor beneath the procedure Main and create a new procedure called GetDatabaseInfo by adding the following code:

```
Sub GetDatabaseInfo(bReport As Boolean, bSheet As Boolean, _
        bPres As Boolean)
    Dim sID As String, sDateTime As String
    Dim sComputer As String
    Dim sgPeriodkWh As Single, sgCost As Single
    Dim rsEnergy As DAO.Recordset
    Dim iCounter As Integer

    Set rsEnergy = m_dbEnergyUsage _
        .OpenRecordset("LabEnergyUsage", dbOpenTable)
End Sub
```

The first three lines of the GetDatabaseInfo procedure declare variables that are set to the data in the database. The next variable declared, rsEnergy, is set to a Data Access Object (DAO), Recordset, which represents the data in a database table. Following the recordset declaration, the variable rsEnergy is set to the recordset found in the table LabEnergyUsage in the Energy.mdb database.

2   Below the Set statement, add the following With...End block containing a Do...Loop:

```
With rsEnergy
    Forms("frmMain").Controls("lblTotalRecords") _
        .Caption = .RecordCount
    Do
        sID = ![Id]
        sDateTime = ![Date and Time]
        sComputer = ![Computer Network]
        Forms("frmMain").Controls("lblCurrentRecord") _
            .Caption = ![Id]
        DoEvents
        .MoveNext
    Loop Until .EOF = True
    .Close
End With
```

The For...Next loop iterates through the recordset, setting the value in each field (Id, Date and Time, and Computer Network) to the declared variables. The last line in the Do...Loop moves to the next record in the recordset, making that record the current record. By default, the first record in the recordset is the current record when the recordset is first opened. When the last record is the current one, the EOF property is set to True and the Do...Loop exits. After the Do...Loop exits, the recordset closes.

181

The two lines within the With...End block that manipulate the Label controls on the form frmMain are used to update the captions of the Label controls so that you have a visual representation of the loop's progress. The keyword DoEvents is a built-in Visual Basic function and is used to make sure that the screen is updated to reflect the changes in the form and in the Label controls.

3 Within the Do...Loop, just before the line moving to the next recordset, .MoveNext, add the following mathematical assignment statements:

```
sgPeriodkWh = m_iWattage * Int(sComputer) / 1000
sgCost = sgPeriodkWh * m_sgCost
g_sgTotalCost = g_sgTotalCost + sgCost
g_iTotalHours = g_iTotalHours + Int(sComputer)
```

4 Just below the lines you added in step 3 and above the line moving to the next recordset, .MoveNext, add the following two If...Then condition blocks:

```
If bReport = True Then
    Call modWord.AddToTable(sID, _
        sDateTime, sComputer, sgPeriodkWh, sgCost)
End If
If bSheet = True Or bPres = True Then
    Call modExcel.AddToSheet(sID, _
        sDateTime, sComputer, sgPeriodkWh, sgCost)
End If
```

Once the data is set to the variables sID, sDataTime, and sComputer, and the appropriate calculations are made, the two condition blocks above determine whether the data is written to the Word report, the Excel workbook, or both. The second If...Then condition block also checks the value of bPres, because creating a presentation in PowerPoint requires that the data first be sent to Excel so that a chart can be created, after which the chart is copied into the presentation.

5 After the With...End block added in step 2, add the following line just after the End With statement and before the End Sub statement:

```
m_dbEnergyUsage.Close
```

This closes the database; you will have retrieved all of the data in it and will no longer need the database in memory.

Close Window

6 Click the Close Window button to close the Module1 Code window and, when Microsoft Access asks if you want to save changes to the module of form Module1, click Yes.

7 In the Save As dialog box, type **modMain** in the Module Name text box and click OK.

The code module modMain contains the procedure Main, which is called by the click event procedure of the cmdOK command button on the form frmMain. The module modMain contains all the code that pertains to opening and retrieving information from the database, as well as the code that determines which Office document to create. In the following sections, you will create code modules that allow you to create each Office document.

Creating a Word Report from Database Information

Most company reports are based on a customized template containing predefined text styles and formatting. In our example, the Access database generates a report by creating a new Word document based on a formatted Word template. (This template, EnerRpt.dot, can be found in the Lesson 8 practice folder.) As shown below, the Energy Report template is a one-row table with preset headers. As each row of data is retrieved from the database, a new row containing the database information and some calculated entries is added to the table. When all the data has been imported to the table, a final row containing the totals from two columns in the table is automatically added.

The EnerRpt.dot file (Energy Management)...

...will be the basis of your report.

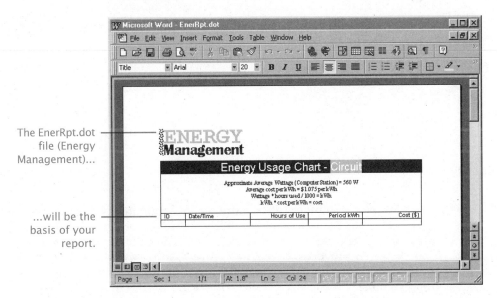

183

Complete a Word document with Access data

1 In the MyEnergy: Database window, in the Modules tab, click New to display a new code module window.

2 Add the following declarations to the code module:

```
Dim m_oWord As New Word.Application
Dim m_oWordDoc As Word.Document
```

The first declaration declares the module-level variable m_oWord as a new instance of the Word Application object. The use of the keyword New in the declaration statement indicates that the first time the variable m_oWord is used in code, a new instance will be created. Thus, you will not need to use the CreateObject function. The m_oWord variable is a module-level variable because it is used in the procedure AddTotalRow to set the Visible property of the Word application window to True once the report has been generated. The AddTotalRow procedure will be created in the section "Format the final row in the Word table."

The second declaration declares the module-level variable m_oWordDoc as a Word Document object, which is used by each of the procedures created in the current code module.

3 Add the following CreateWordDocument procedure, after the variable declarations:

```
Sub CreateWordDocument()
    Set m_oWordDoc = m_oWord.Documents.Add(Template:= _
        g_sFilePath & "EnerRpt.dot", _
        NewTemplate:=False)
    With m_oWordDoc
        .BuiltinDocumentProperties("Subject").Value = g_sCircuit
        .Fields.Update
    End With
End Sub
```

The CreateWordDocument procedure sets the module-level variable m_oWordDoc to the newly added Word Document object. The new Word document is based on the template EnerRpt.dot, which is found in the Lesson 8 practice folder. The first line within the With...End block in the CreateWordDocument procedure sets the built-in document property Subject to the circuit under investigation. In the code module modMain, the public variable g_sCircuit was set to "Computer Network." In the future, you can easily add new circuits to the investigation. The second line (.Fields.Update) in the With...End block updates all of the fields in the Word document. One field, named

Circuit, was added to the Energy Report template, EnerRpt.dot, beside the title "Energy Usage Chart." The field contains the Subject document property.

Add rows and entries in a Word table

1 Move the cursor beneath the procedure CreateWordDocument and create a new procedure called AddToTable by adding the following code:

```
Sub AddToTable(sID As String, sDateTime As String, _
    sComputer As String, sgPeriodkWh As Single, _
    sgCost As Single)

    With m_oWordDoc.Tables(1)
    End With
End Sub
```

Five arguments are passed to the AddToTable procedure. The values of the arguments were set in the GetDatabaseInfo procedure in the code module modMain. The With...End block added within the AddToTable procedure is used to access the first (and only) table in the Word document created in the CreateWordDocument procedure.

2 Add the following With...End block and code within the With...End block added in the preceding step:

```
With .Rows.Last
    .Cells(1).Range.Text = sID
    .Cells(2).Range.Text = sDateTime
    .Cells(3).Range.Text = sComputer
    .Cells(4).Range.Text = sgPeriodkWh
    .Cells(5).Range.Text = Format$(sgCost, "#,##0.00")
End With
```

The With...End block in this code adds values to each cell in the last row of the Word table. Each cell in a row in a table has a text range, represented by the Range object. The Range object allows you to access the Text property so that you can assign a text string to the cell. In the last line within the With...End block, the text string assigned to the cell text is formatted using the built-in Visual Basic function Format$. The Format$ function formats a string according to the second argument in the function. This is similar to formatting cells in Excel.

3 After the With...End block added in the previous step and before the `End With` statement of the table With...End block, add the following line:

```
.Rows.Add
```

After data from the database is added to the cells of the last row in the table, a new row is added so that data from the next record in the database can be added to the table. Your code should match that in the following illustration:

The AddToTable procedure...

...inserts table values in a range of cells.

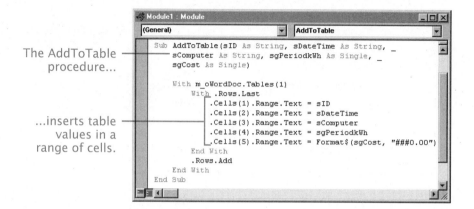

```
Sub AddToTable(sID As String, sDateTime As String, _
    sComputer As String, sgPeriodkWh As Single, _
    sgCost As Single)

    With m_oWordDoc.Tables(1)
        With .Rows.Last
            .Cells(1).Range.Text = sID
            .Cells(2).Range.Text = sDateTime
            .Cells(3).Range.Text = sComputer
            .Cells(4).Range.Text = sgPeriodkWh
            .Cells(5).Range.Text = Format$(sgCost, "###0.00")
        End With
        .Rows.Add
    End With
End Sub
```

Format the final row in the Word table

1 Move the cursor beneath the procedure AddToTable and create a new procedure called AddTotalRow by adding the following code:

```
Sub AddTotalRow()
    With m_oWordDoc.Tables(1).Rows.Last
        .Range.Bold = True
        .Range.Font.Size = 12
        .Borders.Item(wdBorderTop) _
            .LineStyle = wdLineStyleDouble
    End With
End Sub
```

The AddTotalRow procedure contains a With...End block that formats the last row in the Word table. The text range in the cells of the last row are made bold and set to a font size of 12. The border style at the top edge of the cells is set to double lines.

2 Above the End With statement, in the AddTotalRow procedure, add the following code:

```
.Cells(1).Range.Text = "Total"
.Cells(3).Range.Text = g_iTotalHours
.Cells(5).Range.Text = Format$(g_sgTotalCost, "###0.00")
```

The text of the first cell in the last row of the table is "Total." The text of the third cell is set to the total number of hours the stations in the computer network were on. The fifth cell indicates the total energy cost for the period under investigation. The public variables g_iTotalHours and g_sgTotalCost are calculated in the GetDatabaseInfo procedure in the code module modMain.

3 After the With...End block, above `End Sub`, add the following two lines to save the document with the filename "Report" and to display the Word application window:

```
m_oWordDoc.SaveAs g_sFilePath & "Report.doc"
m_oWord.Visible = True
```

*Close
Window*

4 Click the Close Window button to close the Module1 Code window and, when Access asks if you want to save changes to the design of module Module1, click Yes.

5 In the Save As dialog box, type **modWord** in the Module Name text box and click OK.

All the code for creating a Word document based on a predefined template and for adding values to the table within the document is now added. Later, when you run the integrated Office solution and select the item to create a Word report, the document should look like this:

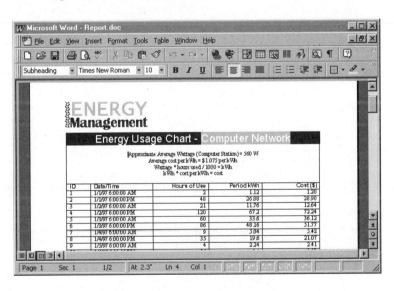

187

Creating an Excel Worksheet and Chart

Microsoft Excel worksheets make it very easy to filter data for analysis as well as to create charts for further study. Adding data to an Excel worksheet is similar to adding values to the cells of a table in Word. Once you populate (or fill in) your worksheet, adding an AutoFilter involves only one line of Visual Basic code. Adding an Excel chart involves a few more steps but is also fairly simple. The chart serves two purposes: to complement the data in the worksheet and to be used in a PowerPoint presentation.

Create an Excel worksheet

1   In the MyEnergy: Database dialog box, in the Modules tab, click New to display a new code module window.

2   Add the following declarations to the code module:

```
Public g_oExcelChart As Excel.Chart
Dim m_oExcel As New Excel.Application
Dim m_oExcelSheet As Excel.Worksheet
Dim m_oExcelBook As Excel.Workbook
```

The first declaration declares the public variable g_oExcelChart as an Excel Chart object. The variable g_oExcelChart is declared as public because it is used in the code module that creates a PowerPoint presentation. The second declaration declares the module-level variable m_oExcel as a new instance of the Excel Application object.

The use of the keyword New in the declaration statement indicates that the first time the variable m_oExcel is used in code, a new instance will be created. Thus, you do not need to use the CreateObject function. The m_oExcel variable is a module-level variable that is used in the CreateChart procedure to set the Visible property of the Excel application window to True once the worksheet and chart have been generated. The CreateChart procedure will be added in the section "Create a chart in Excel" later in this lesson.

3   After the variable declarations, add the following CreateExcelSheet procedure:

```
Sub CreateExcelSheet()
    Set m_oExcelBook = m_oExcel.Workbooks.Add
    Set m_oExcelSheet = m_oExcelBook.Worksheets(1)
End Sub
```

The CreateExcelSheet procedure sets two variables to Excel objects. The first, m_oExcelBook, is set to an Excel Workbook object, which is added to the Workbooks collection of the newly created instance of the Excel

Application object, m_oExcel. Three Worksheets objects are added to a newly created Workbook object unless the setting in the Options dialog box accessed on the Tools menu in Excel indicates otherwise. The first worksheet is set to the module-level variable m_oExcelSheet.

4   After the two Set statements in the CreateExcelSheet procedure, add the following With...End block:

```
With m_oExcelSheet.Rows(1)
    .Font.Bold = True
    .Cells(, 1).Value = "ID"
    .Cells(, 2).Value = "Date/Time"
    .Cells(, 3).Value = "Computer Network"
    .Cells(, 4).Value = "Period kWh"
    .Cells(, 5).Value = "Cost"
End With
```

Within the With...End block, the font in the first row of the worksheet is set to bold. The next five lines add headers to the first five cells in the first row. The Cells property takes two arguments. The first argument is the row index, and the second is the column index. Because the Cells property is accessed from the first row object, the row index does not need to be specified, and only the second argument, the column index, is specified.

A new Excel workbook has been created, and the first worksheet has been formatted. The worksheet is now ready to accept data from the database.

Add entries in an Excel worksheet

1   Move the cursor beneath the procedure CreateExcelSheet and create a new procedure called AddToSheet by adding the following code:

```
Sub AddToSheet(sID As String, sDateTime As String, _
    sComputer As String, sgPeriodkWh As Single, _
    sgCost As Single)

End Sub
```

Five arguments are passed to the AddToSheet procedure. The values of the arguments are set in the GetDatabaseInfo procedure in the code module modMain.

2   Add the following With...End block and code above the `End Sub` statement:

```
With m_oExcelSheet.Rows(Int(sID) + 1)
    .Cells(, 1).Value = sID
    .Cells(, 2).Value = sDateTime
    .Cells(, 3).Value = sComputer
    .Cells(, 4).Value = sgPeriodkWh
    .Cells(, 5).Value = Format$(sgCost, "#,##0.00")
End With
```

The With...End block adds values to each cell in the next available row in the Excel worksheet. Each cell in a row in a worksheet has a value, represented by the Value property. In the last line within the With...End block, the text string assigned to the cell text is formatted using the built-in Visual Basic function Format$, as it is when the same value is added to the Word table you created earlier in this lesson.

Create a chart in Excel

1   Move the cursor beneath the procedure AddToSheet and create a new procedure called CreateChart by adding the following code:

```
Sub CreateChart()
    Set g_oExcelChart = m_oExcelBook.Charts.Add
    With g_oExcelChart
        .ChartType = xlAreaStacked
        .SetSourceData _
            Source:=m_oExcelSheet.Range("C2:C63,E2:E63"), _
            PlotBy:=xlColumns
        .Location Where:=xlLocationAsNewSheet, Name:= _
            "EnergyUsage-" & g_sCircuit
    End With
End Sub
```

The first line of the CreateChart procedure sets the variable g_oExcelChart to a newly created chart in the Excel workbook. The variable is then used in the With...End block to set the chart type, the data source for the chart, and where the chart is to be added in the workbook. The Where argument of the Location method of the Chart object indicates that Excel should add the chart to a newly created chart sheet in the workbook. The tab name of the new sheet will be "EnergyUsage-Computer Network." The sources of the data are the computer network usage column (Column C) and the cost column (Column E) in the first worksheet of the workbook.

2   Within the With...End block, after the Location method and above
`End With`, add the following lines of code:

```
.HasTitle = True
.ChartTitle.Characters _
    .Text = "Energy Usage - " & g_sCircuit
With .Axes(xlCategory, xlPrimary)
    .HasTitle = True
    .AxisTitle.Characters.Text = "Index"
End With
With .Axes(xlValue, xlPrimary)
    .HasTitle = True
    .AxisTitle.Characters.Text = "Cost ($)"
End With
```

The lines above add formatting to the newly created chart. The first
two lines add the title "Energy Usage - Computer Network" to the chart.
The two With...End blocks that follow add a label to the x and y axes
of the chart, respectively.

3   Immediately following the last With...End block added in the
CreateChart procedure, above the `End Sub` statement, add the
following two With...End blocks:

```
With m_oExcelSheet.Range("A:F")
    .Columns.AutoFit
    .AutoFilter
End With

With m_oExcel
    .DisplayAlerts = False
    m_oExcelBook.SaveAs _
        g_sFilePath & "DataAnalysis", xlNormal
    .Visible = True
    .UserControl = True
End With
```

Once AutoFilters are added to the Excel worksheet, the workbook
is saved with the name "DataAnalysis" and the Excel application
window is displayed. The DisplayAlerts property of the Excel Application object is set to False so that a message box is not displayed if the
SaveAs method detects that an Excel file with the same filename
already exists. The UserControl property of the Excel Application
object is set to False when the Excel Application object is created
through Visual Basic. (If the user started Excel, UserControl would be
set to True.)

By setting the UserControl property to True, you are giving control of the Excel Application object you created through Visual Basic to the user. Consequently, the Excel application window remains visible on the screen once the Visual Basic code finishes running. Word, PowerPoint, and Outlook application windows also remain displayed to the user once the Visible property of the respective Application object is set to True.

4   Close the Module1 Code window and, when Access asks if you want to save changes to the design of module Module1, click Yes.

5   In the Save As dialog box, type **modExcel** in the Module Name text box and click OK.

All the code for creating an Excel worksheet and chart is now added. Later, when you run the integrated Office solution and select the item to create an Excel workbook, the worksheet with AutoFilters should look like this:

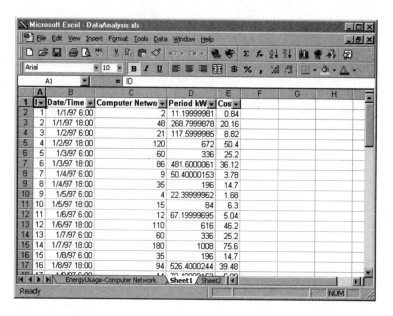

The Excel chart that is simultaneously created should look like this:

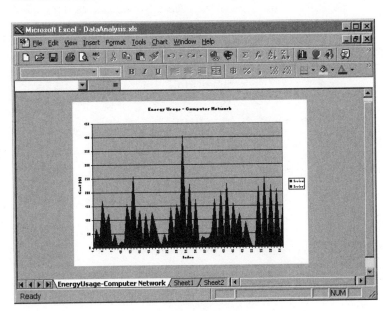

Presenting Results in PowerPoint

Slide presentations are used to communicate information to an audience. PowerPoint presentations are effective because they organize information in screen-size segments that audiences can absorb relatively quickly. Adding the Excel chart to the presentation conveys data results in an easy-to-understand format.

Create a presentation

1   In the MyEnergy: Database window, in the Modules tab, click New to display a new code module window.

2   Add the following CreatePowerPointPres procedure:

```
Sub CreatePowerPointPres()
    Dim oPowerPoint As New PowerPoint.Application
    Dim oPres As PowerPoint.Presentation
    Dim oSlide As PowerPoint.Slide
    Dim sgBottom As Single

    End Sub
```

The first declaration defines the variable oPowerPoint as a new instance of the PowerPoint Application object. The use of the keyword New in the declaration statement indicates that the first time the variable oPowerPoint is used in code, a new instance will be created. The second and third declarations define a Presentation object and a Slide object, respectively. The final declaration in the CreatePowerPointPres procedure defines the variable sgBottom as a Single data type, which is set to the bottom coordinate of the title shape on the first slide.

3 Add the following Set statements and With...End block after the declarations in the CreatePowerPointPres procedure:

```
Set oPres = oPowerPoint.Presentations.Add
Set oSlide = oPres.Slides.Add(1, ppLayoutTitleOnly)
With oSlide.Shapes.Placeholders(1)
    With .TextFrame.TextRange
        .Text = "Energy Usage - " & g_sCircuit
        .Font.Bold = True
        .ChangeCase ppCaseUpper
    End With
    sgBottom = .Top + .Height
End With
```

The new presentation is added to the PowerPoint Application object in the first Set statement, and a new slide is added to the new presentation in the second Set statement. The new slide has the Title only layout, which contains only a Title placeholder and no other preset shapes. The With...End block following the two Set statements accesses the properties of the Title placeholder to set the text, make the font bold, and change the case to uppercase. The last line in the With...End block sets the variable sgBottom to the total of the top coordinate of the Title placeholder plus its height.

4 After the With...End block added in the previous step, add the following With...End block to add the Excel chart to the first slide in the presentation:

```
g_oExcelChart.ChartArea.Copy
With oSlide.Shapes.Paste
    .Top = sgBottom + 20
    .Height = oSlide.Master.Height - sgBottom + 20
    .Left = oSlide.Master.Width / 2 - .Width / 2
End With
```

In order to add the Excel chart to the PowerPoint presentation, the chart area is copied to the Clipboard and pasted into the Shapes collection of the first slide in the presentation. The With...End block then sets the top and left coordinates and the height of the newly pasted chart shape.

5   After the With...End block, above End Sub, add the following two lines to save the presentation with the filename "EnergyPres" and to display the PowerPoint application window:

```
oPres.SaveAs g_sFilePath & "EnergyPres"
oPowerPoint.Visible = True
```

6   Close the Module1 Code window and, when Access asks if you want to save changes to the design of module Module1, click Yes.

7   In the Save As dialog box, type **modPowerPoint** in the Module Name text box and click OK.

All the code for creating a PowerPoint presentation is now added. Later, when you run the integrated Office solution and select the item to create a PowerPoint presentation, the slide should look like this:

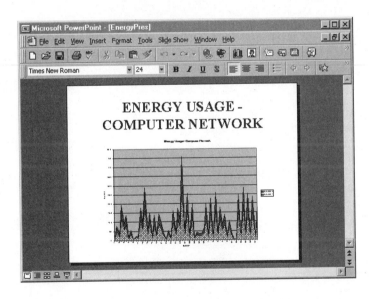

Sending Mail in Outlook

Once all of the Office documents selected in the form frmMain are automatically generated, a mail message created in Outlook can be sent to the appropriate set of people. This link allows you to conveniently update people on the latest information and documents regarding a project.

Create an Outlook mail message

1   In the MyEnergy: Database winddow, in the Modules tab, click New to display a new code module window.

2   Add the following SendMail procedure:

```
Sub SendMail(bReport As Boolean, bSheet As Boolean, _
    bPres As Boolean)
    Dim oOutlook As New Outlook.Application
    Dim oMessage As Outlook.MailItem

    Set oMessage = oOutlook.CreateItem(olMailItem)

End Sub
```

The three Boolean variables passed into the SendMail procedure indicate which check boxes were selected in the form frmMain. These variables are used to determine which file attachments should be added to the mail message. Within the SendMail procedure, two variables are declared. The first, the variable oOutlook, is the declaration of a new instance of the Outlook Application object. The use of the keyword New in the declaration statement indicates that the first time the variable oOutlook is used in code, a new instance will be created. The second, the variable oMessage, declares the variable as an Outlook MailItem object, which is set in the Set statement following the declaration.

3   After the Set statement in the SendMail procedure, add the following With...End block:

```
With oMessage
    .To = "Energy Committee"
    .Subject = "New energy usage documents"
    .Body = "The following documents reflect" & _
        " the energy usage for the circuit: " & _
        g_sCircuit & "." & vbCrLf
    .Display
End With
```

196

The With...End block sets the main properties of the mail message and then displays the message on the screen. If you want to send the mail message automatically, you can replace the Display method with the Send method in the last line of the With...End block. The message will be sent to the alias "Energy Committee."

4 Before the line to display the Outlook message, add the following If...Then condition blocks to add attachments to the message:

```
If bReport = True Then
    .Attachments.Add g_sFilePath & "Report.doc"
End If
If bSheet = True Then
    .Attachments.Add g_sFilePath & "DataAnalysis.xls"
End If
If bPres = True Then
    .Attachments.Add g_sFilePath & "EnergyPres.ppt"
End If
```

The three If...Then condition blocks evaluate the Boolean values representing the items selected in the form frmMain. If an item is selected and the appropriate Office document generated, the document is attached to the mail message.

5 Close the Module1 Code window and, when Access asks if you want to save changes to the design of module Module1, click Yes.

6 In the Save As dialog box, type **modOutlook** in the Module Name text box and click OK.

All the code for creating an Outlook mail message is now added. Later, when you run the integrated Office solution and select the item to create an Outlook mail message along with the other Office documents, the Outlook mail message should look like this:

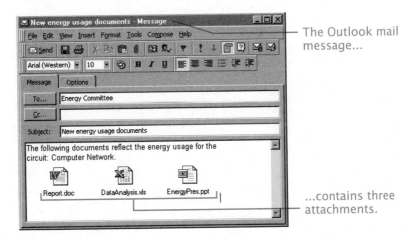

The Outlook mail message...

...contains three attachments.

TIP In the Lesson 8 subfolder of the practice files, the Energy database file contains a procedure in the code module modOutlook that will generate a meeting request in Outlook so that you can schedule a meeting to discuss the results generated by your solution.

See the solution in action

1   In the MyEnergy: Database window, select the item frmMain in the Forms tab of the database and click Open.

The custom Energy Management form is displayed.

2   Select all four check boxes in the Energy Management form and click OK.

A typical Pentium computer system will take about four minutes to run these procedures.

Iterating through the data in the Access database and generating each Office document may take your computer a few minutes, depending on the hardware and software configuration of your computer system. You can watch the progress by reading the Number Of Records Read indicator in the dialog box. Once the Main procedure finishes running, you will see the new Word report, the Excel worksheet and chart, the PowerPoint presentation, and the Outlook mail message with the Office documents attached. Each window displayed on your screen should look similar to the graphic shown at the end of the step-by-step example that created that particular Office document (see pages 187, 192, 195, and 197).

TIP If you code has errors that you cannot easily resolve, or if you did not have time to complete the entire lesson, you can run the solution from the Energy.mdb file provided in the Lesson 8 folder of the practice files. This file contains the complete working code for all the sections in this lesson.

3   Close the Energy database and exit Access.

4   After examining the generated contents in Word, Excel, and PowerPoint, close each application without saving changes.

Lesson Summary

To	Do this
Import data in a text file into an Access database	Click New in the Tables tab in an Access database dialog box, select Import Table from the New Table dialog box, and click OK. In the Import dialog box, select the text file, click OK, and step through the Import Text Wizard.
Create a form in Access	In the Forms tab of an Access database dialog box, click New.
To run a form in Access	In the Forms tab of an Access database dialog box, select a form in the list and click Open.
Add Visual Basic code in Access	In the Modules tab of an Access database dialog box, click New and write Visual Basic procedures within the added code module.

For online information about	Ask the Assistant for help, using the words
Creating forms in Access	"Creating forms"
Databases in general	"Databases"
Importing data into an Access database	"Import data"
Iterating through records in a database	"RecordSet" or "Records"
Access actions in Visual Basic	"Run Access actions from Visual Basic" or "DoCmd"
Manipulating controls on an Access form	"Forms" or "Controls"
Updating the screen to display new information	"Do Events"

Preview of the Next Lesson

In the next lesson, you will learn how to decide where to start writing code for integrated Office solutions. You will then use that information to develop a Visual Basic for Applications add-in for Microsoft Word that generates a Word report from the energy data in the Access database you created in this lesson. After you create your Word add-in, you will learn how to password-protect your code.

Creating Add-Ins for Word

Estimated time
45 min.

In this lesson you will learn how to:

- Decide what type of solution you want to develop.
- Create Visual Basic for Applications add-ins for Word.
- Create user-defined types.
- Password-protect your code.

Before you start building your solution, you need a general plan of what you want to accomplish and what your method will be, taking into consideration what your customer's needs are, where to start, what tools are required, and so forth. As you have seen from previous lessons, you can write Visual Basic code in several different places within Microsoft Office. In addition, each application is unique, storing and displaying information for a distinct audience. So from which application do you base your code? Which offers the best tools to suit your needs and to help deliver your solution to your customers easily?

Deciding Where to Start

When writing Visual Basic code for a business solution that incorporates Microsoft Office, you can store your code in one of three general types of Office projects: document, template, and add-in or wizard. How do you choose where and how to store and deliver your code? The first thing to decide is what type of solution you want to deliver, based on the characteristics of the three types of projects.

Document Projects

Document is used as a collective term to represent all types of Office documents: Word documents, Excel workbooks, PowerPoint presentations, and Access databases. The Visual Basic code you write in the Visual Basic for Applications project of a document commonly provides customizations that are specific to the contents of the document. For example, the code that drives the automatic generation of the Office documents in Lesson 8 was added to an Access database, so you created a document project.

Templates

Template is used as a collective term for all types of Office templates, including Word, Excel, and PowerPoint templates. Writing code in a template is essentially the same as writing code in a document project because the code provides customizations to a document. The difference is that when you apply a template in Excel or PowerPoint, the code is copied into the workbook or presentation. In Word, attaching a template to a document makes the code, along with other Word-specific content such as text styles and AutoText, readily available to the Word document.

Add-Ins and Wizards

Add-ins are tools that you can create to customize and extend the functionality of Word, Excel, PowerPoint, or Access. Microsoft Office add-ins, created using Visual Basic for Applications, come in two main types. The first type is a program you create that conducts a specific task. The second is a wizard add-in that steps you through a series of tasks. Both types of add-ins are commonly accessed through a menu command or toolbar button.

In this lesson, you will create a Visual Basic for Applications add-in for Word that uses the code from the Access database in Lesson 8 to generate a Word document. In the next lesson, you will create Visual Basic for Applications add-ins for Excel and PowerPoint.

Building Word Add-Ins

Microsoft Word templates, or .dot files, are commonly used to store and make available styles, AutoText entries, macros, custom toolbars, menu settings, and shortcut keys to Word documents that are attached to the template. Word templates also serve as Visual Basic for Applications add-ins for Word. In this section, you will create a Word add-in that generates a Word report from the energy data in the Access database in Lesson 8.

Create a Word add-in

1   Start Word, open a new document, and display the Visual Basic Editor.

2   On the Tools menu, click References, and in the Available References list box, select Microsoft DAO 3.5 Object Library and click OK.

> **IMPORTANT**   The procedures in this section require that you have previously installed Data Access Objects for Visual Basic. If the Microsoft DAO 3.5 Object Library does not appear in your Available References list, run the Office Setup program. In the Office 97 Maintenance list, select Data Access, click Change Option, and select Data Access Objects for Visual Basic.

3   Insert a code module, and in the Properties window, type **modWord** to set the Name property.

4   Start Microsoft Access and open the Energy database in the Lesson 8 subfolder of the Office VBA Practice folder.

> **NOTE**   If all your code was working properly at the end of Lesson 8, you can also use the MyEnergy database you created.

5   In the Energy database, copy all of the code in the code module modWord, except for the first line, and paste it into the code module modWord in the Visual Basic Editor in Word.

The first line in the Access code module is Option Compare Database. If the Option Explicit statement is listed twice at the top of the modWord module in Word, remove one of the listings.

6   Insert a new code module, and in the Properties window, type **modMain** to set the Name property.

7   In the Energy database, copy all of the code in the code module modMain, except for the first line, and paste it into the code module modMain in the Visual Basic Editor in Word. If the `Option Explicit` statement is listed twice at the top of the modMain module in Word, remove one of the listings.

8   Remove all non-Word-specific code in the Main procedure in the modMain code module so that the procedure looks like this:

```
Sub Main()
    Set m_dbEnergyUsage = DBEngine.Workspaces(0) _
    .OpenDatabase(g_sFilePath & "Energy.mdb")
    Call modWord.CreateWordDocument
    Call GetDatabaseInfo
    Call modWord.AddTotalRow
End Sub
```

The Main procedure will be called from a custom menu item that your add-in will add to the Menu Bar in Word. In the Energy database, the arguments passed into the Main procedure are used to determine which items are selected in the Access form you created and displayed. The Main procedure then determines which Office documents to create based on the selections in the form. In your Word add-in, however, you are creating only a Word report.

9   Remove the arguments passed to the GetDatabaseInfo procedure so that the beginning of the procedure appears as follows:

```
Sub GetDatabaseInfo()
```

10   Remove all non-Word-specific code, the statements involving the Forms collection, and the DoEvents statement in the GetDatabaseInfo procedure. Then edit the procedure so that only the following line exists after the code in which the variable g_iTotalHours is set and before the MoveNext method of the Recordset object:

```
Call modWord.AddToTable(sID, _
    sDateTime, sComputer, sgPeriodkWh, sgCost)
```

The revised procedure looks like the following:

```
Sub GetDatabaseInfo()
    Dim sID As String, sDateTime As String
    Dim sComputer As String
    Dim sgPeriodkWh As Single, sgCost As Single
    Dim rsEnergy As DAO.Recordset
```

```
    Set rsEnergy = m_dbEnergyUsage _
        .OpenRecordset("LabEnergyUsage", dbOpenTable)
    With rsEnergy
        Do
            sID = ![ID]
            sDateTime = ![Date and Time]
            sComputer = ![Computer Network]
            sgPeriodkWh = m_iWattage * Int(sComputer) / 1000
            sgCost = sgPeriodkWh * m_sgCost
            g_sgTotalCost = g_sgTotalCost + sgCost
            g_iTotalHours = g_iTotalHours + Int(sComputer)
            Call modWord.AddToTable(sID, _
                sDateTime, sComputer, sgPeriodkWh, sgCost)
            .MoveNext
        Loop Until .EOF = True
        .Close
    End With
    m_dbEnergyUsage.Close
End Sub
```

11 Double-click the modWord project item in the Project Explorer to activate the modWord Code window.

12 Remove the keyword New from the module-level declaration of the variable m_oWord, and insert the following line as the first line in the CreateWordDocument procedure:

```
Set m_oWord = Application
```

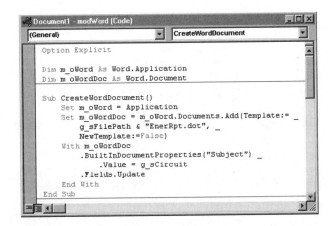

In the Word add-in you are creating, you will call the procedures to create the Word report from within the Word application. To generate the report in the current instance of Word, reference the Word Application object. Or, you could use the GetObject function, which was discussed in Lesson 5.

13 Switch to the Word application window, and on the File menu, click Save As. In the Save As Type drop-down list in the Save As dialog box, select Document Template (*.dot). Change to the folder C:\Program Files\Microsoft Office\Office\Startup, type **MyEnergy** in the File Name text box, and click Save.

Now that you have saved your template (which is now your MyEnergy add-in) into the Startup folder, Word will automatically load your add-in each time Word is started. This process is detailed in the step-by-step example "Load a Word add-in automatically" later in this lesson.

 IMPORTANT The location of the Startup folder is specified in the File Locations tab in the Options dialog box. To determine the current Startup folder for Word, on the Tools menu, click Options to display the Options dialog box, and then click the File Locations tab. If the Startup folder specified in the File Locations tab is different from the location specified above, save the MyEnergy.dot add-in to the correct Startup folder.

14 Exit Access but leave Word open.

The code that creates the Word report from the data in the Access database is now complete. You could run the add-in by placing the cursor in the Main procedure and pressing F5. In the steps below, however, you will create procedures that automatically add a menu item to the Word Menu Bar when your add-in is loaded. With this option, you can generate the report easily by clicking a single menu item.

Creating User-Defined Types

User-defined types are a feature of the Visual Basic programming language that allows you to encapsulate a related set of information, or elements, into a single variable. This is similar in concept to how an object in an Office object model encapsulates a set of related properties and methods into one object. User-defined types are very useful and allow you to write flexible code that can be used in or easily adapted to a variety of situations, as you will see in the following steps.

Add reusable menu item code using user-defined types

As you learned in Lesson 6, the objects, properties, and methods you use to customize menus and toolbars are shared among the Office applications, so you can easily write reusable code. The following procedures will be used in your Word add-in, and you will be able to easily import the same fully functional code into your Excel and PowerPoint add-ins.

1   Switch to the Visual Basic Editor in Word.

2   Insert a code module, and in the Properties window, type **modMenu** to set the Name property.

3   In the Declarations section of modMenu, add the following user-defined type:

```
Public Type MenuItem
    sMenu As String
    sCaption As String
    iBefore As Integer
    sOnAction As String
End Type
```

A user-defined type is created in the Declarations section of a module using the Type statement. In the user-defined type above, you created a type named MenuItem. Within the MenuItem type are four pieces of information, or elements, you will store. The first element is declared as a string value and represents the name of the menu to which you want to add an item. The second is the caption of the menu item, also declared as a string value. The third, an integer value, is the position within the menu where you want to add the custom menu item. The fourth, declared as a string, represents the name of the procedure to be called when the menu item is clicked.

4   Move the cursor beneath the Declarations section of modMenu and add the following AddMenuItem procedure:

```
Sub AddMenuItem(udtMenuItem As MenuItem)
    Dim oCmdCtl As CommandBarControl
End Sub
```

The argument passed to the AddMenuItem procedure represents the MenuItem user-defined type that contains information regarding the menu item you want to add. The benefit of creating and passing menu item information within a user-defined type is that you avoid having to pass each piece of information within the user-defined type as an argument to the AddMenuItem procedure. Otherwise, the AddMenuItem procedure would look something like this:

```
Sub AddMenuItem(sMenu As String, sCaption As String, _
    iBefore As Integer, sOnAction As String)
```

In this case, if you want to set more properties of the custom menu item, you have to add more arguments to the AddMenuItem procedure. In addition, for every call to the AddMenuItem procedure elsewhere in your code, you have to add the argument to the list. On the other hand, if you created a user-defined type as you did above, you can add a new element to the declaration of the user-defined type and not have to worry about adding other arguments to the AddMenuItem procedure or to any calls to the procedure.

5 After the declaration of the variable oCmdCtl, add the following With...End block:

```
With CommandBars(AppMenuBar).Controls(udtMenuItem.sMenu)
End With
```

When Visual Basic runs the With statement, it starts by determining which CommandBar object it needs to access. In this case, you want to access the menu bar of the application. As you learned in Lesson 6, the menu bar in each application within Office varies slightly. The name of the menu bar is set by the Function AppMenuBar, which determines the name of the application that is currently running the code and sets the value of AppMenuBar to the appropriate menu bar name. In step 9 of this example, you will add the function AppMenuBar.

6 Within the With...End block, add the following For Each...Next loop:

```
For Each oCmdCtl In .Controls
    If oCmdCtl.Caption = _
        udtMenuItem.sCaption Then Exit Sub
Next oCmdCtl
```

The For Each...Next loop iterates through the controls on the menu specified by the value udtMenuItem.sMenu, searching for the custom menu item with the caption equal to udtMenuItem.sCaption. If the custom menu item is found, Visual Basic runs the Exit statement and no more code runs in the AddMenuItem procedure. The code for the AddMenuItem procedure is shown in the following illustration:

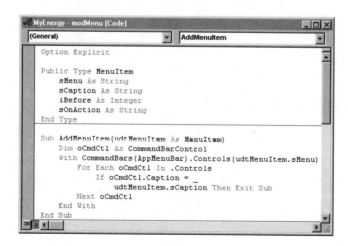

7   After the For Each...Next loop and above the `End With` statement, add the following lines of code:

```
Set oCmdCtl = .Controls.Add( _
    Type:=msoControlButton, _
    Before:=udtMenuItem.iBefore)
oCmdCtl.Caption = udtMenuItem.sCaption
oCmdCtl.OnAction = udtMenuItem.sOnAction
```

If the menu item is not found after the For Each...Next loop finishes, a new menu item control is added and set to the variable oCmdCtl, which was declared as a CommandBarControl object. The Caption and OnAction properties for the newly created control are set just after the control is added. The properties are set to the value contained within the user-defined type. When you type udtMenuItem and then add a period, the Auto List Members drop-down list will be displayed, listing each of the elements within the MenuItem user-defined type.

8   Move the cursor beneath the AddMenuItem procedure and add the following RemoveMenuItem procedure:

```
Sub RemoveMenuItem(udtMenuItem As MenuItem)
    Dim oCmdCtl As CommandBarControl

    With CommandBars(AppMenuBar).Controls(udtMenuItem.sMenu)
        For Each oCmdCtl In .Controls
            If oCmdCtl.Caption = udtMenuItem.sCaption Then
                oCmdCtl.Delete
                Exit Sub
            End If
        Next oCmdCtl
    End With
End Sub
```

The RemoveMenuItem procedure iterates through the controls on the menu specified by udtMenuItem.sMenu, searching for the custom menu item with the caption equal to udtMenuItem.sCaption. If the menu item is found, the control is deleted and the procedure is exited.

You can see an additional benefit of passing menu item information within a user-defined type to a procedure by examining the RemoveMenuItem procedure above. You can use the same user-defined type that you did to pass to the AddMenuItem procedure, but the code within the procedure does not need every element within the user-defined type, nor does each element in the user-defined type have to be explicitly set. If the elements are not set explicitly, they keep their default values, as discussed in Lesson 3. For example, when you declare a string variable, the value is set to an empty string, or "", while an integer value, when declared, is given the value of 0.

9 Move the cursor beneath the procedure RemoveAddItem and add the following AppMenuBar function:

```
Function AppMenuBar() As String
    Select Case Application.Name
    Case "Microsoft Word"
        AppMenuBar = "Menu Bar"
    Case "Microsoft Excel"
        AppMenuBar = "Worksheet Menu Bar"
    Case "Microsoft PowerPoint"
        AppMenuBar = "Menu Bar"
    End Select
End Function
```

The AppMenuBar function is declared as returning a string value. The function contains a Select Case condition block that examines the name of the Application object and sets the value of AppMenuBar to the appropriate menu bar name. This function is necessary because Excel has two built-in menu bars: Worksheet Menu Bar and Chart Menu Bar. Word and PowerPoint also have a built-in menu bar, named Menu Bar. Although you're using Word now, the AppMenuBar function allows you to insert the modMenu code module in Word, Excel, or PowerPoint without making modifications to the code.

10 Right-click the modMenu item in the Project Explorer, and click Export File on the shortcut menu.

Right-click the modMenu item...

...then click Export File.

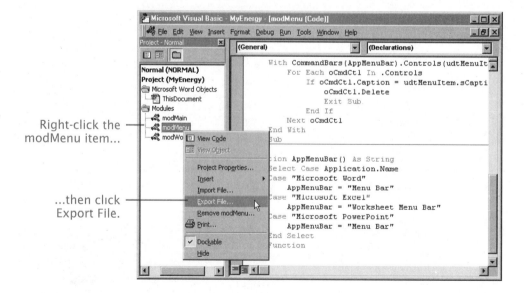

11 In the Export File dialog box, change to a folder where the code module modMenu can be stored and easily accessed. The default filename displayed in the File Name text box is the same as the name of the module, modMenu. Accept this name and click Save.

The modMenu item can now be imported and reused easily within other Visual Basic for Applications add-ins or solutions that need to add or remove menu items. You will use the modMenu item in Lesson 10 when you create add-ins for Excel and PowerPoint.

Add a menu item that creates a report

When you add custom commands to a menu or toolbar in Word, the customizations must be saved in a particular file or template that is currently open in Word. If you click Customize on the Tools menu and then click the Commands tab in the Customize dialog box, the Save In drop-down list in the lower area of the dialog box displays the file in which a menu or toolbar customization is stored.

In addition to using the Customize dialog box to add menu and toolbar customizations, you can also use Visual Basic for Applications code while you are developing your MyEnergy template. When you run a procedure that creates a menu item or toolbar button from within an open template, the customization will be saved in the open template. In the steps below, you will create a procedure that adds a menu item to be saved with the MyEnergy template.

1 In the Project Explorer, double-click the modMain project item to activate its Code window.

2 Move the cursor beneath the Declarations section of modMain, above Main, and add the following AddCustomItem procedure:

```
Sub AddCustomItem()
    Dim udtMenuItem As MenuItem
    With udtMenuItem
        .sMenu = "Tools"
        .sCaption = "Energy &Report"
        .iBefore = 1
        .sOnAction = "Main"
    End With
    Call modMenu.AddMenuItem(udtMenuItem)
End Sub
```

The AddCustomItem procedure above declares a variable udtMenuItem as the user-defined type MenuItem. The With...End block sets the four elements of the MenuItem user-defined type.

A custom menu item with the caption "Energy Report" will be added at the top of the Tools menu. When the menu item is clicked, it will call the Main procedure. Once the elements are set, the AddMenuItem

211

procedure within the code module modMenu is called and the variable udtMenuItem is passed to the AddMenuItem procedure in the modMenu module.

3   Move the cursor beneath the AddCustomItem procedure and add the following RemoveCustomItem procedure:

```
Sub RemoveCustomItem()
    Dim udtMenuItem As MenuItem
    With udtMenuItem
        .sMenu = "Tools"
        .sCaption = "Energy &Report"
    End With
    Call modMenu.RemoveMenuItem(udtMenuItem)
End Sub
```

The RemoveCustomItem procedure declares a variable udtMenuItem as the user-defined type MenuItem and sets only two of the four elements. The custom menu item Energy Report will be removed from the Tools menu. Once the elements are set, the RemoveMenuItem procedure within the code module modMenu is called and the variable udtMenuItem is passed.

4   Place the cursor in the AddCustomItem procedure and press F5 to run the procedure.

5   Switch to the Word application window and click the Tools menu to see the Energy Report menu item added to the top of the menu.

6   On the File menu, click Save to save the template MyEnergy, and then exit Word.

The Energy Report custom menu item is saved with the MyEnergy.dot add-in. Each time the MyEnergy template is loaded, the custom menu item Energy Report automatically appears on the Tools menu. When the MyEnergy template is unloaded, the Energy Report menu item automatically disappears. If you want to remove the custom menu item while you are developing the template, place the cursor in the RemoveCustomItem procedure and press F5. Then save the template, as in step 6 above. In this case, the custom menu item will not be saved with the template.

Run procedures automatically when a template is loaded

If you create a procedure named AutoExec in a template, Word automatically runs the procedure when the template is loaded. Similarly, if you create a procedure named AutoExit in a template, Word automatically runs the procedure when the template is unloaded. As you will learn in Lesson 10, Excel and PowerPoint each provide similar procedures, called Auto_Open and Auto_Close, that run automatically when an Excel or PowerPoint add-in is loaded or unloaded.

In Lesson 10, the names of the AddCustomItem and RemoveCustomItem procedures added in the preceding steps will be changed to Auto_Open and Auto_Close, respectively, so that menu customizations can be added or removed when the Excel or PowerPoint add-in is loaded or unloaded. Unlike Word, menu customizations in Excel and PowerPoint cannot be saved in an add-in. Thus, you will need to use the procedures that automatically run in Excel and PowerPoint in order to add or remove menu customizations.

Load a Word add-in automatically

To load a Word add-in automatically, you must save the Word add-in file in the Startup folder C:\Program Files\Microsoft Office\Office\Startup or in the location specified in the File Locations tab of the Options dialog box, as you did in the last step of "Create a Word add-in" at the beginning of this lesson. When Word is started, it iterates through the template files in the Startup folder and loads each one. Once Word loads a particular template, it searches for the AutoExec procedure and, if it exists, runs the procedure.

IMPORTANT When you want a template from the Startup folder to load automatically, you must first exit all running instances of Microsoft Word and then restart Word. If you are using Word as your e-mail editor, you must also exit your e-mail application, such as Microsoft Exchange or Microsoft Outlook, so that Word is no longer loaded anywhere in memory.

1   Restart Word and click the Tools menu to display the list of menu items.

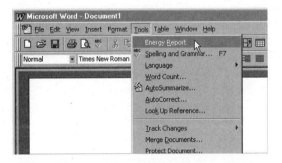

The addition of the custom menu item Energy Report to the Tools menu indicates that Word loaded the template. You can also display the Templates And Add-Ins dialog box to see what add-ins are currently loaded and available.

2   On the Tools menu, click Templates And Add-Ins.

In the Templates And Add-Ins dialog box, the MyEnergy.dot template is listed in the Global Templates and Add-Ins list. (Your list of other available add-ins may be different.)

3   Click Cancel to close the Templates And Add-Ins dialog box.

4   On the Tools menu, click Energy Report to create a report.

This may take a minute or so, depending on the hardware and software configuration of your computer. Once the procedure finishes running, you will see the new report in the Word application window, and the filename in the title bar should be Report.doc.

5   Exit Word without saving changes.

When you exit Word, all templates are unloaded, including MyEnergy.dot. The Energy Report custom menu item is removed automatically from the Tools menu. If you start Word again, the custom menu item is automatically added back to the Tools menu.

Load a Word add-in manually

1   In Windows Explorer, change to the folder C:\Program Files\Microsoft Office\Office\Startup and move the file MyEnergy.dot to the folder C:\Office VBA Practice\Lesson9.

2   Start Word and click the Tools menu to display the list of menu items.

Energy Report should not be displayed because the MyEnergy.dot template is not loaded.

3   On the Tools menu in Word, click Templates And Add-Ins.

4   In the Templates And Add-Ins dialog box, click Add, change to the Lesson 9 folder, select MyEnergy.dot in the Add Template dialog box, and click OK.

This adds the template to the Global Templates And Add-Ins list box. The check box beside the template item in the list box indicates two things: whether it is currently loaded, and whether it will load automatically the next time you start Word. That is, if the check box is selected, the add-in will be or is already loaded in the current session of Word. If you haven't cleared the check mark before you exit Word, the add-in loads automatically the next time you start Word.

5   Click OK to close the Templates And Add-Ins dialog box.

The Energy Report menu item should now be displayed on the Tools menu, which indicates that the MyEnergy template was loaded.

6   If you want to create a report, on the Tools menu, click Energy Report.

7   Exit Word.

TIP   When you want to open the MyEnergy template to make modifications to the Visual Basic code saved with it, click Open on the File menu in Word and change to the file; or, right-click the filename MyEnergy.dot in Windows Explorer and then click Open on the shortcut menu.

Password-Protecting Your Code

When you distribute your Visual Basic for Applications solution, you may not want others to modify or tamper with the functionality of your program. To secure your code, the Visual Basic Editor in Microsoft Word, Excel, and PowerPoint provides password protection for your program. If you lock your project and assign a password to it, when you later double-click the project in the Project Explorer of the Visual Basic Editor, a dialog box appears asking you for the password before you can view the contents.

You can password-protect any Visual Basic for Applications project in Word, Excel, or PowerPoint, no matter whether it's a document, template, or add-in project. As you will learn in Lesson 13, you can password-protect code that you add to a custom Outlook form as well. In Access, if you save your database as an MDE file, Access removes editable Visual Basic code and protects code modules, forms, and reports. For more information about securing Access databases and your Visual Basic code, in Access, ask the Assistant for help using the words "About MDE Files."

Add a password to your project

When you open the MyEnergy template you created earlier to make modifications to the Visual Basic code, the Visual Basic for Applications project of the template will be listed in the Project Explorer in the Visual Basic Editor. If the project is not password-protected, all of the project items will be listed and any module can be opened. To prevent the project from expanding and displaying the project items in the Project Explorer, you need to add a password.

1   Start Word. On the File menu, click Open. Change to the Lesson 9 folder and open MyEnergy.dot.

It is important that you open the template by clicking Open on the File menu in Word, navigating to the file, and clicking Open. If you load the template by using the Template And Add-Ins dialog box, you are unable to edit the Visual Basic for Applications project of the MyEnergy template.

2   Switch to the Visual Basic Editor and note the appearance of the MyEnergy project and its project items in the Project Explorer. (You can open the Modules folder to see relevant items.)

3   On the Tools menu, click Project Properties to display the Project Properties dialog box and then click the Protection tab.

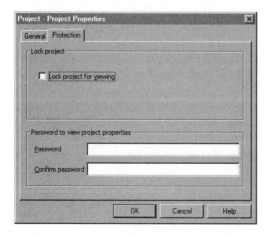

4 In the Protection tab of the Project Properties dialog box, select Lock Project For Viewing.

5 In the Password text box, enter a password and then enter it again in the Confirm Password text box. Click OK.

 IMPORTANT Remember the password you assign to the project. If you forget it, the Visual Basic Editor does not provide a way to retrieve the contents from the project. The password you provide is also case-sensitive, so make sure you remember the exact syntax you use.

6 Switch to the Word application window, save MyEnergy.dot, and exit Word.

7 Restart Word and open MyEnergy.dot.

Switch to the Visual Basic Editor and note that the MyEnergy project is not expanded in the Project Explorer.

8 Double-click the MyEnergy project item in the Project Explorer.

The Project Password dialog box is displayed, prompting you to enter a password.

9 Enter the password you assigned to the project and click OK.

The MyEnergy project in the Project Explorer should now be expanded. You can also display the Project Properties dialog box again and change the password or remove password protection from the project.

10 Exit Word.

217

Adding passwords to your project does not affect the functionality of the Visual Basic code you write. It is usually a good practice to add a password to your project just before you distribute your solution to ensure that others cannot tamper with your code and that your program works as intended.

 IMPORTANT You may want to remove the Energy Report custom menu item. You can do this by starting Word, opening the MyEnergy.dot template, opening the Visual Basic Editor, placing the cursor in the RemoveMenuItem procedure located in the modMenu module, and pressing F5. When Visual Basic displays the Macros dialog box, select RemoveCustomItem and click Run.

Lesson Summary

To	Do this
Create a Word add-in	Create a new Word document, add your code, and save the document as a Word Template file (*.dot) using the Save As dialog box.
Automatically load a Word add-in	Place the Word add-in file in the C:\Program Files\Microsoft Office\Office\Startup folder.
Manually load a Word add-in	On the Tools menu in Word, click Templates And Add-Ins, click Add in the dialog box, select the add-in, and click OK twice.
Manually unload a Word add-in	On the Tools menu in Word, click Templates And Add-Ins, select the add-in in the Global Templates And Add-Ins list, and click Remove; or, clear the item in the list and click OK.
Automatically run code in a Word add-in when Word opens	Create the procedure AutoExec in your add-in.
Automatically run code in a Word add-in when Word closes	Create the procedure AutoExit in your add-in.
Create user-defined variables	Use the Type statement in the Declarations section of a module.
Password-protect your Visual Basic code in the Visual Basic Editor	In the Editor, on the Tools menu, click Project Properties, and in the Protection tab, select Lock Project For Viewing and add a password.

For online information about	Ask the Assistant for help, using the words
Procedures that are automatically run in Word	"Auto Macros"
Creating user-defined variables	"User-defined types"
Password protection for an Applications project in the Visual Basic Editor	"Protection tab"
Password protection for Visual Basic code in Access databases	"MDE" (with the Access window active)

Preview of the Next Lesson

In the next lesson, you will use the code from the Energy database you created in Lesson 8 to create Visual Basic for Applications add-ins for both Excel and PowerPoint. You will also see how you can run the procedures in an Excel add-in from a PowerPoint add-in and thus avoid duplication of code.

Creating Add-Ins for Excel and PowerPoint

Estimated time
45 min.

In this lesson you will learn how to:

■ Create Visual Basic for Applications add-ins for Excel and PowerPoint.

■ Reuse code modules from other projects.

■ Run procedures in an Excel add-in from a PowerPoint add-in.

Ever since Microsoft Excel version 5.0, developers have been creating custom solutions for Excel with Visual Basic for Applications add-ins. Now Microsoft PowerPoint 97 exposes the necessary tools for creating Visual Basic for Applications add-ins for PowerPoint. The model PowerPoint uses to create add-ins is similar to that of Excel, so as you learn the Excel add-in model, you learn the PowerPoint add-in model.

Once you develop add-ins for Word, Excel, PowerPoint, or Access, you can easily run procedures in one add-in from another. Although an add-in may serve a purpose for a specific application, you can use the functionality you create in one add-in from within another add-in, thus avoiding duplication of code in multiple projects.

Building Excel Add-Ins

When you develop Visual Basic for Applications add-ins for Microsoft Excel, you start by creating a new workbook. Once you add your custom code to the workbook, you can save the workbook as an Excel add-in. In this section, you will create an Excel add-in that generates an Excel workbook containing a spreadsheet and chart filtered from the energy data in the Microsoft Access database in Lesson 8.

Create an Excel add-in

1   Start Excel and display the Visual Basic Editor.

2   On the Tools menu, click References, select the item Microsoft DAO 3.5 Object Library in the Available References list box, and click OK.

3   Insert a code module, and in the Properties window, type **modExcel** to set the Name property.

4   Start Microsoft Access and open the Energy database in the Lesson 8 practice folder.

 NOTE   If all your code was working properly at the end of Lesson 8, you can also use the MyEnergy database you created.

5   In the Energy database, copy all of the code in the code module modExcel except for the first line and paste it into the code module modExcel in the Visual Basic Editor in Excel.

The first line in the Access code module is Option Compare Database. If the Option Explicit statement is listed twice at the top of the modExcel module in Excel, remove one of the listings.

6   Insert a new code module, and in the Properties window, type **modMain** to set the Name property.

7   In the Energy database, copy all of the code in the code module modMain except for the first line and paste it into the code module modMain in the Visual Basic Editor in Excel. If the Option Explicit statement is listed twice at the top of the modMain module in Excel, remove one of the listings.

8   Remove all non-Excel-specific code in the Main procedure in the modMain code module so that the procedure looks like this:

```
Sub Main()
    Set m_dbEnergyUsage = DBEngine.Workspaces(0) _
        .OpenDatabase(g_sFilePath & "Energy.mdb")
```

```
        Call modExcel.CreateExcelSheet
        Call GetDatabaseInfo
        Call modExcel.CreateChart
    End Sub
```

The Main procedure will be called from a custom menu item that your add-in will add to the Worksheet Menu Bar in Excel.

9 Remove the arguments passed to the GetDatabaseInfo procedure so that the beginning of the procedure appears as follows:

```
Sub GetDatabaseInfo()
```

10 Remove all non-Excel-specific code in the GetDatabaseInfo procedure, the statements involving the Forms collection, and the `DoEvents` statement in the GetDatabaseInfo procedure. Then edit the procedure so that only the following line exists after the code in which the variable g_iTotalHours is set and before the MoveNext method of the Record-set object:

```
Call modExcel.AddToSheet(sID, _
    sDateTime, sComputer, sgPeriodkWh, sgCost)
```

The revised procedure looks like this:

```
Sub GetDatabaseInfo()
    Dim sID As String, sDateTime As String
    Dim sComputer As String
    Dim sgPeriodkWh As Single, sgCost As Single
    Dim rsEnergy As DAO.Recordset
    Set rsEnergy = m_dbEnergyUsage _
        .OpenRecordset("LabEnergyUsage", dbOpenTable)
    With rsEnergy
        Do
            sID = ![Id]
            sDateTime = ![Date and Time]
            sComputer = ![Computer Network]
            sgPeriodkWh = m_iWattage * Int(sComputer) / 1000
            sgCost = sgPeriodkWh * m_sgCost
            g_sgTotalCost = g_sgTotalCost + sgCost
            g_iTotalHours = g_iTotalHours + Int(sComputer)
            Call modExcel.AddToSheet(sID, _
                sDateTime, sComputer, sgPeriodkWh, sgCost)
            .MoveNext
        Loop Until .EOF = True
        .Close
    End With
    m_dbEnergyUsage.Close
End Sub
```

11 Double-click the modExcel project item in the Project Explorer to activate the modExcel Code window.

12 Remove the keyword New from the module-level declaration of the variable m_oExcel, and insert the following line as the first line in the CreateExcelSheet procedure:

```
Set m_oExcel = Application
```

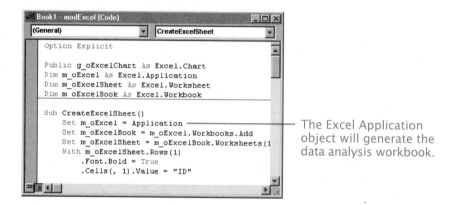

The Excel Application object will generate the data analysis workbook.

In the Excel add-in you are creating, you will call the procedures to create the Excel data analysis workbook from within the Excel application. To generate the workbook in the current instance of Excel, reference the Excel Application object. Or, you could use the GetObject function, which was discussed in Lesson 5.

13 Switch to the Excel application window, and on the File menu, click Save As. In the Save As Type drop-down list in the Save As dialog box, select Microsoft Excel Workbook (*.xls). Change to the folder C:\Office VBA Practice\Lesson10, type **MyEnergy** in the File Name text box, and click Save.

By saving the workbook, you are saving the source code of your add-in.

14 Exit Access but leave Excel open.

The code that creates the Excel data analysis workbook from the data in the Access database is now complete. You could run the add-in by placing the cursor in the Main procedure and pressing F5. In the steps below, however, you will create procedures that automatically add a menu item to the Excel Worksheet Menu Bar when your add-in is loaded. With this option, you can generate the data analysis workbook easily by clicking a single menu item.

Add a menu item in Excel

If you create a procedure named Auto_Open in an Excel workbook or add-in, Excel automatically runs the procedure when the file is loaded. Similarly, if you create a procedure named Auto_Close, Excel automatically runs the procedure when the file is unloaded. You can use these two procedures to automatically add and remove custom menu items and toolbars so that you can access functionality in your add-in from the user interface.

1   Switch to the Visual Basic Editor of Excel.

2   In the Project Explorer, right-click the VBAProject (MyEnergy.xls) project, and click Import File on the shortcut menu.

3   In the Import File dialog box, change to the Lesson 9 folder, select the file modMenu.bas, and click Open.

 NOTE   Recall that in Lesson 9 you created your own version of modMenu.bas. If you prefer, you can change to the folder where you exported that code module in the Lesson 9 section "Add reusable menu item code using user-defined types," and then open that version.

The project modMenu should now be listed in the Project Explorer in the Modules folder under the project VBAProject (MyEnergy.xls).

4   In the Project Explorer, double-click the modMain project item to activate its Code window. Move the cursor beneath the Declarations section of modMain and add the following Auto_Open procedure:

```
Sub Auto_Open()
    Dim udtMenuItem As MenuItem
    With udtMenuItem
        .sMenu = "Tools"
        .sCaption = "E&nergy Analysis"
        .iBefore = 1
        .sOnAction = "Main"
    End With
    Call modMenu.AddMenuItem(udtMenuItem)
End Sub
```

When you start Excel, Excel automatically runs the Auto_Open procedure just after your add-in is loaded into memory. The contents of the Auto_Open procedure here are virtually the same as that of the AddCustomItem procedure created for your Word add-in in Lesson 9. The only differences are the name of the procedure and the menu caption.

TIP The code within the Auto_Open and Auto_Close procedures in Excel workbooks or add-ins can be pasted into the Open and Close event procedures of the Excel Workbook object instead. When Excel loads a workbook or add-in, it runs the Workbook_Open event procedure in the ThisDocument module just before it runs the Auto_Open procedure. When Excel unloads a workbook or add-in, it runs the Workbook_BeforeClose event procedure in the ThisDocument module just before it runs the Auto_Close procedure. The Auto_Open and Auto_Close procedures run automatically only if they are added to a standard code module.

5 Move the cursor beneath the Auto_Open procedure and add the following Auto_Close procedure:

```
Sub Auto_Close()
    Dim udtMenuItem As MenuItem
    With udtMenuItem
        .sMenu = "Tools"
        .sCaption = "E&nergy Analysis"
    End With
    Call modMenu.RemoveMenuItem(udtMenuItem)
End Sub
```

If you don't remember how to use user-defined types, you may want to review them in Lesson 9.

When you exit Excel, Excel automatically runs the Auto_Close procedure just before your workbook or add-in is unloaded. The Auto_Close procedure above declares a variable udtMenuItem as the user-defined type MenuItem and sets two of the four elements. The custom menu item Energy Analysis will be removed from the Tools menu.

Once the elements are set, the RemoveMenuItem procedure within the code module modMenu is called and the variable udtMenuItem is passed. The contents of the Auto_Close procedure here are virtually the same as that of the RemoveCustomItem procedure created for your Word add-in in Lesson 9. The only differences are the name of the procedure and the menu caption.

Save a workbook as an Excel add-in

1 Switch to the Excel application window, and on the File menu, click Save to save the workbook MyEnergy.xls.

Saving the MyEnergy.xls file saves your source code before you create the actual Excel add-in.

2 On the File menu, click Save As, and in the Save As Type drop-down list in the Save As dialog box, select Microsoft Excel Add-In (*.xla). Change to the folder C:\Office VBA Practice\Lesson10, type **MyEnergy** in the File Name text box, and click Save.

When you save the workbook MyEnergy.xls as an Excel add-in, Excel copies the contents of the MyEnergy.xls workbook and creates a new file on your computer system with the file extension *xla*. The MyEnergy.xls file is still displayed in the Excel application window. The .xla file allows you to easily recognize the file as an Excel add-in.

Determine whether a workbook is an add-in

The MyEnergy.xls and MyEnergy.xla files are exactly the same except that the worksheets in the MyEnergy.xla file are not displayed in the Excel application window when the MyEnergy.xla file is loaded. You can avoid tracking two separate files by setting the IsAddIn property of the workbook to True, as the following step-by-step example will show. Preserving the .xla file, however, allows you and your users to recognize an Excel add-in more readily in Windows Explorer.

1 Switch to the Visual Basic Editor, and in the Project Explorer, click the ThisWorkbook project item in the Microsoft Excel Objects folder under the project VBAProject (MyEnergy.xls).

   The properties of the workbook project item are listed in the Properties window. The title bar caption of the Properties window is Properties – ThisWorkbook.

2 In the Properties window, scroll to the IsAddIn property and set its value to True.

   Excel now treats the MyEnergy.xls workbook as an Excel add-in; the worksheets of the workbook are not displayed in the Excel application window.

3 Switch to the Excel application window.

   The worksheets of the MyEnergy.xls file are no longer displayed and the title bar of Excel no longer displays the filename MyEnergy.xls, but the worksheets have not been deleted.

4 To make the worksheets visible again, set the IsAddIn workbook property to False. (Switch back to the Editor, double-click the ThisWorkbook project item, and in the Properties window, set IsAddIn to False.)

5 Close the file MyEnergy.xls without saving changes and exit Excel.

Load an Excel add-in automatically

To automatically load an Excel add-in, you have to save the Excel add-in file in the folder C:\Program Files\Microsoft Office\Office\XlStart. When Excel is started, it iterates through the add-in files in the XlStart folder and loads each one. Once Excel loads a particular add-in, it searches for the Auto_Open procedure and, if it exists, runs the procedure.

IMPORTANT When you want an add-in from the XlStart folder to load automatically, you must first exit all running instances of Microsoft Excel and then restart Excel.

1   Use Windows Explorer to move the file MyEnergy.xla from the folder C:\Office VBA Practice\Lesson10 to the folder C:\Program Files\ Microsoft Office\Office\XlStart.

2   Restart Excel and click the Tools menu to display the list of menu items.

The addition of the custom menu item to the Tools menu indicates that Excel loaded the MyEnergy add-in.

 NOTE In the Add-Ins dialog box, which is displayed by clicking Add-Ins on the Tools menu, the Energy add-in is not listed in the Add-Ins Available list. Add-ins loaded from the XlStart folder are not listed in the Add-Ins dialog box.

3   On the Tools menu, click Energy Analysis to create a data analysis workbook.

Once the code in the add-in finishes running, you will see the new workbook in the Excel application window, and the filename in the title bar should be DataAnalysis.xls.

4   Exit Excel without saving changes.

When you exit Excel, all add-ins are unloaded, including the MyEnergy add-in. The Auto_Close procedure in MyEnergy.xla runs automatically, and the Energy Analysis custom menu item is removed from the Tools menu. Of course, you can't verify this functionality yet because the Auto_Open procedure is run when you restart Excel.

5   To verify that the custom menu item was removed from the Tools menu, use Windows Explorer to move the MyEnergy.xla file from the XlStart folder back to the folder C:\Office VBA Practice\Lesson10 and restart Excel.

The Energy Analysis custom menu item should no longer be displayed on the Tools menu.

Load an Excel add-in manually

1 On the Tools menu, click Add-Ins.

2 In the Add-Ins dialog box, click Browse. In the Browse dialog box, change to the Lesson 10 practice folder, select MyEnergy.xla, and click OK.

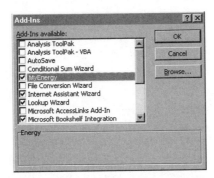

This adds the add-in to the Add-Ins Available list box. (Your list of available add-ins may be different.) The check box beside the add-in item in the list box indicates two things: whether or not it is currently loaded, and whether it will be automatically loaded the next time you start Excel. That is, if the check box is selected, the add-in will be or is already loaded in the current session of Excel. If you don't clear the check mark before you exit Excel, the add-in will load automatically the next time you start Excel.

3 Click OK to close the Add-Ins dialog box.

The Energy Analysis menu item should now be displayed on the Tools menu, indicating that the MyEnergy.xla add-in file was loaded.

 NOTE When you load the MyEnergy.xls file, the Auto_Open procedure runs automatically, just as it did when the MyEnergy.xla file was loaded. Thus, even though the MyEnergy.xla add-in file may not be currently loaded, the Energy Analysis menu item may be displayed, because the Auto_Open procedure in the MyEnergy.xls file adds it to the Tools menu.

4 On the Tools menu, click Energy Analysis to create a data analysis workbook.

5 Exit Excel.

Building PowerPoint Add-Ins

When you develop Visual Basic for Applications add-ins for Microsoft PowerPoint, you start by creating a new presentation. Once you add your custom code to the presentation, you can save the presentation as a PowerPoint add-in. In this section, you will create a PowerPoint add-in that generates a PowerPoint presentation containing an Excel chart filtered from the energy data in the Microsoft Access database in Lesson 8.

Create a PowerPoint add-in

1   Start PowerPoint, open a new presentation, and display the Visual Basic Editor.

2   On the Tools menu, click References, and in the Available References list box, select Microsoft DAO 3.5 Object Library, and select the adjacent check box so that a check appears in the box.

3   In the Available References list box, select Microsoft Excel 8.0 Object Library as well, and select the adjacent check box. Click OK.

4   Insert a code module, and in the Properties window, type **modPowerPoint** to set the Name property.

5   Start Microsoft Access and open the Energy database in the Lesson 8 subfolder of the practice files.

 NOTE   If all your code was working properly at the end of Lesson 8, you can also use the MyEnergy database you created.

6   In the Energy database, copy all of the code in the code module modPowerPoint except for the first line and paste it into the code module modPowerPoint in the Visual Basic Editor in PowerPoint.

The first line in the Access code module is `Option Compare Database`. If the `Option Explicit` statement is listed twice at the top of the modPowerPoint module in PowerPoint, remove one of the listings.

7   Insert a code module, and in the Properties window, type **modMain** to set the Name property.

8   In the Energy database, copy all of the code in the code module modMain except for the first line and paste it into the code module modMain in the Visual Basic Editor in PowerPoint. If the `Option Explicit` statement is listed twice at the top of the modMain module in PowerPoint, remove one of the listings.

9   Exit Access.

Call an Excel add-in from PowerPoint

The code in the Energy database from Lesson 8 created a PowerPoint presentation by copying the chart generated in Excel. To do the same thing with your PowerPoint add-in, you would need to copy the Excel code. However, rather than copying all of the code from the Excel add-in to create the chart, you can use the Run method of the Excel Application object to run a procedure within an Excel add-in or workbook. If the procedure you specify has arguments passed into it, the Run method allows you to pass arguments to the specified procedure.

1   In the Visual Basic Editor in PowerPoint, in the Declarations section of modMain, add the following two declarations:

```
Public g_oExcelChart As Excel.Chart
Dim m_oExcel As New Excel.Application
```

2   Change the Main procedure in the modMain code module so that the procedure looks like this:

```
Sub Main()
    Set m_dbEnergyUsage = DBEngine.Workspaces(0) _
        .OpenDatabase(g_sFilePath & "Energy.mdb")

    With m_oExcel
        .Workbooks.Open "C:\Office VBA Practice\Lesson10\" _
            & "MyEnergy.xla"
        .Run "MyEnergy.xla!modExcel.CreateExcelSheet"
        Call GetDatabaseInfo
        .Run "MyEnergy.xla!modExcel.CreateChart"
        Set g_oExcelChart = .Workbooks(1).Charts(1)
        Call modPowerPoint.CreatePowerPointPres
        .Quit
    End With
End Sub
```

Using the Open method of the Excel Workbooks object, the With...End block above opens the Excel add-in to make sure it is loaded into memory. Once the add-in is loaded, the Run method of the Excel Application object is used to call the procedure CreateExcelSheet in the Excel add-in. The GetDatabaseInfo procedure is then called to fill the Excel worksheet. After the data has been copied into the worksheet, the CreateChart procedure in the Excel add-in is called.

The CreatePowerPointPres procedure in the PowerPoint add-in is called after the public variable g_oExcelChart is set to the chart created by the CreateChart procedure in the Excel add-in. The g_oExcelChart variable is used by the CreatePowerPointPres procedure to copy the chart and paste it into a PowerPoint slide. Last, the instance of Excel used to import the data and create the chart is exited using the Quit method of the Excel Application object.

3   Remove the arguments passed to the GetDatabaseInfo procedure so that the beginning of the procedure looks like this:

```
Sub GetDatabaseInfo()
```

4   In the GetDatabaseInfo procedure, remove all non-Excel-specific lines, the statements involving the Forms collection, and the DoEvents statement in the GetDatabaseInfo procedure. Then edit the procedure so that only the following line exists after the variable g_iTotalHours is set and before the MoveNext method of the Recordset object:

```
Call modExcel.AddToSheet(sID, _
    sDateTime, sComputer, sgPeriodkWh, sgCost)
```

5   Change the line above to the following:

```
m_oExcel.Run _
    "MyEnergy.xla!modExcel.AddToSheet", _
    sID, sDateTime, sComputer, _
    sgPeriodkWh, sgCost
```

Because the procedure AddToSheet does not exist in the PowerPoint add-in, you use the Run method of the Excel Application object to call the procedure AddToSheet in the Excel add-in. The first argument of the Run method, which is named Macro, is the procedure you want to call. The standard syntax of the Macro argument has three parts: *<Filename>!<Module name>.<Procedure name>*.

The filename can be the name of any Excel workbook or add-in. If the filename is not specified, Excel will search through all currently loaded Excel files to find and run the specified procedure. The filename and module name are separated by an exclamation point (!). If the filename is not specified, the exclamation point is not required.

The module name is the name of the module containing the procedure, specified by the procedure name. The module name does not need to be specified as long as there is only one procedure with the specified name in the Excel file. The module and procedure names are separated by a period. The arguments following the Macro module name argument in the Run method represent the arguments that must be passed to the specified procedure.

The revised procedure looks like the following:

```
Sub GetDatabaseInfo()
    Dim sID As String, sDateTime As String
    Dim sComputer As String
    Dim sgPeriodkWh As Single, sgCost As Single
    Dim rsEnergy As DAO.Recordset

    Set rsEnergy = m_dbEnergyUsage _
        .OpenRecordset("LabEnergyUsage", dbOpenTable)
    With rsEnergy
        Do
            sID = ![Id]
            sDateTime = ![Date and Time]
            sComputer = ![Computer Network]

            sgPeriodkWh = m_iWattage * Int(sComputer) / 1000
            sgCost = sgPeriodkWh * m_sgCost
            g_sgTotalCost = g_sgTotalCost + sgCost
            g_iTotalHours = g_iTotalHours + Int(sComputer)

            m_oExcel.Run _
                "MyEnergy.xla!modExcel.AddToSheet", _
                sID, sDateTime, sComputer, _
                sgPeriodkWh, sgCost

            .MoveNext
        Loop Until .EOF = True
        .Close
    End With
    m_dbEnergyUsage.Close
End Sub
```

TIP Word, Excel, PowerPoint, and Access each provide the Run method for their Application object. The syntax of the first argument is the same across all four applications. To find out about a specific difference between the Run methods of any of these applications, in the Visual Basic Editor of the application in question, ask the Assistant for help using the words "Run method." Using the Project Explorer, switch to the modPowerPoint Code window.

6 Double-click the modPowerPoint module in the Project Explorer window.

7 Remove the keyword New from the procedure-level declaration of the variable oPowerPoint, and insert the following line just after the procedure-level declarations in the CreatePowerPointPres procedure:

```
Set oPowerPoint = Application
```

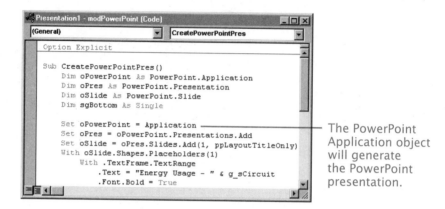

The PowerPoint Application object will generate the PowerPoint presentation.

In the PowerPoint add-in you are creating, you will call the procedures to create the PowerPoint presentation.

8 Switch to the PowerPoint application window, and on the File menu, click Save As. In the Save As Type drop-down list in the Save As dialog box, select Presentation (*.ppt). Change to the folder C:\Office VBA Practice\Lesson10, type **MyEnergy** in the File Name text box, and click Save.

By saving the presentation, you are saving the source code.

The code to create a PowerPoint presentation from the data in the Access database is now complete. You can run the add-in by placing the cursor in the Main procedure and pressing F5. Just as you did for the Excel add-in earlier in this lesson, however, you now create procedures that automatically add a menu item to the PowerPoint Menu Bar when your add-in is loaded. With this option, you can generate the PowerPoint presentation easily by clicking a single menu item.

Add a menu item in PowerPoint

If you create a procedure named Auto_Open in a PowerPoint add-in, PowerPoint automatically runs the procedure when your add-in is loaded. Similarly, if you create a procedure named Auto_Close, PowerPoint automatically runs the procedure when your add-in is unloaded. Unlike Excel, however, these two procedures do not run automatically if they are in a presentation and the presentation is loaded. (In Excel, the Auto_Open and Auto_Close procedures run automatically if they are in a workbook or add-in.)

1   Switch to the Visual Basic Editor.

2   In the Project Explorer, right-click the VBAProject (MyEnergy.ppt) project, and click Import File on the shortcut menu.

3   In the Import File dialog box, change to the Lesson 9 subfolder, select the file modMenu.bas, and click Open.

 NOTE   Recall that in Lesson 9 you created your own version of modMenu.bas. If you prefer, you can change to the folder where you exported that code module in the Lesson 9 section "Add reusable menu item code using user-defined types."

The project modMenu should now be listed in the Project Explorer in the Modules folder under the project VBAProject (MyEnergy.ppt).

4   In the Project Explorer, double-click the modMain project item to activate its Code window. Move the cursor beneath the Declarations section of modMain and add the following Auto_Open procedure:

```
Sub Auto_Open()
    Dim udtMenuItem As MenuItem
    With udtMenuItem
        .sMenu = "Tools"
        .sCaption = "E&nergy Presentation"
        .iBefore = 1
        .sOnAction = "Main"
    End With
    Call modMenu.AddMenuItem(udtMenuItem)
End Sub
```

When you start PowerPoint, it automatically runs the Auto_Open procedure just after your add-in is loaded into memory.

5   Move the cursor beneath the Auto_Open procedure and add the following Auto_Close procedure:

```
Sub Auto_Close()
    Dim udtMenuItem As MenuItem
    With udtMenuItem
        .sMenu = "Tools"
        .sCaption = "E&nergy Presentation"
    End With
    Call modMenu.RemoveMenuItem(udtMenuItem)
End Sub
```

When you exit PowerPoint, it automatically runs the Auto_Close procedure just before your add-in is unloaded.

Save a presentation as a PowerPoint add-in

1   Switch to the PowerPoint application window, and on the File menu, click Save to save the presentation MyEnergy.ppt.

Saving the MyEnergy.ppt file saves your source code before you create a PowerPoint add-in.

2   On the File menu, click Save As, and in the Save As Type drop-down list in the Save As dialog box, select PowerPoint Add-In (*.ppa). Navigate to the folder C:\Office VBA Practice\Lesson10, type **MyEnergy** in the File Name text box, and click Save.

When you save the presentation MyEnergy.ppt as a PowerPoint add-in, PowerPoint removes all slides from the presentation and saves only the Visual Basic code you wrote in the file MyEnergy.ppa.

TIP   If an error occurs when you click Save to save the presentation as a PowerPoint add-in, switch to the Visual Basic Editor and click Compile VBAProject on the Debug menu. When PowerPoint saves the presentation as an add-in, PowerPoint tries to compile the code in the Visual Basic for Applications project. When you click Compile VBAProject on the Debug menu, the Visual Basic for Applications project will be compiled. If an error occurs while the code is being compiled, Visual Basic for Applications will display an alert indicating the error, and the line where the error occurred will be highlighted. The Compile VBAProject menu item is available in the Visual Basic Editor in both Word and Excel. Access provides a set of compiling options on the Debug menu when a code module (standard or class) is active.

3   Close the file MyEnergy.ppt and exit PowerPoint. You do not need to save changes.

NOTE   The source code and the compiled add-in are provided for you in the Lesson 10 subfolder of the Office VBA Practice folder. The files are Energy.ppt and Energy.ppa, respectively.

Load a PowerPoint add-in

To automatically load a PowerPoint add-in, you first have to manually load the add-in. Unlike Word and Excel, PowerPoint does not have a Startup folder through which it iterates when it starts. Instead, PowerPoint iterates through a set of keys in the Windows Registry. To register a PowerPoint add-in, you must add it manually to the Available Add-Ins list in the Add-Ins dialog box in PowerPoint.

When PowerPoint is started, it iterates through the registered add-in files and loads any add-in that is selected to be loaded automatically. Once Powerpoint loads a particular add-in, it searches for the Auto_Open procedure and, if it exists, runs the procedure.

 TIP If you are an advanced user who knows how to use a setup program that can write to the Windows Registry, then under HKEY_CURRENT_USER\Software\Microsoft\Office\8.0\PowerPoint\AddIns you can add a new add-in key. The two values you need to add under the new add-in key are the DWORD value AutoLoad and the string value Path. AutoLoad can be set to 0 or 1; a value of 1 indicates that the add-in will load automatically when PowerPoint is started. Path indicates the file path of the PowerPoint add-in. Each time you use the Add-Ins dialog box in PowerPoint, these two values are created.

1 Start PowerPoint and open a blank presentation. Click the Tools menu to display the list of menu items.

Energy Presentation should not be displayed because the MyEnergy.ppa add-in is not loaded.

2 On the Tools menu, click Add-Ins.

3 In the Add-Ins dialog box, click Add New. In the Add New PowerPoint Add-Ins dialog box, change to the C:\Office VBA Practice\Lesson10 folder, select MyEnergy.ppa, click OK, and then click Close.

If PowerPoint displays a warning about macros that may contain viruses, click the Enable Macros button.

This adds the add-in to the Available Add-Ins list box. The "x" beside the add-in item in the list box indicates two things: whether the add-in is currently loaded, and whether it will load automatically the next time you start PowerPoint.

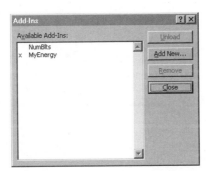

4 Click Close to close the Add-Ins dialog box.

Energy Presentation should now be displayed on the Tools menu, indicating that the MyEnergy.ppa add-in was loaded.

5 On the Tools menu, click Energy Presentation to create a PowerPoint presentation based on the Energy data.

This may take a minute or so, depending on the hardware and software configuration of your computer. Once the procedure finishes running, you will see the new presentation in the PowerPoint application window, and the filename in the title bar should be EnergyPres.

6 Exit PowerPoint.

Lesson Summary

To	Do this
Create an Excel add-in	Create a new Excel workbook, add your code, and save the workbook as an Excel add-in file (*.xla) using the Save As dialog box.
Automatically load an Excel add-in	Place the Excel add-in file in the C:\Program Files\Microsoft Office\Office\XlStart folder.
Manually load an Excel add-in	On the Tools menu in Excel, click Add-Ins, click Browse in the Add-Ins dialog box, search for the add-in on your system, and click OK twice.
Manually unload an Excel add-in	On the Tools menu in Excel, click Add-Ins, select the add-in in the Add-Ins Available list, clear the item, and click OK.
Automatically run code in a workbook or an Excel add-in when Excel opens	Create the procedure Auto_Open in a standard code module in your add-in; or, add code to the Workbook_Open event procedure.
Automatically run code in a workbook or an Excel add-in when Excel closes	Create the procedure Auto_Close in a standard code module in your add-in; or, add code to the Workbook_BeforeClose event procedure.
Create a PowerPoint add-in	Open a new PowerPoint presentation, add your code, and save the presentation as a PowerPoint Add-In file (*.ppa) using the Save As dialog box.
Automatically load a PowerPoint add-in	On the Tools menu in PowerPoint, click Add-Ins, and add the add-in file to the Available Add-Ins list. If the add-in has no "x" beside it, select it, click Load, and click Close.
Manually load a PowerPoint add-in	On the Tools menu in PowerPoint, click Add-Ins, click Add New in the Add-Ins dialog box, search for the add-in on your system, and click OK twice.

To	Do this
Manually unload a PowerPoint add-in	On the Tools menu in PowerPoint, click Add-Ins, select the add-in in the Available Add-Ins list, click Unload, and click Close.
Automatically run code in a PowerPoint add-in when PowerPoint opens	Create the procedure Auto_Open in your add-in.
Automatically run code in a PowerPoint add-in when PowerPoint closes	Create the procedure Auto_Close in your add-in.
Run procedures in Word, Excel, or PowerPoint add-ins from other add-ins	Use the Run method of the Application object in Word, Excel, or PowerPoint.

For online information about	Ask the Assistant for help, using the words
Procedures that are automatically run in Excel	"Open event" and "BeforeClose event"
Running procedures in other add-ins and Office documents	"Run method"

Preview of the Next Lesson

In the next lesson, you will create an Office wizard similar in look and style to the Fax Wizard in Word and the AutoContent Wizard in PowerPoint. You will also learn how to use common Windows dialog boxes such as the Browse For Folder and Open dialog boxes in your add-ins, and how to take advantage of functions built into the Visual Basic programming language.

Developing Office Wizards

Estimated time
120 min.

In this lesson you will learn how to:

- Create an Office wizard similar in style to the Fax Wizard in Word and the AutoContent Wizard in PowerPoint.
- Add navigation buttons to your wizard and create a "subway map."
- Integrate the Office Assistant into your wizards.
- Use common Windows dialog boxes such as the Browse For Folder dialog box and the Open dialog box.
- Add your Word wizard to the New dialog box.

Wizards have become standard features for many software applications. Wizards guide you through a series of tasks and often help you save time creating documents. They step you through many prebuilt content templates and provide you with ideas, starter text, formatting, and organization for your work. The new style of Microsoft Office wizards now allows you to navigate more easily, both backward and forward, through the steps. It also allows you to visually track your progress through the task steps so that you have a sense of where you are and where you are going.

Integrating the Office Assistant with wizards makes it even easier to create helpful steps. The Assistant gives you tips and hints for going through the steps efficiently as well as visual examples and step-by-step instructions for specific tasks.

IMPORTANT This lesson requires that you install the optional wizards and reports available to Microsoft Word 97. To install them, run the Office Setup program. Click Add/Remove, select Microsoft Word, click Change Option, select Wizards And Templates, click Change Option, and click Select All. Click OK twice and then click Continue. Once they are installed, click OK to end the Setup program.

Wizard Look and Style

The wizard dialog box has three main features: navigation buttons, a subway map, and tab pages. The subway map is optional but is provided in many Office wizards. You can make your wizard work equally well without the subway map, as you will see later in this lesson.

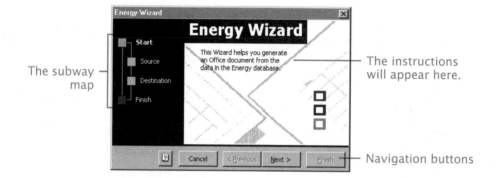

The Energy Wizard you will create in this lesson will allow you to specify the location of the Energy database used by the Word Energy add-in you created in Lesson 9. It will also allow you to specify where the generated Word report should be saved to.

The Energy Wizard has the same look and style as the Fax Wizard in Word. To access the Fax Wizard, click New on the File menu in Word, and in the Letter And Faxes tab, select the Fax Wizard icon, and click OK. (The details of the AutoContent Wizard in PowerPoint differ slightly from those of the Word wizards, but the look and style of the two wizard types are the same.) In this lesson, you will use the details of the Fax Wizard in Word as the model. The code for the wizard UserForm will be very generic so that you can easily plug the same code into a Microsoft Word, Excel, or PowerPoint wizard.

 NOTE The Office wizard that you create in this lesson will be developed for Word. In the Lesson 11 practice folder, you'll find Excel and PowerPoint versions of the wizard. All project items in the wizard that you create in this lesson are available in the Lesson 11 practice folder.

Set up a multiple-step wizard dialog box

You can easily build dialog boxes with multiple steps by using the MultiPage control. The MultiPage control is a container of controls within a collection of pages. As you will see, the MultiPage control makes it simple to design each page because you can add controls to one page and easily display the controls of another page.

MultiPage control

1 Start Microsoft Word. Display the Visual Basic Editor and insert a new UserForm.

2 In the Properties window, change the default name in the Name property of the new UserForm from UserForm1 to **frmWizard**.

3 In the Toolbox, click the MultiPage control and then click the UserForm frmWizard.

4 In the Properties window, change the default name in the Name property from MultiPage1 to **mpgSteps**. (The prefix *mpg* represents "multipage.")

5 Right-click the first tab of the mpgSteps control and click New Page on the shortcut menu.

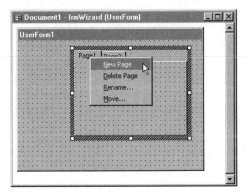

This adds a new page to the mpgSteps control. The tab caption of the new page is Page3.

6 Click the tab with the caption Page1 and change the Name property in the Properties window to **pgStart**. (The prefix *pg* represents "page.") Change the Caption property from Page1 to **Start**.

7 Click the tab with the caption Page2 and change the Name property to **pgStep1**. Change the Caption property to **Step1**.

8 Click the tab with the caption Page3 and change the Name property to **pgFinish**. Change the Caption property to **Finish**.

Your MultiPage control has three pages. The first page is the Start screen, or the screen that is first shown when the wizard is displayed. The last page is the Finish screen, which is displayed once the user completes all the steps in the wizard. The page between the first and last pages will become the step in the wizard where the user sets options and types information that the wizard needs to complete its overall task. Each subsequent step in the wizard requires its own page. In the section "Add a new step in the wizard," you will learn how to easily add another new page and, hence, another new step in your wizard.

The style of the MultiPage control, by default, is set to the enumeration value fmTabStyleTabs, which represents a value of 0. Later in this lesson, when you start adding controls to each page in the control, you will set the Style property of the MultiPage control to fmTabStyleNone so that the tabs are not displayed in the wizard dialog box. Some wizards display tabs, but the style you are creating in this lesson does not display tabs.

Add navigation buttons

Most well-designed wizards provide a set of common navigation buttons along the lower edge of the wizard dialog box. These navigation buttons are Cancel, Previous, Next, and Finish. With the introduction of the Office Assistant, you can add another button that allows you to display tips or instructions from the Assistant.

1 Move the MultiPage control mpgSteps to the upper-right area of the UserForm frmWizard.

2 Resize the UserForm to slightly increase its width. Double-click the CommandButton control in the Toolbox, and then click four times in the lower area of the UserForm, working from left to right, to create four command buttons. Use the following illustration as a guide:

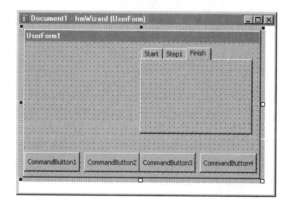

NOTE   By double-clicking a control in the Toolbox, you can add more than one of a particular control to a UserForm without having to continuously click the control in the Toolbox. You cannot resize or select any control in the UserForm until you click the Select Objects arrow in the Toolbox.

Select Objects arrow

3   Click the Select Objects arrow in the Toolbox so that you can select the controls in the UserForm, and then change the properties of the CommandButton controls to the following:

Control	Property	Value
CommandButton1	Name	cmdCancel
CommandButton1	Caption	Cancel
CommandButton1	Cancel	True
CommandButton2	Name	cmdPrevious
CommandButton2	Caption	< Previous
CommandButton2	Accelerator	P
CommandButton3	Name	cmdNext
CommandButton3	Caption	Next >
CommandButton3	Accelerator	N
CommandButton4	Name	cmdFinish
CommandButton4	Caption	Finish
CommandButton4	Accelerator	F

The Cancel property of the Cancel button should be set to True so that the user can press ESC to cancel the wizard dialog box. Allowing the user to cancel a dialog box by pressing ESC is a standard Windows programming practice.

4   Double-click the Previous button and add the following line to the cmdPrevious_Click event procedure:

```
mpgSteps.Value = mpgSteps.Value - 1
```

The Value property of the MultiPage control mpgSteps is an integer that indicates the currently active page. A value of 0 represents the first page in the control. The maximum value of this property is the number of pages minus 1. Each time you click the Previous button, the value of the mpgSteps control is decreased by 1 and the previous step is displayed.

Remember, because the code belongs exclusively to an object (the frmWizard UserForm), the code is contained in a class module. If a module does not belong to an object, it is referred to as a code module (or as a standard module in newer versions of Visual Basic).

5 In the Object drop-down list of the frmWizard Code window, select cmdNext and add the following line to the cmdNext_Click event procedure:

```
mpgSteps.Value = mpgSteps.Value + 1
```

Each time you click the Next button, the value of the mpgSteps control is increased by one and the next step is displayed.

6 In the Object drop-down list of the frmWizard Code window, select cmdCancel and add the following line to the cmdCancel_Click event procedure:

```
Unload Me
```

The Visual Basic keyword Me is an implicit reference to the UserForm in which the code is currently running. Thus, Me represents the UserForm frmWizard. When you click the Cancel button or press ESC, the dialog box is closed and unloaded from memory.

7 In the Object drop-down list of the frmWizard Code window, select cmdFinish and add the following line to the cmdFinish_Click event procedure:

```
Unload Me
```

For now, the Finish button closes the UserForm. Later in this lesson, however, you will add code to the cmdFinish_Click event procedure that checks the values entered in the steps in the wizard and then calls a number of procedures to perform the wizard's overall task before the dialog box is unloaded from memory.

8 In the Object drop-down list, select mpgSteps and add the following lines to the mpgSteps_Change event procedure:

```
Select Case mpgSteps.Value
Case 0
    cmdNext.Enabled = True
    cmdPrevious.Enabled = False
    cmdFinish.Enabled = False
Case m_iTotalSteps - 1
    cmdNext.Enabled = False
    cmdPrevious.Enabled = True
    cmdFinish.Enabled = True
Case Else
    cmdNext.Enabled = True
    cmdPrevious.Enabled = True
    cmdFinish.Enabled = False
End Select
```

When the value of the MultiPage control mpgSteps is changed by the cmdNext_Click or cmdPrevious_Click event procedure, the Change event of the mpgSteps control is triggered. The Select Case statement you added evaluates the current value of the mpgSteps control and determines the appropriate course of action. If the value is 0, the Start page is displayed and the Previous button is disabled because there are no more pages before the Start.

If the value is equal to the module-level variable m_iTotalSteps minus one, the Finish page is displayed and the Next button is disabled because there are no more pages after the Finish. In this case, the Finish button is enabled. The variable m_iTotalSteps is declared in step 10 and represents the total number of pages in the mpgSteps control. If the value of the mpgSteps control is neither the first nor last page, both the Previous and Next buttons are enabled.

9 In the Object drop-down list of the frmWizard Code window, select UserForm. In the Procedure drop-down list of the module, select Initialize and add the following lines to the UserForm_Initialize event procedure:

```
m_iTotalSteps = mpgSteps.Pages.Count
mpgSteps.Value = 0
Call mpgSteps_Change
```

Before the dialog box is displayed, you first need to initialize the state of some controls and then set the value of the variable m_iTotalSteps. This is done in the UserForm_Initialize event procedure, which is run just before the dialog box is displayed on the screen. In the Initialize event procedure of the UserForm frmWizard, m_iTotalSteps is set to the number of pages in the mpgSteps control.

The value of the mpgSteps control is set to 0 so that the Start page is shown when the UserForm is displayed. Despite the fact that the value of the mpgSteps control is set, the mpgSteps_Change event procedure may not run if the value of the mpgSteps is 0 while you are designing the UserForm. Thus, you explicitly call the mpgSteps_Change event procedure so that the navigation button is also initialized.

10 In the Declarations section of the frmWizard Code window (just above the first procedure), add the following module-level declaration:

```
Dim m_iTotalSteps As Integer
```

 TIP If the Option Explicit statement is not included at the beginning of the frmWizard Code window, you should add it there. If you want the Option Explicit statement to be added to any code module by default, on the Tools menu in the Visual Basic Editor, click Options, and then click Require Variable Declaration in the Editor tab of the Options dialog box. See "Do I Need to Declare My Variables and Constants?" in Lesson 3 for more information.

11 In the frmWizard UserForm, resize and move the navigation CommandButton controls, using the following illustration as a guide. Then press F5 to display the dialog box.

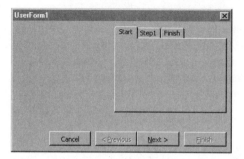

The Finish and Previous buttons are disabled, and the first page (the Start page) in the MultiPage control is shown when the wizard is displayed. Click the Next and Previous buttons to see the pages of the MultiPage control being activated and the navigation buttons being enabled and disabled.

12 Click Cancel, and then in the Project Explorer, right-click the frmWizard project item located in the Forms folder. Click Export File on the shortcut menu.

13 In the Export File dialog box, change to the Lesson 11 subfolder in the Office VBA Practice folder, type the name **frmWizardTemplateBasic** in the File Name text box, and click Save.

14 Switch to the Word application window. On the File menu, click Save As. In the Save As Type drop-down list in the Save As dialog box, select Document Template (*.dot). Change to the folder C:\Program Files\Microsoft Office\Templates\Reports. Type **Energy Wizard** in the File Name box and click Save.

This saves the work you've done so far.

This step-by-step example gave you the basics of setting up a wizard dialog box. In steps 12 and 13, you exported the UserForm so that you can use it as a starting point when you create a new wizard. In the next step-by-step example, you will continue building onto your wizard by adding the subway map panel on the left side of the UserForm.

Create a subway map

The "subway map" is a new style of Office wizard that allows for easy navigation through the wizard's steps by giving a visual representation of where you are within the wizard. Each "station" on the subway map represents a step in the wizard, and the current station, or step, is green. If you want to skip a step or jump to a certain step, you can easily do so by using the subway map panel.

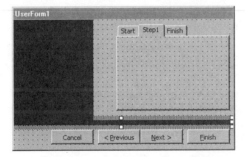

Image
control

1 In the Editor, in the Project Explorer, double-click the frmWizard project item. In the Toolbox, click the Image control, and then click in the upper-left area of the UserForm. In the Properties window, change the name of the Image control from Image1 to **imgLeftPane**.

2 Click the Image control in the Toolbox again and click the UserForm just below the imgLeftPane control. Change the name of the Image control from Image1 to **imgBottomStripe**.

3 To change the color of the Image controls you just inserted, select both Image controls by first selecting either one and then holding down the CTRL key to select the other. In the Properties window, click the value of the BackColor, and then click the arrow. Click the Palette tab and select the color black.

4 Move and resize the imgLeftPane and imgBottomStripe controls so that the UserForm looks like the following illustration:

5 Click the Image control in the Toolbox and then click the imgLeftPane control. Change the name of the newly inserted Image control to **imgSubway**.

You are placing imgSubway on top of imgLeftPane.

6 In the Properties window, change the BackStyle property of the imgSubway control to 0 – fmBackStyleTransparent. Change the BorderColor property by clicking the arrow, clicking the Palette tab, and selecting light gray. The value &H00C0C0C0& appears, which represents light gray.

7 Add another Image control and place it in the upper-left corner of the imgSubway control. Change the name to **imgStart** and set the BorderStyle property to 0 – fmBorderStyleNone. Resize the control so that it looks like the following illustration:

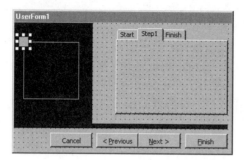

8 Click the imgStart control. On the Edit menu, click Copy. On the Edit menu, click Paste twice to create two copies of the control. In the Properties window, select Image1 from the drop-down list and change its name to **imgStep1**. Similarly, change the name of Image2 to **imgFinish**.

9 Move the imgStep1 and imgFinish controls so that they are on the border of the imgSubway control.

If the imgStep1 and imgFinish controls are underneath the mpgSteps control, select the selection border around the mpgSteps control and move the control temporarily out of the way. Also, if one image is underneath the other, select one by clicking its name in the drop-down list in the Properties window and then clicking the same control on the UserForm.

10 In the Toolbox, click the Label control, and then click the UserForm just beside the imgStart control. Set the following properties for the Label control:

Property	Value
Name	lblStart
BackStyle	0 – fmBackStyleTransparent
Caption	Start
ForeColor	&H00FFFFFF& (or white in the Palette tab)

11 Select the lblStart control by clicking any other control and then clicking the lblStart control. (If you initially click only the lblStart control, you will select the caption of the control, not the control itself.) On the Edit menu, click Copy, and then paste the control twice.

12 Move one of the pasted Label controls beside the imgStep1 control, name it **lblStep1**, and set the Caption property to **Step1**. Move the second pasted Label control beside the imgFinish control, name it **lblFinish**, and set the Caption property to **Finish**.

13 Move and resize the controls so that the UserForm looks like the following illustration:

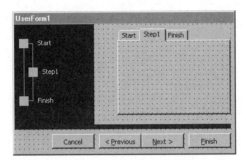

Make sure the label controls are slightly wider than the text they contain.

14 Select the controls imgStart, lblStart, imgStep1, lblStep1, imgFinish, and lblFinish, and then in the ControlTipText property in the Properties window, type **To skip to this step, click here.** Each subway map image and label has the same ToolTip text, which is the same as that in the Fax Wizard in Microsoft Word.

The layout of the subway map is now complete. What remains is to add the code that allows you to use the subway map to navigate through the steps.

Indicate active and visited steps in the subway map

The subway map must indicate which step is currently active and which steps you have visited. The currently active step is indicated by setting two properties of the controls in the subway map. First, set the BackColor property of the Image control, or station, to light green. Second, set the font of the station label to bold. Once you move on to another step in the wizard, the BackColor property of the Image control of the previous station is set to dark gray to indicate that you have previously visited there.

View Code

1 In the Project Explorer, select the frmWizard project item and click the View Code button, which is the leftmost button on the Project Explorer toolbar.

2 At the top of the module, just after the module-level declaration m_iTotalSteps, add the following module-level declaration:

```
Dim m_sCurStep As String
```

The variable m_sCurStep is the name of the current step, and it is used to keep track of the current step. Once you move to another step, you can use the value in the variable m_sCurStep to determine what the previous step was and to reset its properties so that the previous step appears visited.

3   In the Object drop-down list of the frmWizard Code window, select mpgSteps so that the mpgSteps_Change event procedure appears. Add the following procedure call just before the Select Case statement so that the call is the first line of the mpgSteps_Change event procedure:

```
Call SetSubwayMap
```

Every time the mpgSteps_Change event procedure runs, the SetSubwayMap procedure is called so that the images and labels of the map can be initialized.

4   At the bottom of the module, create the SetSubwayMap procedure by adding the following code:

```
Sub SetSubwayMap()
    Controls("img" & m_sCurStep).BackColor = &H808080
    Controls("lbl" & m_sCurStep).Font.Bold = False

    Select Case mpgSteps.Value
    Case 0
        m_sCurStep = "Start"
    Case m_iTotalSteps - 1
        m_sCurStep = "Finish"
    Case Else
        m_sCurStep = "Step" & mpgSteps.Value
    End Select
    Controls("img" & m_sCurStep).BackColor = vbGreen
    Controls("lbl" & m_sCurStep).Font.Bold = True
End Sub
```

The SetSubwayMap procedure performs three tasks. The first task is to use the m_sCurStep value to determine what the previous step is. The SetSubwayMap procedure is called when the value of the mpgSteps control has been changed. Before you update the value of m_sCurStep to reflect the current step, you reset the control properties of the previous step so that it appears visited. This is done by setting the BackColor property of the Image control to dark gray (&H808080) and the font of the Label control to roman (not bold).

For the second task of the procedure, the Select Case statement evaluates the current value of the mpgSteps control and sets the variable m_sCurStep to the name of the current step. The value of m_sCurStep is then used to set the BackColor property of the current Image control to light green (vbGreen). The third task of the procedure is to set the font of the associated Label control to bold. The Visual Basic color enumeration vbGreen represents the value &HFF00.

5   In the Object drop-down list of the frmWizard Code window, select UserForm. In the Procedure drop-down list in the upper-right area of the Code window, select Initialize and add the line:

```
m_sCurStep = "Start"
```

The UserForm_Initialize event procedure should now look like this:

```
Private Sub UserForm_Initialize()
    m_iTotalSteps = mpgSteps.Pages.Count
    m_sCurStep = "Start"
    mpgSteps.Value = 0
    Call mpgSteps_Change
End Sub
```

View Object

6   In the Project Explorer, select the frmWizard project item and click the View Object button, which is just to the right of the View Code button on the Project Explorer toolbar.

7   Select the imgFinish control on the frmWizard UserForm. In the Properties window, change the BackColor property to red in the Palette tab (a value of &H000000FF&).

The color red is used as an initial indicator that this step is the last one in the wizard (or the last station on the subway map).

8   Click anywhere on the frmWizard UserForm and press F5 to run the UserForm.

The Start square is green.

The Finish square is red.

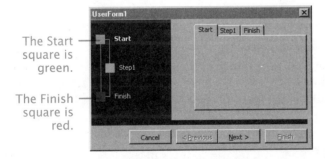

Click the Next and Previous buttons to see the pages of the MultiPage control being activated, the navigation buttons being enabled and disabled, and the properties of the Image and Label controls of the subway map being updated. The last remaining task is to add the code that allows you to click the controls on the subway map to navigate between the steps.

Add code to the subway map

1 Close and unload the frmWizard UserForm by clicking the Cancel or Finish button.

2 Double-click the imgStart control of the subway map and add the following line to the imgStart_Click event procedure:

```
mpgSteps.Value = 0
```

3 In the Object drop-down list, select lblStart and add the following line to the lblStart_Click event procedure:

```
mpgSteps.Value = 0
```

4 In the Object drop-down list, select imgStep1 and add the following line to the imgStep1_Click event procedure:

```
mpgSteps.Value = 1
```

5 In the Object drop-down list, select lblStep1 and add the following line to the lblStep1_Click event procedure:

```
mpgSteps.Value = 1
```

6 In the Object drop-down list, select imgFinish and add the following line to the imgFinish_Click event procedure:

```
mpgSteps.Value = m_iTotalSteps - 1
```

7 In the Object drop-down list, select lblFinish and add the following line to the lblFinish_Click event procedure:

```
mpgSteps.Value = m_iTotalSteps - 1
```

8 Press F5 to run the UserForm.

Click the Image and Label controls on the subway map to see the Previous and Next buttons being enabled and disabled, and the pages of the MultiPage control being activated.

Add a new step in the wizard

The naming convention used for the controls of the subway map is essential for writing flexible code so that a new step can be added easily. The following step-by-step example shows how to set up your code to add more steps as needed.

1   Close and unload the frmWizard UserForm by clicking the Cancel or Finish button.

2   In the frmWizard UserForm, select the imgStep1 control. With the CTRL key pressed, select the lblStep1 control adjacent to it.

3   On the Edit menu, click Copy and then click Paste.

   A copy of imgStep1 and a copy of lblStep1 are pasted into the center of the UserForm. Both copies of the controls are selected.

4   Click the selection border of either one of the controls and drag the two controls so that the imgStep1 control sits on the border of the imgSubway control.

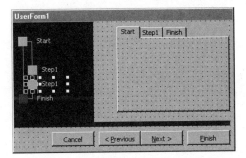

5   Rename the pasted Image control to **imgStep2** and the Label control to **lblStep2**. Change the Caption of lblStep2 to **Step2**.

6   Move imgStep1, lblStep1, imgStep2, and lblStep2 so that these controls are evenly spaced on the border of the imgSubway control.

7   Click the mpgSteps MultiPage control and then right-click any of the tabs. On the shortcut menu, click New Page.

   A new page is added to the control with the default tab caption Page1.

8   In the Properties window, change the Caption property of Page1 to **Step2** and then change the Name property to **pgStep2**.

9   Right-click any tab in the MultiPage control. On the shortcut menu, click Move.

The Page Order dialog box, which lists the pages within the MultiPage control, is displayed.

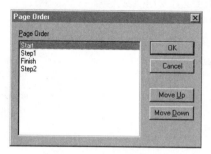

10 In the Page Order dialog box, select Step2 in the Page Order list and click the Move Up button to move the Step2 page after the Step1 page and before the Finish page. Click OK.

11 Double-click the imgStep2 control. In the imgStep2_Click event procedure, add the following line:

```
mpgSteps.Value = 2
```

12 In the Object drop-down list, select lblStep2 and add the following line to the lblStep2_Click event procedure:

```
mpgSteps.Value = 2
```

13 Press F5 to run the UserForm.

Click the Next button, or click the label Step2 to navigate and activate the second step in the wizard.

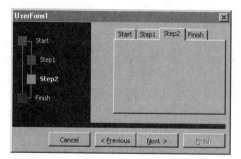

14 Close and unload the frmWizard UserForm by clicking the Cancel or Finish button.

15 Right-click the frmWizard project item in the Project Explorer and then click Export File on the shortcut menu. In the Export File dialog box, change to the Lesson 11 practice folder, and in the File Name text box, type the name **frmWizardTemplateSubway** and click Save.

16 Click the Save button on the toolbar to save the work you've done so far.

Save

The wizard UserForm with its subway map is now complete. In step 15, you exported the UserForm so that you can use it as a starting point when you create a new wizard with a subway map. The final process in setting up the wizard UserForm is to add the new element that all wizards in Microsoft Office 97 can include: the Office Assistant.

> **NOTE** None of the code in the UserForm you have created so far is specific to Word, Excel, or PowerPoint, so you can import the wizard UserForm into a Visual Basic for Applications project in any one of the three applications. You cannot import UserForms created in the Visual Basic Editor in Word, Excel, and PowerPoint into Microsoft Access. You can, however, use the techniques described in the previous step-by-step example to create the same type of wizard in Access.

Integrating the Office Assistant into Wizards

Most of the wizards in Microsoft Office now provide a toggle button alongside the Cancel, Previous, Next, and Finish navigation buttons in the wizard dialog box. When the toggle button is pressed, the Office Assistant is displayed, revealing a tip in its balloon for the current step in the wizard. Tips are often helpful the first few times you use a wizard; but once you are familiar with a wizard, you may no longer need the assistance of tips. The Assistant provides an easy method for creating helpful steps by displaying tips that you do not have to add directly on the wizard UserForm. Hence, using the Assistant helps prevent your wizard from appearing cluttered.

Add the Assistant button

View Object

1 Click the frmWizard project item and then click the View Object button in the Project Explorer.

2 Click the ToggleButton control in the Toolbox and then click the frmWizard UserForm to the left of the Cancel button.

ToggleButton control

3 In the Properties window, remove the text from the Caption property so that no caption is displayed, and change the Name property to **tglAssistant**. (The prefix *tgl* represents "toggle.")

257

Ellipsis

4 Click the Picture property, and then click the ellipsis button in the right column to display the Load Picture dialog box. Change to the Lesson 7 practice folder and select the bitmap file Assistnt.bmp. Click Open.

5 Resize the tglAssistant ToggleButton control so that its height is the same as that of the other navigation buttons and its width is equal to its height, as shown in the illustration:

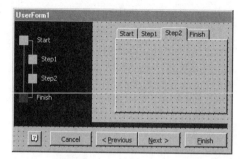

6 Run the UserForm and click the tglAssistant ToggleButton control. When it is first clicked, the control stays pressed. To return the toggle button to its initial state, click the toggle button again.

Now that the Assistant toggle button is added to your wizard, you need to write the code that will determine the current step in the wizard and display the appropriate tip when the Assistant button is clicked.

Make the Assistant display a tip

1 Close and unload the frmWizard UserForm by clicking the Cancel or Finish button.

2 In the Project Explorer, right-click the Energy Wizard project, and click Import File on the shortcut menu. In the Import File dialog box, change to the Lesson 11 practice folder and select the file modAsst.bas. Click Open.

The file modAsst.bas contains all of the code that will display tips in the Assistant balloon as well as close the Assistant balloon whenever necessary. In the following steps, you will add calls to procedures in the standard code module you just imported. The module name is modAssistant.

3 Select the frmWizard project item and then click the View Code button in the leftmost corner of the Project Explorer toolbar.

View Code

4   In the Object drop-down list of the frmWizard Code window, select UserForm. In the UserForm_Initialize event procedure, add the call to the VisibleCheck procedure so that the UserForm_Initialize procedure appears as follows:

```
Private Sub UserForm_Initialize()
    m_iTotalSteps = mpgSteps.Pages.Count
    m_sCurStep = "Start"
    mpgSteps.Value = 0
    Call mpgSteps_Change
    Call modAssistant.VisibleCheck
End Sub
```

Before the wizard is displayed, the visible state of the Assistant is determined in the VisibleCheck procedure in the modAssistant module. This procedure also contains code that handles cases where the Assistant is not installed; if this is the case, the Assistant button is disabled.

5   On the frmWizard UserForm, double-click the tglAssistant ToggleButton control. In the tglAssistant_Click event procedure, add the following code:

```
Private Sub tglAssistant_Click()
    Call modAssistant.ToggleAssistant
End Sub
```

The ToggleAssistant procedure determines the value of the tglAssistant ToggleButton control and then decides whether to display or hide the Assistant.

6   In the Object drop-down list of the frmWizard Code window, select mpgSteps. In the mpgSteps_Change event procedure, add the following If...Then condition block after the call to the SetSubway procedure:

```
If tglAssistant.Value = True Then
    Call modAssistant.SetBalloonText
End If
```

Each time the page changes in the wizard, the value of the Assistant button is evaluated. If the button is clicked, the SetBalloonText procedure is called and the tip for the current step is displayed in the Assistant balloon.

7 Finally, add the following code to both the cmdCancel_Click and cmdFinish_Click event procedures, just before line unloading the wizard UserForm. The cmdCancel_Click event procedure would appear as follows:

```
Private Sub cmdCancel_Click()
    If tglAssistant.Value = True Then
        Call modAssistant.CloseBalloon
    End If
    Unload Me
End Sub
```

The cmdFinish_Click event procedure is exactly the same except for the name of the procedure. The If...Then condition block determines whether the Assistant balloon is displaying a wizard tip by evaluating the value of the tglAssistant ToggleButton control. If the toggle button is clicked (in the up position), the Assistant balloon is closed.

8 Press F5 to run the wizard and then click the Assistant button to display the tip for the current step.

The Assistant balloon should appear and the tip "Start" should appear, which represents the tip for the currently active step. Click the Next button to see the next tip and continue through the steps to see the Assistant balloon being updated to reflect the current step.

The current step... 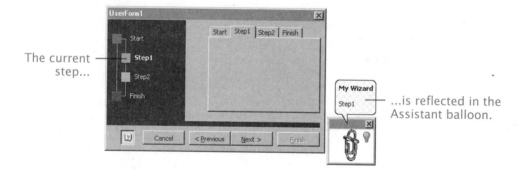 ...is reflected in the Assistant balloon.

9 Close and unload the frmWizard UserForm by clicking the Cancel or Finish button.

10 Right-click the frmWizard project item in the Project Explorer and then click Export File on the shortcut menu. In the Export File dialog box, change to the Lesson 11 practice folder, and in the File Name text box, type the name **frmWizardTemplateAssistant** and click Save.

11 Click the Save button to save the work you've done so far.

Save

260

The wizard UserForm with navigation buttons, subway map, and Assistant integration is now complete. In step 10, you exported the UserForm so that you can use it as a starting point when you create a new wizard with a subway map and the Office Assistant.

 TIP The contents of all three UserForms that you saved in this lesson—frmWizardTemplateBasic, frmWizardTemplateSubway, and frmWizardTemplateAssistant—are also provided in the Lesson 11 practice folder of the practice files CD-ROM. The files are named frmBasic, frmSubway, and frmAsst.

Customizing Wizard Steps

In Lesson 9, the paths for the Energy database file and the Word Energy template that you needed to generate the Word report from the Energy database in Access were specified directly in your code. If the scenario was real, however, you might have to change the location of the two files often, thus causing your wizard code to produce an error when it tries to find the files in the original location. By adding some controls to your wizard, and with the help of two common Microsoft Windows dialog boxes, you can specify directly in the wizard UserForm the Energy database file and the Word Energy template. The wizard then uses the paths you entered when automatically generating a Word report from the data in the Energy database.

Prepare the wizard Start screen

1 On the frmWizard UserForm, click the first tab in the mpgSteps MultiPage control to activate the first page.

Make sure that the text "pgStart Page" appears in the drop-down list at the top of the Properties window.

Ellipsis

2 In the Properties window, click the Picture property and then click the ellipsis button in the right column. In the Load Picture dialog box, change to the Lesson 11 practice folder and select the file Start.bmp. Click Open.

The background of the first page of the MultiPage control now displays a bitmap similar in look and style to that of the Fax Wizard in Word and the AutoContent Wizard in PowerPoint.

3 Set the PictureSizeMode property value to 1 – fmPictureSizeModeStretch.

4 Click the selection border of the MultiPage control.

The text "mpgSteps MultiPage" appears in the drop-down list at the top of the Properties window.

5   Scroll down the Properties window and change the Style property from
0 – fmTabStyleTabs to 2 – fmTabStyleNone.

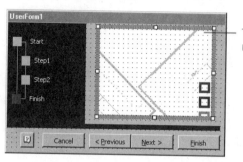

The MultiPage control
now has no tabs.

The pages have not disappeared, only the tabs have. Switching between
the pages of the MultiPage control is not as simple as clicking the tab of
the specific page. To navigate the pages of the MultiPage control, click
anywhere within the MultiPage control to activate the current page and
use the drop-down list at the top of the Properties window to activate the
specific page. You should work without the tabs in the MultiPage control
so that you can precisely place controls within the pages.

6   Resize the mpgSteps MultiPage control so that it fills the space between
the controls imgLeftPane and imgBottomStripe and the right side of the
UserForm.

7   Click the Image control in the Toolbox and then click in the upper-left
area of the first page of the mpgSteps control. Add a Label control just
below the Image control and set the properties as follows:

*Image
control*

Control	Property	Value
Image1	Name	imgTitleBack
Image1	BackColor	&H00000000& (or black from the Palette tab)
Label1	Name	lblTitle
Label1	Caption	Energy Wizard
Label1	BackStyle	0 – fmBackStyleTransparent
Label1	Font	Set the Font Style to Bold and the Font Size to 20.
Label1	ForeColor	&H00FFFFFF& (or white in the Palette tab)

8   Move the lblTitle control onto the imgTitleBack control.

9   Add a Label control under the lblTitle control and slightly to the right, set its Name to **lblStartDescription**, set its BackStyle to 0 – fmBackStyleTransparent, and set its caption to **This Wizard helps you generate an Office document from the data in the Energy database.** Move and size the controls using the following illustration as a guide:

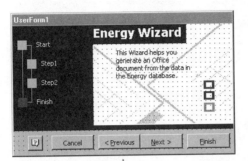

The page that first appears when you first load the wizard is now complete.

Add controls for each step in the wizard

1   Click within the MultiPage control and select pgStep1 Page from the drop-down list in the Properties window. The second page in the mpgSteps MultiPage control is activated.

2   Click the Label control in the Toolbox and click in the upper area of the second page of the mpgSteps control. Add a TextBox control below the Label control and a CommandButton control below the TextBox control.

3   Set the properties of the controls added to the second page. If you followed the steps throughout the lesson, the default names for the controls added will be the same as those listed below:

Control	Property	Value
Label1	Name	lblSource
Label1	Caption	Energy Database:
Label1	Accelerator	E
TextBox1	Name	txtDataSource
CommandButton1	Name	cmdBrowse
CommandButton1	Caption	Browse...
CommandButton1	Accelerator	B

The accelerator keys for controls on the pages in the MultiPage control should never be P, N, or F because these values are reserved for the navigation buttons Previous, Next, and Finish, respectively, at the bottom of the wizard UserForm.

4 Add a Label control below the Browse button. Add a TextBox control below the Label control and a CommandButton control below the TextBox control. Set the properties of the controls added as follows:

Control	Property	Value
Label1	Name	lblTemplate
Label1	Caption	Energy Template:
Label1	Accelerator	n
TextBox1	Name	txtTemplate
CommandButton1	Name	cmdBrowseTemplate
CommandButton1	Caption	Browse...
CommandButton1	Accelerator	r

5 Resize and move the controls on the second page so that the UserForm appears similar to the following illustration:

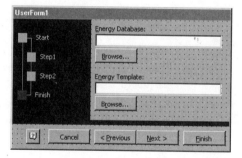

6 Click within the MultiPage control and select pgStep2 Page from the drop-down list in the Properties window. The third page in the mpgSteps MultiPage control is activated.

7 Click the Label control in the Toolbox and click at the top of the second page of the mpgSteps control. Add a TextBox control below the Label control and a CommandButton control below the TextBox control. Set the properties of the controls as listed below:

Control	Property	Value
Label1	Name	lblDestination
Label1	Caption	Destination folder:
Label1	Accelerator	D
TextBox1	Name	txtDestination
CommandButton1	Name	cmdBrowseFolder
CommandButton1	Caption	Browse...
CommandButton1	Accelerator	B

8   Change the Caption property of lblStep1 and lblStep2 on the subway map to **Source** and **Destination**, respectively. Adjust the width of both label controls so that the caption text fits, leaving some extra space so that when the text is made bold, the caption still fits within the width of the control. Move and size the controls using the following illustration as a guide:

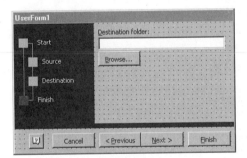

Prepare the wizard Finish screen

1   Click within the MultiPage control and select pgFinish Page from the drop-down list in the Properties window. The last page in the mpgSteps MultiPage control is activated.

Ellipsis

2   In the Properties window, click the Picture property and then click the ellipsis button in the right column. In the Load Picture dialog box, change to the Lesson 11 practice folder and select the file Finish.bmp. Click Open.

3   Set the PictureSizeMode property value to 1 – fmPictureSizeModeStretch.

4 Click the Image control in the Toolbox and click in the upper-left of the first page of the mpgSteps control. Add a Label control just below the Image control and set the properties as follows:

Control	Property	Value
Image1	Name	imgFinishTitleBack
Image1	BackColor	&H00000000& (or black from the Palette tab)
Label1	Name	lblFinishTitle
Label1	Caption	Energy Wizard
Label1	BackStyle	0 – fmBackStyleTransparent
Label1	Font	Set the Font Style to Bold and the Font Size to 16.
Label1	ForeColor	&H00FFFFFF& (or white in the Palette tab)

5 Add a Label control under the lblFinishTitle control and slightly to the right, set its Name to **lblFinishDescription**, its BackStyle to 0 – fmBackStyleTransparent, and its caption to **You are now ready to generate the Office document. Click Finish.**

6 Move the lblFinishTitle control onto the imgFinishTitleBack control and resize the controls so that the wizard UserForm appears as follows:

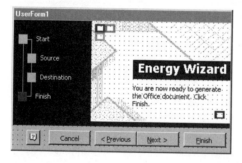

7 Click the Save button to save the work you've done so far.

Save

The page that appears when you have finished going through the steps in the wizard is now complete, as is each step in the wizard. In the next section below, you will add code that will allow you to interact with the controls you've added to your wizard.

Using Dialog Boxes from Microsoft Windows

Microsoft Windows provides a set of common dialog boxes so that developers writing applications for Windows do not need to create certain dialog boxes from scratch. Some of the common dialog boxes are the File dialog box, which is used to open, save, or browse for files on your computer or computer network; the Browse For Folder dialog box, which is used to specify a folder name; and the Color dialog box, which allows you to choose a specific color.

In the wizard you are creating, you will take advantage of the File and Browse For Folder dialog boxes. The code provided in the practice files allows you to easily use these dialog boxes without knowing too much about the code itself, which uses more advanced Windows-based programming techniques. To learn more about the specifics of this code and Windows programming using the Visual Basic programming language, consult books on the Visual Basic and Windows application programming interfaces (APIs).

Add a common Windows dialog box to your wizard

1   In the Project Explorer, right-click the Energy Wizard project, and click Import File on the shortcut menu. In the Import File dialog box, change to the Lesson 11 practice folder and select the file modFlDlg.bas. Click Open.

The file modFlDlg.bas contains code that allows you to display the Microsoft Windows system File dialog box, which is the same dialog box as the Import File dialog box you just used. The name of the imported standard module is modFileDialog, and this module also contains a user-defined type that you can use to set properties such as the caption in the title bar of the File dialog box.

2   Click within the MultiPage control and select pgStep1 Page from the drop-down list in the Properties window. Double-click the first Browse button and add the following code to the cmdBrowse_Click event procedure:

```
Private Sub cmdBrowse_Click()
    Dim sFileName As String
    Dim udtFileDialog As FileDialog

    With udtFileDialog
        .sFilter = "Access Database (*.mdb)" & _
            Chr$(0) & "*.mdb" & Chr$(0) & Chr$(0)
        .sDefaultExt = "*.mdb"
        .sTitle = "Browse"
        sFileName = modFileDialog _
            .WinFileDialog(udtFileDialog, 1)
```

```
        End With
        If Len(sFileName) > 0 Then
            txtDataSource.Text = sFileName
        End If
    End Sub
```

The variable udtFileDialog is declared as the user-defined type FileDialog, which is declared as public in the modFileDialog module. For more information on user-defined types, see Lesson 9. The user-defined type is used to set the filters that are displayed in the Files Of Type drop-down list in the File dialog box.

The default extension is then set to the filter extension that is to be initially displayed in the Files Of Type drop-down list. The filter used when you click the cmdBrowse control is the Access Database type. The title bar caption of the File dialog box is set to the text "Browse."

The value of sFileName is then set to the value returned by the function WinFileDialog, which displays the File dialog box. The If...Then condition block determines whether you clicked Cancel in the File dialog box or selected a valid file and clicked Open. If a valid file was selected, its full path is entered in the txtDataSource text box. If you clicked Cancel, the value of sFileName is an empty string.

3   In the Object drop-down list of the module, select cmdBrowseTemplate and copy the same code to the cmdBrowseTemplate_Click event procedure that you added in the previous step to the cmdBrowse_Click event procedure. Change the two lines setting the value of sFilter and sDefaultExt to the following:

```
.sFilter = "Document Template (*.dot)" & _
    Chr$(0) & "*.dot" & Chr$(0) & Chr$(0)
.sDefaultExt = "*.dot"
```

The filters used when you click the cmdBrowseTemplate control are of the Document Template type.

4   Change the line `txtDataSource.Text = sFileName` in the cmdBrowseTemplate_Click event procedure to:

```
txtTemplate.Text = sFileName
```

If a valid file was selected, its full path is entered in the txtDataSource text box.

5   Select pgStep2 Page from the drop-down list in the Properties window and then select cmdBrowseFolder from the drop-down list in the Proper-

ties window. Add the following code to the cmdBrowseFolder_Click event procedure:

```
Private Sub cmdBrowseFolder_Click()
    Dim sPath As String
    sPath = modBrowseFolder.BrowseForFolder
    If Len(sPath) > 0 Then
        txtDestination.Text = sPath
    End If
End Sub
```

The function BrowseForFolder in the modBrowseFolder module displays the Microsoft Windows system Browse For Folder dialog box. (Your Browse For Folder dialog box will look different.)

6   In the Project Explorer, right-click the Energy Wizard project and click Import File on the shortcut menu. In the Import File dialog box, change to the Lesson 11 practice folder and select the file modBrwse.bas. Click Open.

The file modBrwse.bas contains code that allows you to display the Microsoft Windows system Browse For Folder dialog box. The name of the imported standard module is modBrowseFolder.

View Object

7   Click the frmWizard project item and then click the View Object button in the Project Explorer to display the wizard UserForm.

8   Press F5 to run the wizard.

Save

9   Click the Save button to save the work you've done so far.

Step through the wizard and click each of the Browse buttons in the steps. The wizard allows you to find the Energy database file and the Word Energy template to be used to generate a Word report from the data in the Energy database.

Adding Wizards to the New Dialog Box

In the application window of Word, Excel, PowerPoint, or Access, you can make your wizards accessible to users in two basic ways. The first way is to add a custom menu item or toolbar button that, when clicked, displays your wizard. The second is to provide access to your wizards through the New dialog box, displayed by clicking New on the File menu. The New dialog box displays a set of tabs that correspond to the folders in the path C:\Program Files\Microsoft Office\Templates. Any folder in this path that contains templates or wizards specific to an application is listed in the New dialog box.

The Energy Wizard you have created in this lesson can now be easily integrated with the Word Energy add-in you created in Lesson 9. With a few modifications, you can create a fully functional Energy Wizard that you can access from the New dialog box.

Integrate your wizard with the Word Energy add-in

1   In the Project Explorer, right-click the Energy Wizard project and click Import File on the shortcut menu. In the Import File dialog box, change to the Lesson 11 practice folder and select the file modWord.bas. Click Open. Import the file modMain.bas from the same folder as well.

    The files modWord.bas and modMain.bas are exported copies of the modules you created in Lesson 9.

2   If the modMain Code window is not active, double-click the modMain project item in the Modules folder in the Project Explorer. In modMain, remove the public constant declaration g_sFilePath:

    ```
    Public Const g_sFilePath As String = _
        "C:\Office VBA Practice\Lesson8\"
    ```

    You no longer need this constant because you will replace every use of it with the path specified in the Energy Wizard you created in this lesson.

3   In the Main procedure, replace the line setting the module-level database object variable with:

    ```
    Set m_dbEnergyUsage = DBEngine.Workspaces(0) _
        .OpenDatabase(frmWizard.txtDataSource.Text)
    ```

    Instead of specifying the exact path in your code, you will use the file-name specified in the txtDataSource text box in the wizard UserForm.

4   Double-click the modWord project item in the Project Explorer to activate the modWord Code window. In the CreateWordDocument

procedure, replace the line setting the module-level object variable m_oWordDoc with:

```
Set m_oWordDoc = m_oWord.Documents.Add(Template:= _
    frmWizard.txtTemplate.Text, _
    NewTemplate:=False)
```

Instead of specifying the exact path in your code, you will use the filename specified in the txtTemplate text box in the wizard UserForm.

5   In the AddTotalRow procedure in modWord, replace the line that saves the generated Word document using the SaveAs method with the following code:

```
m_oWordDoc.SaveAs frmWizard.txtDestination.Text _
    & "\" & "Report.doc"
```

Instead of specifying the exact path in your code, you will use the path specified in the txtDestination text box in the wizard UserForm.

6   In the modMain module, remove the AutoExec and AutoExit procedures.

The wizard you are creating will be started from the File New dialog box rather than from a click on a menu item. Thus, the AutoExec and AutoExit procedures are no longer needed for adding and removing a custom menu item.

7   In the Project Explorer, double-click the ThisDocument project item in the Microsoft Word Objects folder to activate the Code window. In the Object drop-down list, select Document. Add code to the Document_New event procedure so that it appears as follows:

```
Private Sub Document_New()
    Dim oDoc As Document
    Set oDoc = ActiveDocument
    frmWizard.Show
    oDoc.Close savechanges:=False
End Sub
```

When you select the wizard in the New dialog box and click OK, Word creates a new document based on the template. When this event occurs, the Document_New event procedure in the wizard runs automatically. In the Document_New event procedure, the added document, which became the active document in the Word application window, is set to the object variable oDoc.

The Energy Wizard UserForm is then displayed by using the Show method of the UserForm object. If the UserForm is not currently loaded, the Show method loads the UserForm first and then displays it. Once the wizard is finished running or is unloaded, the last line in the Document_New event procedure closes the initial document created by Word without saving any changes.

8   In the Project Explorer, double-click the frmWizard UserForm. Double-click the Finish button. Add the following If...Then condition block above the Unload Me statement in the cmdFinish_Click event procedure:

```
If txtDataSource.TextLength > 0 And _
        txtDestination.TextLength > 0 Then
    Call Main
End If
```

If both a source and a destination are specified, the Main procedure is called, and the data that the wizard has gathered will be made available to the code in other modules.

9   On the Tools menu, click References, select the check box next to Microsoft DAO 3.5 Object Library in the Available References list box, and click OK.

Save

10 Click the Save button to save the work you've done so far.

11 Close the file Energy Wizard.dot.

Create a Word wizard in the New dialog box

Recall that the Energy Wizard template file is saved in the folder C:\Program Files\Microsoft Office\Templates\Reports. You must now change the template to a wizard file.

1   Start the Windows Explorer if it is not already open. Change to the folder C:\Program Files\Microsoft Office\Templates\Reports, right-click the Energy Wizard.dot file, and click Rename on the shortcut menu. Change the file extension from *dot* to **wiz** and press ENTER. Click Yes when Microsoft Windows asks you to confirm renaming the file.

2   Switch to Word. On the File menu, click New. In the New dialog box, click the Reports tab and double-click the Energy Wizard icon to start the wizard.

3   Step through the wizard and browse for the Energy.mdb database and the EnerRpt.dot template (both are in the Lesson 8 folder), and then the folder in which you want to save the generated report. Click Finish.

The Energy Wizard will generate the report and then unload itself. The new document that was created just as the wizard started closes without saving any changes before the wizard is unloaded.

4   Exit Word.

Lesson Summary

To	Do this
Create a multistep wizard dialog box	Add a MultiPage control to a UserForm and add the controls required for each step of the wizard within each page of the MultiPage control.
Create a set of navigation buttons at the bottom of a wizard dialog box	Add four CommandButton controls with the labels Cancel, Previous, Next, and Finish. In the Click event procedure for the Previous and Next buttons, decrement and increment, respectively, the value of the MultiPage control by one. Each time the value of the MultiPage control changes, use a Select Case condition block within the Change event procedure for the MultiPage control to determine which navigation buttons should be enabled.
Allow users to navigate to nonsequential steps within a wizard	Create a "subway map" on the left side of the MultiPage control in the wizard dialog box. The subway map should consist of Image and Label controls that indicate "stations," or steps in the wizard.
Indicate active and visited steps in the wizard	Set the BackColor property of an Image control in the subway map to light green if the station, or step, is active. If the step is inactive, set the BackColor to dark gray.

For online information about	Ask the Assistant for help, using the words
Using the MultiPage control	"MultiPage"
Setting colors	"Color properties"
Creating Assistant balloons	"Balloons"

Preview of the Next Lesson

In the next lesson you will learn how to use hyperlinks to easily tie together information within a single document or among several documents, and to connect hyperlinks on a page to the World Wide Web.

Getting More From Microsoft Office

Lesson 12
Weaving the Office Web   277

Lesson 13
Designing Custom Microsoft Outlook Forms   299

Weaving the Office Web

Estimated time
90 min.

In this lesson you will learn how to:

■ Add hyperlinks in Office documents.

■ Connect hyperlinks to a page on the World Wide Web.

■ Find text in an Excel workbook and insert a hyperlink into a cell.

■ Search for a style in a Word document and add a hyperlink to a file.

Hyperlinks have become an effective tool for content creation because they allow you to conveniently tie together information within a single document or among several documents. Instead of adding lengthy or ambiguous descriptions on where to find more information, you can provide direct access to the information via a single mouse click. Connecting content within or between Microsoft Office documents, or from Office documents to graphics and video files, the Internet, or pages on the World Wide Web, can be achieved easily through the use of hyperlinks.

You can go even further by adding and manipulating hyperlinks in an Office document with Visual Basic for Applications and the Hyperlink object model. As your Office documents grow in size and in number of hyperlinks, you may find it an arduous task to find and then replace or remove a hyperlink. The destination of a hyperlink can change often, but with Visual Basic for Applications, you can create programs to help manage the hyperlinks in your Office documents.

IMPORTANT In Microsoft Office, you can specify hyperlinks that jump to sites on the Internet and World Wide Web, even if you do not have access to the Internet from your computer. In order for such hyperlinks to succeed when clicked, however, your computer must have access to the Internet as well as an internet browser installed.

Adding Hyperlinks

To insert a hyperlink into a Microsoft Word document, Excel workbook, or PowerPoint presentation, you select a string of text, a range of cells, or a shape, and then click Hyperlink on the Insert menu. In Microsoft Access, you select either the control or the text in a Label, TextBox, Command Button, or Image control and then click Hyperlink on the Insert menu. Microsoft Outlook does not provide an equivalent hyperlink feature.

In the Insert Hyperlink dialog box, you can specify a link to another file or to a URL, or to a specific location within your document. Using the Insert Hyperlink dialog box, however, you have to insert hyperlinks one at a time. For example, if you want to add a hyperlink to every occurrence of a company's name, you would have to use the Find dialog box in Word, Excel, or PowerPoint to search for the text, and then insert each hyperlink manually.

In Visual Basic for Applications, you can easily create an add-in that quickly iterates through the content of a document and searches for the text to which you want to add a hyperlink. In this section, you will create a custom Add Hyperlink UserForm that allows you to specify the text to be searched for. When text matching the criteria is found, a hyperlink is added to the text and is set to the URL specified in the custom Add Hyperlink UserForm.

 TIP The Add Hyperlink UserForm and the add-in that searches for hyperlinks will be created using Excel, but you can export the UserForm and reuse it in an add-in for Word or PowerPoint. Word and PowerPoint add-ins equivalent to the Excel add-in created in this lesson are provided in the Lesson 12 practice folder. The filename for the Word add-in is HyprLink.dot; for PowerPoint, it is HyprLink.ppt. An add-in for Access is not provided, but the Hyperlink object used in this lesson can be applied to Access also.

Search for text in an Excel workbook and add a hyperlink

1   Start Microsoft Excel. Display the Visual Basic Editor, and insert a UserForm into the blank workbook project.

2   In the Toolbox, click the Label control and then click in the upper-left area of the UserForm. Click the TextBox control and then click just below the Label control on the UserForm. Add a second Label control below the TextBox control, and then add a ComboBox control below the second Label control.

3   Add a CommandButton control to the upper-right area of the UserForm and then add a second CommandButton control just below the first one. The UserForm should look like the following illustration:

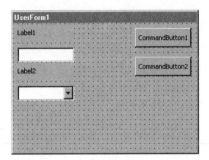

4   Set the properties of the UserForm and inserted controls as follows:

Control	Property	Value
Label1	Name	lblFind
Label1	Caption	Find what:
Label1	Accelerator	F
TextBox1	Name	txtFindWhat
Label2	Name	lblHyperlink
Label2	Caption	Add hyperlink:
Label2	Accelerator	A
ComboBox1	Name	cboHyperlinks
CommandButton1	Name	cmdOK
CommandButton1	Caption	OK
CommandButton2	Name	cmdClose
CommandButton2	Caption	Close

Control	Property	Value
CommandButton2	Accelerator	C
CommandButton2	Cancel	True
UserForm1	Name	frmAddHyperlink
UserForm1	Caption	Add Hyperlink

5 Resize the controls and UserForm so that they appear as follows:

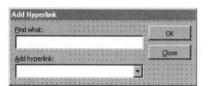

6 Double-click the cmdOK CommandButton control. In the cmdOK_Click event procedure, add the following multiple-declaration code so that the procedure looks like this:

```
Private Sub cmdOK_Click()
    Dim sFindWhat As String, sHyperlink As String
End Sub
```

Two string variables are declared in the first line of the event procedure. The first variable is used to hold the text entered in the txtFindWhat TextBox control, and the second is used to hold the text entered in the cboHyperlinks ComboBox control.

7 After the procedure-level declarations, add the following assignment statements and If...Then condition blocks:

```
sFindWhat = txtFindWhat.Text
If Len(Trim$(sFindWhat)) < 1 Then
    MsgBox "Please enter search text.", _
        vbOKOnly + vbInformation
    Exit Sub
End If

sHyperlink = cboHyperlinks.Text
If Len(Trim$(sHyperlink)) = 0 Then
    MsgBox "Please enter a hyperlink.", _
        vbOKOnly + vbInformation
    Exit Sub
End If
```

The line before each If...Then condition block sets the value of the two declared variables. Each condition block then evaluates the length of the string set to each variable by using the Len function, which is a built-in Visual Basic function. If the Len function returns a value of 0, no text was entered in the text box or the combo box, and a message box will be displayed. To make sure that you did not insert a space in the text box or the combo box, the Visual Basic built-in function Trim$ first removes any leading or trailing spaces from a string variable. The Len function then evaluates the trimmed string variable.

TIP In Visual Basic, the Trim function and some of the built-in string manipulation functions can appear with or without the dollar-sign ($) suffix. If you do not use a dollar-sign suffix, the function returns a Variant data type. If you do use a suffix, the function returns a String data type. It is common to use the String version of a function so that you work with exact data types.

8   After the second If...Then condition block, add the following two lines:

```
Call AddHyperlinks(sFindWhat, sHyperlink)
Unload Me
```

The AddHyperlinks procedure, created in the next step-by-step example, iterates through the worksheet cells in the active workbook and searches for the text specified in the sFindWhat variable. If the text in a cell is equivalent to the value of sFindWhat, a hyperlink that has the address specified in the sHyperlink variable is added to the cell. Once the AddHyperlinks procedure runs, the frmAddHyperlink UserForm is unloaded.

9   In the Object drop-down list, select cmdClose. In the cmdClose_Click event procedure, add the following line:

```
Unload Me
```

10   In the Object drop-down list, select UserForm. In the Procedures drop-down list, select Initialize. In the UserForm_Initialize event procedure, add the following call to the FillHyperlinkList procedure so that it looks like this:

```
Private Sub UserForm_Initialize()
    Call FillHyperlinkList(cboHyperlinks)
End Sub
```

The FillHyperlinkList procedure, created in one of the next step-by-step examples, iterates through the Hyperlinks collection object in each worksheet of the active workbook and fills the cboHyperlinks ComboBox control passed to the FillHyperlinkList procedure with the hyperlinks found in the active workbook.

11   Switch to the Excel application window. On the File menu, click Save As, change to the Lesson 12 practice folder, and save the workbook as MyHyperlink.xls.

Find text in an Excel worksheet

1   Switch to the Visual Basic Editor and insert a standard code module. In the Properties window, change the module name from Module1 to modSearchXl.

2   Add the procedure AddHyperlinks with the following arguments and declarations:

```
Sub AddHyperlinks(sFindWhat As String, _
    sHyperlink As String)
    Dim oRange As Range
    Dim sFirstAddress As String
    Dim oSheet As Worksheet
End Sub
```

The AddHyperlinks procedure accepts two arguments. The first argument is the text specified in the txtFindWhat text box in the frmAddHyperlink UserForm. The second is the text from the cboHyperlinks combo box. These two values are assigned to the variables sFindWhat and sHyperlink, respectively. The object variable oRange is declared as a Range type.

The variable oRange will be used to store the cell range in the worksheet with text that matches the value of sFindWhat. The variable sFirstAddress is used to store the value of the cell address where the first instance of the text specified by sFindWhat is found on a worksheet. The object variable oSheet is used to specify the worksheet where the search for the text is currently being conducted.

3   Below the procedure-level declarations, add this For Each...Next loop:

```
For Each oSheet In ActiveWorkbook.Worksheets
    Set oRange = oSheet.Range("A:IV").Find( _
        What:=sFindWhat, LookIn:=xlValues, _
        MatchCase:=True)
Next oSheet
```

The For Each...Next loop iterates through the Worksheets collection of the active workbook and implicitly assigns the object variable oSheet to the next Worksheet object in the collection. Within the loop, the Set statement assigns the object variable oRange to the cell range returned by the Find method. The Find method searches through the specified cell range for the value specified by the first argument, *What*.

The What argument is set to the value of sFindWhat. The LookIn argument indicates that the Find method should conduct its search in the value of the cell. The MatchCase argument is set to True so that the search looks for only those values that match the case of the value specified by sFindWhat.

4 Within the For Each...Next loop, after the Set statement, add the following If...Then condition block:

```
If Not oRange Is Nothing Then
    sFirstAddress = oRange.Address
End If
```

If the Find method does not find a cell that contains the value specified by sFindWhat, the object variable oRange is set to Nothing. This indicates that the worksheet specified by oSheet does not contain the value specified by sFindWhat. If the Find method does find a match, the object variable oRange is set to the cell containing the sFindWhat value and the If...Then condition block is entered. The first line in the If...Then condition block assigns the address of the cell containing the sFindWhat value to the sFirstAddress variable.

5 Within the If...Then condition block, after the line setting the variable sFirstAddress, add the following Do...Loop statement:

```
Do
    Set oRange = oSheet.Range("A:IV").FindNext(oRange)
Loop While oRange.Address <> sFirstAddress
```

The FindNext method uses the same conditions specified in the Find method to search for the next cell matching the conditions. In the FindNext method, you specify the After argument so that the search continues after a specified cell range. If a cell is found, FindNext returns a Range object, which is assigned to the object variable oRange. To continue the search started with the Find method through the remainder of the worksheet, the Do...Loop statement is used.

When the search reaches the end of the cell range (in this case, it's the last row in column IV), the search starts from the beginning of the cell range again (the first row in column A). To ensure that the search does not continue endlessly, a While condition block is added to the Do...Loop statement to check whether the cell range address returned by the FindNext method is the same as the cell range address where the first cell was found by the Find method. If they are the same, the loop is exited.

6 Within the Do...Loop statement, before the Set statement, add the following If...Then condition block:

```
If Trim$(oRange.Text) = sFindWhat Then
    oRange.Hyperlinks.Add Anchor:=oRange, _
        Address:=sHyperlink
End If
```

If the trimmed value of the cell found by the Find or FindNext method is equal to the sFindWhat value, a hyperlink is added to the cell. The Add method of the Hyperlinks object accepts three arguments. The first argument, *Anchor,* represents the text range or shape where the hyperlink is to be anchored. The second argument represents the hyperlink address, which can be a filename or URL, and is the same value that is entered in the Link To File Or URL text box in the Insert Hyperlink dialog box. The optional third argument is SubAddress, which is the value entered in the Named Location In File text box in the Insert Hyperlink dialog box and is not specified here.

The procedure is now complete and should look like the following code:

```
Sub AddHyperlinks(sFindWhat As String, _
        sHyperlink As String)
    Dim oRange As Range
    Dim sFirstAddress As String
    Dim oSheet As Worksheet

    For Each oSheet In ActiveWorkbook.Worksheets
        Set oRange = oSheet.Range("A:IV").Find( _
            What:=sFindWhat, LookIn:=xlValues, _
            MatchCase:=True)
        If Not oRange Is Nothing Then
            sFirstAddress = oRange.Address
            Do
                If Trim$(oRange.Text) = sFindWhat Then
                    oRange.Hyperlinks.Add _
                        Anchor:=oRange, _
                        Address:=sHyperlink
                End If
                Set oRange = oSheet _
                    .Range("A:IV").FindNext(oRange)
            Loop While oRange.Address <> sFirstAddress
        End If
    Next oSheet
End Sub
```

Save

7   Click the Save button to save the work you've done so far.

Search through an Excel workbook for existing hyperlinks

1   In the Visual Basic Editor, beneath the AddHyperlinks procedure, add the procedure FillHyperlinksList with the following argument and declarations:

```
Sub FillHyperlinkList(oCombo As MSForms.ComboBox)
    Dim i As Integer, sAddress As String
    Dim bNotInList As Boolean, oHLink As Hyperlink
    Dim oSheet As Worksheet
End Sub
```

Recall that you added a call to the FillHyperlinks procedure in the UserForm_Initialize event procedure. You passed the cboHyperlinks ComboBox control to the FillHyperlinks procedure so that the procedure can fill the combo box with the hyperlinks found in the active workbook. In the FillHyperlinks procedure, the combo box is assigned to the object variable oCombo.

2   Below the procedure-level declarations, add the following nested For Each...Next loops:

```
For Each oSheet In Worksheets
    For Each oHLink In oSheet.Hyperlinks
        sAddress = oHLink.Address
        bNotInList = True


    Next oHLink
Next oSheet
```

The outer loop iterates through the Worksheets collection of the active workbook and implicitly sets the object variable oSheet to the next worksheet in the collection. The For Each...Next loop within the first loop iterates through the Hyperlinks collection of the worksheet specified by the oSheet object variable. Each Worksheet object in Excel contains a Hyperlinks collection. In PowerPoint, the Hyperlinks collection can be accessed from the Slide object; in Word, the Hyperlinks collection can be accessed from the Document object.

Within the For Each...Next loop iterating through the Hyperlinks collection, the string variable sAddress and the Boolean variable bNotInList are set each time the loop continues to the next hyperlink. The address of the hyperlink is assigned to sAddress and the Boolean variable bNotInList is set to True because you are assuming that the hyperlink address does not exist in the list of the cboHyperlinks ComboBox control.

3   To determine whether the address of the hyperlink is already added to the list of the cboHyperlinks ComboBox control, add the following For...Next loop below the line setting the value of bNotInList to True:

```
For i = 0 To oCombo.ListCount - 1
    If oCombo.List(i) = sAddress Then
        bNotInList = False
        Exit For
    End If
Next i
```

To iterate through the list in the cboHyperlinks combo box, you need to start the For...Next loop at 0 and end the loop at the number of items in the list minus 1. To check the value of each item in the list, use the List property of the ComboBox control. If the item in the list matches the address of the hyperlink assigned to oHLink, the loop is exited just after the Boolean variable bNotInList is set to False, indicating that the item is in the list.

4   Below the For...Next loop you added in step 3, add the following If...Then condition block:

```
If bNotInList = True Then
    oCombo.AddItem sAddress
End If
```

When the Do...Loop statement has iterated through each item in the cboHyperlinks combo box or is exited early by the Exit For statement, the Boolean variable bNotInList is evaluated. If the value of the Boolean variable was not changed in the Do...Loop statement, the address of the hyperlink specified by oHLink was not in the list and will be added using the AddItem method of the cboHyperlinks ComboBox control.

5   After the line Next oSheet and before the line End Sub, add the following If...Then condition block:

```
If oCombo.ListCount > 0 Then
    oCombo.ListIndex = 0
End If
```

If the cboHyperlinks combo box contains at least one item, the value shown as the text of the combo box when the UserForm is initially displayed is the first item in the combo box. To set this property, you use the ListIndex property. A value of 0 indicates the first item.

6   In the Project Explorer, right-click the MyHyperlink.xls project, and click Import File on the shortcut menu. In the Import File dialog box, change to the Lesson 12 practice folder and select the file modTBar.bas. Click Open.

The file modTBar.bas contains code that will create a custom Hyperlinks toolbar and allow you to display the frmAddHyperlinks UserForm. The second button on the toolbar, Replace Hyperlink, will be used in the next step-by-step example of this lesson.

7   Switch to the Excel application window. On the File menu, click Save to save the MyHyperlink.xls workbook. To create an Excel add-in from the current workbook, on the File menu, click Save As, change to the Lesson 12 practice folder, select Microsoft Excel Add-In (*.xla) in the Save As Type drop-down list, and click Save.

8   Close and save the MyHyperlink.xls workbook. (Despite your having saved the workbook in step 7, Excel asks if you want to save changes again. Click Yes.)

Use the custom Hyperlinks add-in in Excel

1   Create a new Excel workbook. Type **Microsoft** randomly in several of the cells of the active sheet, and then type **Excel** randomly.

2   On the Tools menu, click Add-Ins. In the Add-Ins dialog box, click Browse, change to the Lesson 12 practice folder, select the file MyHyperlink.xla, and click OK twice.

The custom Hyperlinks toolbar should now be displayed.

3   Click the Add Hyperlink button on the custom Hyperlinks toolbar. In the Add Hyperlink dialog box, type **Microsoft** in the Find What text box. Type **http://www.microsoft.com/** in the Add Hyperlink combo box.

You will search for this text...

...and create this hyperlink.

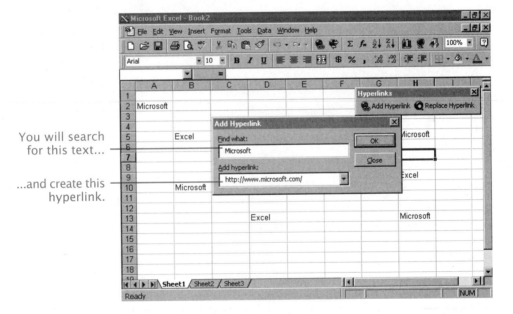

4   Click OK to add the hyperlink http://www.microsoft.com/ to each cell in the active workbook containing the value Microsoft.

287

The active worksheet now contains a hyperlink in cells containing the value Microsoft. The cells with hyperlinks are indicated by a blue font color and underlined text. If you place the cursor over the hyperlink, a tip window is displayed revealing the destination of the hyperlink.

The underlined words are hyperlinks.

When the cursor is over a hyperlink, the URL is shown.

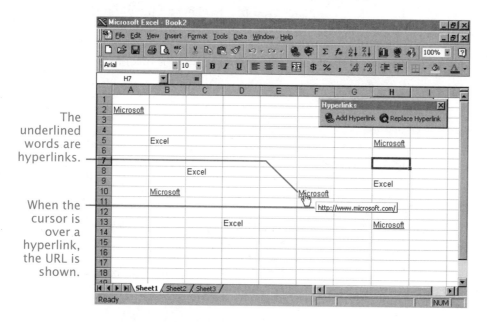

Replacing Hyperlinks

The destinations of hyperlinks often change. Changing every hyperlink in the Excel workbook from the preceding step-by-step example may be a tedious task, depending on the number of text matches found. Using the Hyperlinks collection of the Worksheet object and the Address property of the Hyperlink object, you can easily change the destination of a hyperlink at all occurrences.

The method of replacing a hyperlink varies slightly between Word and Excel and PowerPoint. In Excel and PowerPoint, you can change the destination of a hyperlink by resetting the Address property. In Word, the Address property is read-only. That is, you cannot set it, so to change the hyperlink, you need to add the new hyperlink to a text range or shape using the Add method of the Hyperlinks collection object.

TIP In this section, you will create a procedure to replace the hyperlinks in the Excel workbook from the preceding step-by-step example. The equivalent procedures that accomplish the same task in Word and PowerPoint are found in the practice files HyprLink.dot and HyprLink.ppt, respectively, in the Lesson 12 practice folder. The equivalent Excel file is HyperLink.xls.

Replace a hyperlink in an Excel workbook

1   In the Excel application window, on the Tools menu, click Add-Ins. In the Add-Ins dialog box, clear the Myhyperlink check box and click OK.

2   Open the MyHyperlink.xls workbook and switch to the Visual Basic Editor.

3   In the Project Explorer, right-click the MyHyperlink.xls project, and click Import File on the shortcut menu. In the Import File dialog box, change to the Lesson 12 practice folder and select the file frmReplc.frm. Click Open.

    The file frmReplc.frm contains code in a custom UserForm that displays a list of hyperlinks in the current workbook and a text box so that you can specify the new address of the hyperlink selected in the list. You can see the UserForm by double-clicking frmReplaceHyperlink in the Forms folder in the MyHyperlink project.

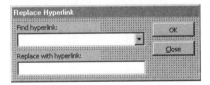

If Visual Basic automatically adds a new End Sub *statement when you delete the single quotation mark in front of Sub DisplayReplaceForm, delete this super-fluous statement.*

4   In the Project Explorer, double-click the modTBar project item to activate its Code window. Scroll almost to the end of the module and uncomment (remove the initial single quotation mark from) the lines of the DisplayReplaceForm procedure.

    The DisplayReplaceForm procedure is called by the Replace Hyperlink button on the custom Hyperlinks toolbar. The OnAction property of the Replace Hyperlink button was set to DisplayReplaceForm in the AddToolBar procedure in the modTBar module.

5 In the Project Explorer, double-click the modSearchXl project item to activate its Code window. After the FillHyperlinkList procedure, add the ReplaceHyperlinks procedure with the following arguments and declarations:

```
Sub ReplaceHyperlinks(sOldAddress As String, _
        sNewAddress As String)
    Dim oHLink As Hyperlink
    Dim oSheet As Worksheet
End Sub
```

The ReplaceHyperlinks procedure iterates through the Hyperlinks collection of each worksheet in the active workbook and for each hyperlink replaces the address stored in the string variable sOldAddress with the address stored in the string variable sNewAddress.

The ReplaceHyperlinks procedure accepts two arguments. The first argument is the text specified in the cboHyperlinks combo box in the frmReplaceHyperlink UserForm. The second is the text from the txtHyperlink text box. These two values are assigned to the variable sOldAddress and sNewAddress, respectively.

6 Below the procedure-level declarations, add the following nested For Each...Next loops:

```
For Each oSheet In ActiveWorkbook.Worksheets
    For Each oHLink In oSheet.Hyperlinks

    Next oHLink
Next oSheet
```

The outer loop iterates through the Worksheets collection of the active workbook and implicitly sets the object variable oSheet to the next worksheet in the collection. The inner For Each...Next loop iterates through the Hyperlinks collection of the worksheet specified by the oSheet object variable.

7 To determine whether the address of the hyperlink assigned to the object variable oHLink is the same as the address you want to replace, add the following If...Then condition block within the For Each...Next loop that iterates through the Hyperlinks collection:

```
If oHLink.Address = sOldAddress Then
    oHLink.Address = sNewAddress
End If
```

If the hyperlink address matches the address specified in the Replace Hyperlink UserForm, the hyperlink address is changed to the new address.

8 Switch to the Excel application window. On the File menu, click Save to save the MyHyperlink.xls workbook. To re-create the MyHyperlink Excel add-in from the current workbook, click Save As on the File menu, and in the Lesson 12 practice folder, select Microsoft Excel Add-In (*.xla) in the Save As Type drop-down list and click Save. Click Yes when asked if you want to replace the existing file.

9 Close and save the MyHyperlink.xls workbook.

10 On the Tools menu in Excel, click Add-Ins. In the Add-Ins dialog box, select Myhyperlinks and click OK.

11 On the custom Hyperlinks toolbar, click the Replace Hyperlink button. In the Replace Hyperlink dialog box, select http://www.microsoft.com/ from the Find Hyperlink drop-down list and, in the Replace With Hyperlink text box, type **http://www.msn.com/**.

12 Click OK.

The active worksheet now contains a hyperlink in cells containing the value Microsoft. If you place the cursor over the hyperlink, a tip window is displayed revealing the hyperlink destination of http://www.msn.com/.

13 Exit Excel without saving changes.

Creating Hyperlinks

To prevent a Word document that contains a lot of graphics from becoming too large in size, you can store the graphics files in the same folder as the Word document and add a *relative hyperlink* to the graphics file. A relative hyperlink searches the path of the file containing the hyperlink for the specified destination of the hyperlink. This allows you to move the file containing the hyperlink, along with other supporting files, to a different folder without breaking any hyperlinks.

By following this practice, you can maintain a smaller Word document, filled only with text, for faster loading and saving. All supporting files are maintained outside of the document, usually in the same file folder. Using this scheme, you can easily pass around the document for revisions and comments, and change graphics independently. Once the report is final, you or a production team can then incorporate the graphics into the document.

Search for a text style in a Word document and add a relative hyperlink

In this example, you will create a procedure that iterates through the paragraphs of a Word document and searches for paragraphs with the style named Graphic. In the Graphic-style paragraphs, a description is provided of the graphic and a filename is listed in brackets. The procedure retrieves the filename in the brackets and adds a relative hyperlink to the file from the filename provided in the text.

1   Start Word and display the Visual Basic Editor.

2   Insert a standard code module in the Visual Basic for Applications project for Document1. In the Properties window, change the module name to **modFileLink**.

3   Add the procedure FindStyle with the following declarations:

```
Sub FindStyle()
    Dim oPara As Paragraph
    Dim oTxtRange As Range
End Sub
```

The first declaration of the object variable oPara is declared as a Paragraph object. The second declaration of the object variable oTxtRange is declared as a Range object.

4   Add a For Each...Next loop that iterates through the paragraphs of the active document and evaluates the style of each paragraph using an If...Then condition block.

```
For Each oPara In ActiveDocument.Range.Paragraphs
    If oPara.Style = "Graphic" Then

    End If
Next oPara
```

The For Each...Next loop sets the object variable oPara to the next paragraph in the active document each time a loop completes. The If...Then condition block evaluates the text style of the paragraph. If the style is Graphic, it passes the text range of the paragraph to the ParseText function, which you will add below.

5   Within the If...Then condition block, add the following lines of code:

```
Set oTxtRange = ParseText(oPara.Range)
If Not oTxtRange Is Nothing Then
    oTxtRange.Hyperlinks.Add oTxtRange, oTxtRange.Text
End If
```

The Set statement accomplishes two things. When Visual Basic first runs the code in the Set statement, the program will note that ParseText is a function and that the text range of the paragraph with the style Graphic is being passed to the function. The ParseText function returns a text range representing the filename specified in the paragraph, and the range is then assigned to the object variable oTxtRange.

If the value of oTxtRange is not Nothing (that is, a filename was returned by the ParseText function), a hyperlink to the file is added to the text range. The anchor of the hyperlink is the range returned by the ParseText function, and the hyperlink address is the actual text of the range returned by the ParseText function.

6 Place the cursor beneath the FindStyle procedure and add the ParseText function:

```
Function ParseText(oTxtRange As Range) As Range
    Dim iLParen As Integer, iRParen As Integer
    Dim sFileName As String, sText As String
    Dim iStart As Integer, iEnd As Integer
End Function
```

The argument passed to the ParseText function is the Range object representing the paragraph with the style Graphic. The ParseText function is declared as a Range object.

7 After the procedure-level declarations, add the following code:

```
sText = oTxtRange.Text
iLParen = InStr(1, sText, "(", vbTextCompare)
iRParen = InStr(1, sText, ")", vbTextCompare)
```

The text of the range object passed to the ParseText function is assigned to the string variable sText. The two lines after the variable assignment use the Visual Basic built-in function InStr. The InStr function searches for a specified string within another string and returns a long value representing the position of the first occurrence.

Four arguments are passed to the InStr function. The first argument indicates where in the string to start the search. The second, the string in which the search is to be conducted. The third, the string for which you are searching. And the fourth, the type of comparison between the two specified strings. The Visual Basic enumeration value vbTextCompare indicates a textual, non-case-sensitive comparison. If the InStr functions find the specified strings (left and right parentheses), the positions of each search string are returned and assigned to the integer variables iLParen and iRParen, respectively.

8 Add an If...Then condition block to determine whether the InStr functions returned a value:

```
If iLParen > 0 And iRParen > 0 And _
    iLParen < iRParen Then
    sFileName = Mid$(sText, iLParen + 1, _
        iRParen - iLParen - 1)
End If
```

If the InStr functions in step 7 return a value greater than 0, the search string was found and the position was assigned to integer variables iLParen and iRParen. The If...Then statement evaluates the value of iLParen and iRParen, checking to see whether the position of the left parenthesis is less than (that is, to the left of) the position of the right parenthesis. If all three conditions within the If...Then statement are met, the line in the If...Then condition block sets the string variable sFileName to the text between the left and right parentheses. The Mid$ function is used to return only the text between the parentheses.

9 Below the line assigning a value to the sFileName string variable, add the following code:

```
iStart = oTxtRange.Start + iLParen
iEnd = iStart + Len(sFileName)
Set ParseText = ActiveDocument _
    .Range(iStart, iEnd)
```

To set a Range object variable to a range in a Word document, you can use the Range method of the Document object. Two arguments are specified in the Range method. The first argument is the starting position, and the second is the ending position of the range you want to set to an object variable. To determine the starting position of the range of text between the parentheses found in step 7, you use the starting position of the paragraph that was passed to the ParseText function.

The value of iLParen is then added because iLParen represents the position of the left parenthesis with respect to the beginning of the text passed into the ParseText function. The ending position of the range of text between the parentheses found in step 7 is determined by adding the length of the text found between the parentheses to the value of iStart.

10 Switch to the Word application window, and on the File menu, click Save As. Change to the C:\Program Files\Microsoft Office\Office\Startup folder and save the document as a Word template with the filename **MyFileLink.dot**.

You did not add any toolbars or menu items to access the FindStyle procedure, but you can still run the procedure from the Macro dialog box, as you will do in subsequent steps.

TIP The FileLink.dot Word add-in solution included in the Lesson 12 practice folder contains a toolbar that is saved with the add-in. When the add-in was created, the code to create the toolbar was run and the toolbar was saved in the FileLink.dot file. When the file is loaded, the toolbar is automatically displayed. See Lesson 9 for more information on creating and storing menu and toolbar customizations in Word files.

11 Exit and then restart Word.

12 Open the Word file Sample.doc in the Lesson 12 practice folder.

13 On the Tools menu, point to Macro, and then click Macros on the shortcut menu. In the Macros dialog box, select MyFileLink.dot in the Macros In drop-down list. In the Macro Name list, select the FindStyle procedure. Click Run.

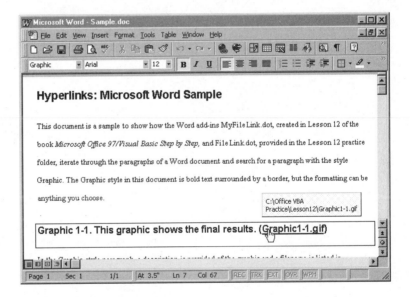

The filenames specified in the Graphic-style paragraphs now contain hyperlinks to the graphics file on disk. The hyperlink is a relative link, so wherever the sample document is saved along with the graphics files in the same folder, the hyperlinks will remain valid.

14 Click the hyperlinks in the Sample document.

The graphics file associated with the hyperlink you clicked in the Sample document will be loaded and displayed in the application that is registered to display .gif files. (If you installed Microsoft PhotoEditor with Microsoft Office 97, Microsoft PhotoEditor will be loaded and will display the graphics file.)

15 Exit Word without saving changes to the Sample.doc or MyFileLink.dot file.

Lesson Summary

To	Do this
Add a hyperlink to text in Word, a cell in Excel, or a shape in PowerPoint	In Word and Excel, use the Add method of the Hyperlinks collection object. In the first argument of the Add method, named *Anchor*, specify the range to which you want to add a hyperlink as the anchor object. For example, in Excel: ```Set oRange = ActiveSheet.Cells(1, 1)``````ActiveSheet.Hyperlinks.Add _`````` Anchor:=oRange, _`````` Address:="Error! Bookmark not defined."``` In PowerPoint, use the ActionSetting object to set the action to ppActionHyperlink and then set the hyperlink destination using the Address property of the Hyperlink object.
Change the destination of an existing hyperlink in Excel	Use the Address property of the Hyperlink object.
Find a cell with specific text in Excel	Use the Find method of the Range object. In the first Find method argument, named *What*, specify the text you want to find. For example, to search for the word *Microsoft* in column A of the active worksheet and set the font to bold: ```Dim oRange As Range``````Set oRange = ActiveSheet _`````` .Range("A:A") _`````` .Find(What:="Microsoft")``````If Not oRange Is Nothing Then`````` oRange.Font.Bold = True End If```

To	Do this
Search for a text style used by a paragraph in a Word document	Loop through the Paragraphs collection and use the Style property of the Range object. For example: ```\nIf ActiveDocument.Range _\n .Paragraphs(1) _\n .Style = "Heading 1" Then\n MsgBox "Heading 1"\nEnd If\n```
Find text in a Word document	Use the members of the Find object to set the conditions of the search and then use the Execute method of the Find object to conduct the search.
Change the destination of an existing hyperlink in Word	Use the Add method of the Hyperlinks object to reassign the address of the hyperlink. (In Word, the Address property is read-only, unlike in Excel.)
Find text in a PowerPoint document	Use the Find method of the TextRange object. Specify the conditions of the search in the arguments of the Find method.
Change the destination of an existing hyperlink in PowerPoint	Use the Address property of the Hyperlink object. The Hyperlink object can be accessed from the ActionSetting object. For example: ```\nWith ActivePresentation.Slides(1) _\n .Shapes(1).ActionSettings(1) _\n .Action = ppActionHyperlink\n .Hyperlink.Address = _\n "Error! Bookmark not defined."\nEnd With\n```
Search for specific text in a string	Use the Visual Basic built-in InStr function. The InStr function returns the position of the text matching the criteria in the string.
Determine the length of a string	Use the Visual Basic built-in function Len.
Remove leading and trailing spaces from a variable	Use the Visual Basic built-in function Trim, RTrim, or LTrim.

For online information about	Ask the Assistant for help, using the words
Removing leading and trailing spaces from a variable	"Trim," "RTrim," or "LTrim"
Returning the character length of a string variable	"Len"
Searching for text in a string	"InStr"

Preview of the Next Lesson

In the next lesson, you will learn how to use the design editor in Outlook to create custom forms. The basics of the Form Design Editor will be discussed so that you can easily create, write code for, and publish custom Outlook forms to a local or public folder in your company.

Designing Custom Microsoft Outlook Forms

In this lesson you will learn how to:

- Use the Forms Designer in Outlook.
- Customize a form using ActiveX controls.
- Add code to a form using Microsoft Visual Basic, Scripting Edition.
- Publish a custom form to a personal folder or public folder.
- Set form properties and password-protection.

Estimated time
90 min.

Electronic mail has progressed rapidly from plain, unformatted messages to highly formatted messages filled with graphics, attachments, hyperlinks, and controls leading to more interaction. In Microsoft Outlook, every form you use to send a mail message, schedule a meeting, complete a task request, or compose a journal entry can be customized. You can add a company logo, voting buttons, and question and feedback boxes to forms. Custom forms serve to perform tasks that you once may have conducted via paper memo, simple e-mail messages, or other specialized applications.

A mail message, meeting request, task request, journal entry, or any other form that Outlook provides is referred to as an Outlook *item*, and each item represents a foundation from which you can create your own custom forms. In this lesson, you will create a custom questionnaire form by using an Outlook mail message item. The controls and some of the code used to create the questionnaire will be similar to that used in the wizard you created in Lesson 11, so you can easily leverage your experience from previous lessons.

Using the Outlook Forms Designer

Microsoft Outlook does not support the Visual Basic Editor provided by Microsoft Word, Excel, and PowerPoint or many of the advanced programming tools found in the Visual Basic Editor and in Microsoft Access. Creating custom forms in Outlook, however, is similar to building UserForms in the Visual Basic Editor or forms in Access. In all cases of creating forms, you simply drag controls from a toolbox onto the form and then set the properties of each control using a Properties window.

Display the Outlook Forms Designer

1   Start Microsoft Outlook and open the Inbox folder.

2   On the File menu, point to New, and then click Mail Message on the submenu.

    A new mail message is displayed.

3   On the Tools menu of the active mail message window, click Design Outlook Form.

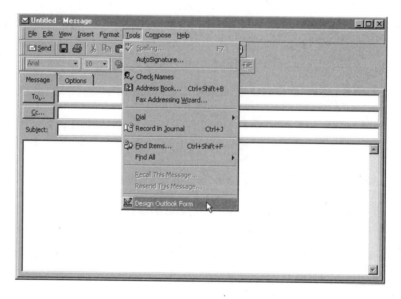

The Design Outlook Form menu item appears on the Tools menu of every Appointment, Meeting Request, Contact, Task, Task Request, or

Journal Entry form in Outlook. When you select Design Outlook Form, Outlook places the active form in design mode.

If Design appears in parentheses in the title bar, the form is in design mode.

Two new menus appear...

...as does a Design toolbar...

...and the Field Chooser dialog box.

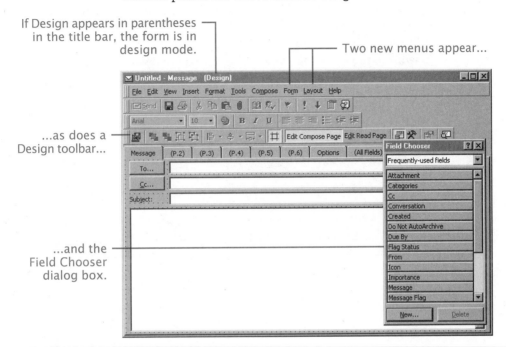

When the form is in design mode, the word *Design* appears in parentheses in the form's title bar. Two new menus appear on the Menu Bar of the form: the Form and Layout menus. A Design toolbar appears to help you create your custom form, while most (or all) of the controls on the Standard and Formatting toolbars in the form are disabled. The Field Chooser dialog box is displayed, providing you with a list of fields that you commonly see in built-in Outlook forms, such as the To, Cc, and Subject fields.

Display and hide pages in an Outlook form

When your mail message form is in design mode, Outlook displays 10 tabbed pages. The first six pages are customizable, including the Message page. When you use a built-in mail message form to compose an e-mail message, you see the Message and Options pages displayed. You can choose to display or hide any page in a custom form except for the Properties and Actions pages, which are always hidden. Hidden pages are indicated by parentheses around the name of the page on the tab.

1 Click the Options tab.

2 On the Form menu, click Display This Page (if it is currently selected) to clear this menu item.

You cleared the Display This Page menu item so that the Options page will not be displayed when the form is not in design mode. By clicking the menu item, the visible state of the active page is toggled. Parentheses now appear around the name Options on the tab.

You must display or hide each page individually. For each page you want to hide, click the tab to activate the page and then click the Display This Page menu item to clear the check box beside the menu item.

3 On the Tools menu, click Design Outlook Form to run the form.

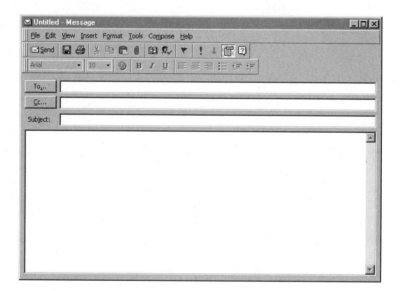

If only one page in a form is displayed, the tab is not shown. When more than one page is shown, the tabs are displayed, allowing you to switch between the pages.

Rename a page in a form

1 On the Tools menu, click Design Outlook Form to put the form in design mode.

2 With the Message page active, click Rename Page on the Form menu.

The Rename Page dialog box is displayed.

3 In the Page Name text box, type **Questionnaire** and click OK.

The text "Questionnaire" appears in the tab of the first page in the form. The Questionnaire page is where you will add the necessary controls to display your questions and to allow the message recipient to enter comments.

Customizing Forms with Controls

You can add the common field controls Outlook provides by using the Field Chooser dialog box or by selecting controls from the Toolbox. The Toolbox in Outlook is similar to the Toolbox in the Visual Basic Editor of Microsoft Word, Excel, and PowerPoint, and you can use it to add the same controls you added to your wizard in Lesson 11. To add and remove controls from the Toolbox, see Lesson 4.

The Field Chooser dialog box provides a list of fields commonly used in built-in Outlook forms. To use one of these fields, select the field in the Field Chooser dialog box and drag the field to the page of the form where you want to place it. The AutoLayout feature of Outlook will automatically size the field. If the field you want doesn't appear in the Field Chooser dialog box, select a different field set from the drop-down list in the upper part of the Field Chooser dialog box.

Add controls to your custom Outlook form

1 To make room for controls that will be used to display the questions of your questionnaire, click the Message text field on the form and press DELETE. Select and delete the Cc button and the adjacent text box. Select and delete the To button but not the adjacent text box.

Your form should look similar to the following illustration:

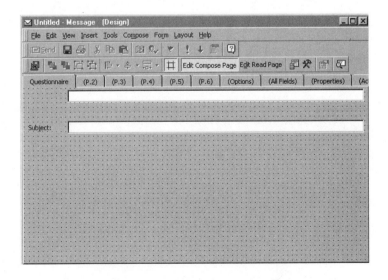

2 Move the Subject label and the adjacent text box beneath the text box that was adjacent to the To button.

 TIP To move the controls as a unit, select one, hold down CTRL, and select the other.

3 Click the Control Toolbox button on the Design Mode toolbar.

4 In the Toolbox, click the Label control and then, on the form, click to the left of the text box that was adjacent to the To button.

Control Toolbox

5 Right-click the new Label control and then click Advanced Properties on the shortcut menu.

Label control

The Properties window displayed is similar to the window provided in the Visual Basic Editor except that the Properties window in the Outlook Forms Designer does not provide a drop-down list of controls available on the active form. The drop-down list is replaced by a text box in which you enter the value of the property listed in the Properties window. Likewise, you cannot edit the value of a property in the field next to the property's name; instead, you must enter the value in the text box.

6 Select the Caption property in the Properties window, and, in the text box, type **To:** and click Apply (or, you can press ENTER). Scroll down the list of properties and select the Name property. In the text box, type **lblTo** and click Apply.

7 In the Toolbox, click the Image control and click just below the Subject label. Resize the Image control so that its height is approximately the same as that of the text box adjacent to the Subject label.

Image control

8 In the Properties window for the Image control, change the Name property to **imgLogo**. Select the Picture property in the Properties window and then click the button with the ellipsis, at the upper-right corner of the Properties window. In the Load Picture dialog box, change to the Lesson 13 practice folder, select Logo2.wmf, and click Open.

Ellipsis

If the Advanced Properties window isn't visible, right-click the Image control and then click Advanced Properties on the shortcut menu.

9 In the Properties window, select the PictureSizeMode property, and, in the drop-down list in the upper part of the Properties window, select 1 – Stretch.

10 In the Toolbox, click the MultiPage control and then click below the Image control on the form. In the Properties window for the MultiPage control, change the Name property from MultiPage1 to **mpgSteps**.

MultiPage control

11 Right-click any tab in the MultiPage control and then click Insert on the shortcut menu.

A new page is added to the MultiPage control.

12 Add three CommandButton controls below the MultiPage control.

In the Properties window, change the properties of the inserted controls to the following:

Control	Property	Value
CommandButton1	Name	cmdPrevious
CommandButton1	Caption	< Previous
CommandButton1	Accelerator	P
CommandButton2	Name	cmdNext
CommandButton2	Caption	Next >
CommandButton2	Accelerator	N
CommandButton3	Name	cmdFinish
CommandButton3	Caption	Finish
CommandButton3	Accelerator	F

13 Move and size the controls using the following illustration as a guide:

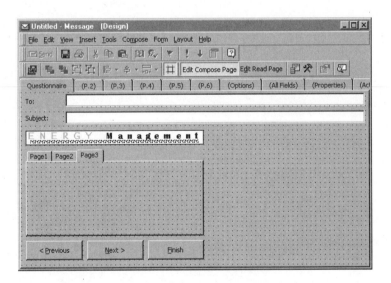

The general layout of the form is complete, but the controls that will display the questions and allow a user to enter comments have yet to be added. You will add these controls to the MultiPage control in the following steps.

Add controls to the MultiPage control

To make sure you select the MultiPage control, not the page within it, display the Advanced Properties window and notice the control name.

1 Click the first tab of the MultiPage control, Page1, and then click the selection border of the MultiPage control. In the Toolbox, click the Label control, and then click in the top-left area of the MultiPage control.

 IMPORTANT When you click the Page1 tab of the MultiPage control, the Toolbox may disappear. In addition, your cursor may not change back to the shape it had before you inserted the Label control. To change the cursor back to the Normal Select style, click the selection border of the MultiPage control. The Toolbox should automatically reappear as well. This may happen each time controls are added to the MultiPage control in the following steps.

TextBox control

2 In the Toolbox, click the TextBox control and drag the control onto the first page of the MultiPage control, just below the Label control. Size the controls using the following illustration as a guide:

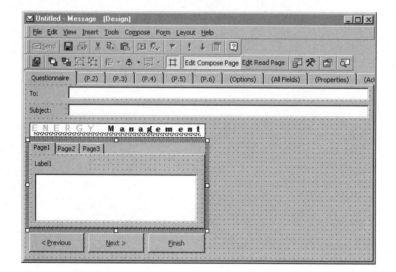

3 Right-click the Label control on the first page of the MultiPage control, and then click Advanced Properties on the shortcut menu. In the Properties window, change the Name property to **lblQues1**. Change the

Caption property to **Question 1: Please comment on the results**. Select the TextBox control just below the lblQues1 label and change the Name property of the control to **txtQues1**.

Label control

4   Click the second tab, Page2, of the MultiPage control. Click the selection border of the MultiPage control. In the Toolbox, click the Label control and then click in the top-left area of the MultiPage control. If necessary, click the selection border of the MultiPage control to change the cursor back to the Normal Select style.

5   In the Toolbox, click the TextBox control and drag the TextBox control onto the second page of the MultiPage control, just below the Label control.

6   Right-click the Label control on the second page of the MultiPage control, and then click Advanced Properties on the shortcut menu. In the Properties window, change the Name property to **lblQues2**. Change the Caption property to **Question 2: Did the results meet your expectations?** Select the TextBox control just below the lblQues2 label and change the Name property of the control to **txtQues2**.

7   Click the third tab, Page3, of the MultiPage control. Click the selection border of the MultiPage control. In the Toolbox, click the Label control and then click in the top-left area of the MultiPage control. If necessary, click the selection border of the MultiPage control to change the cursor back to the Normal Select style.

8   In the Toolbox, click the TextBox control and drag the TextBox control onto the third page of the MultiPage control, just below the Label control.

9   Right-click the Label control on the third page of the MultiPage control, and then click Advanced Properties on the shortcut menu. In the Properties window, change the Name property to **lblQues3**. Change the Caption property to **Question 3: How can the process be improved?** Select the TextBox control just below the lblQues3 label and change the Name property of the control to **txtQues3**.

10 Right-click the selection border of the MultiPage control and then click Advanced Properties on the shortcut menu. Scroll down the Properties window and select the Style property. In the drop-down list in the upper

part of the Properties window, select 2 – None. Move and size the controls using the following illustration as a guide:

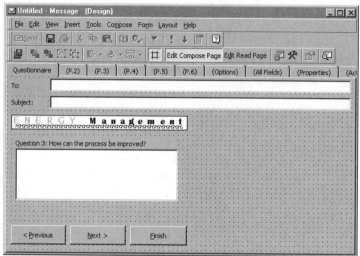

The page now looks like what users will see and use when they load the questionnaire onto their computers. After they answer the questions, they will click Finish to send the form to the alias specified on the To line of the Questionnaire page. You may, however, want the people who receive the completed questionnaire forms to see something different: Rather than showing the same controls and layout you used to ask the questions, you may want to summarize the answers in a normal mail message page.

Display different controls, depending on who is viewing the form

You can add controls to a custom form in two different page views: Edit Compose Page and Edit Read Page. When your custom form is in design mode, you can toggle between the Edit Compose Page and Edit Read Page layouts by clicking the corresponding entry on the Form menu.

1 On the Form menu, click Edit Read Page.

The layout of the controls on the Edit Read Page view is the same as the layout of the original mail message form before you customized it. Only the Edit Compose Page view layout was customized.

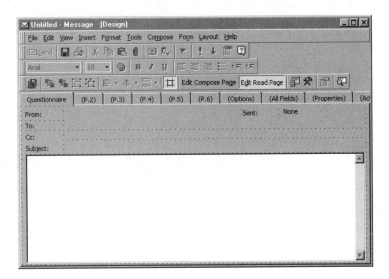

2   On the Form menu, click Edit Compose Page to display the customized layout.

The Form menu contains a Separate Read Layout menu item, which is selected by default when a custom form is in design mode. When the Separate Read Layout menu item is selected, as it is in your custom form, the Edit Compose Page layout will be displayed when the user opens the custom form. When the user completes the form and sends it on, the next recipient then sees the contents of the Edit Read Page.

 TIP   Microsoft Outlook installs a set of Outlook template files within the folder C:\Program Files\Microsoft Office\ Templates\Outlook. A good example of a custom form with different Edit Compose Page and Edit Read Page views is the While You Were Out template. To display this template in design mode, on the File menu in Outlook, point to New and then click Choose Template on the submenu. In the Choose Template dialog box, select While You Were Out in the Outlook tab and click OK. On the Tools menu of the form, click Design Outlook Form and toggle between the Edit Compose Page and Edit Read Page views. This template is also a good example of a custom form created without writing Visual Basic script.

Using Microsoft Visual Basic, Scripting Edition, you can populate (fill in) the message control in the Edit Read Page view with the answers users enter in the text boxes in the Edit Compose Page view. Thus, the recipients of the completed questionnaires will see a summary of the comments.

Writing Code for a Custom Form

Microsoft Outlook supports Microsoft Visual Basic, Scripting Edition, also known as VBScript, which is a subset of the Visual Basic programming language.

TIP Visual Basic, Scripting Edition, does not support a few of the common conventions that you may frequently use in Visual Basic programming. For the latest information and full documentation for Microsoft Visual Basic, Scripting Edition, visit the Web site http://www.microsoft.com/vbscript on the Internet.

Using Visual Basic, Scripting Edition, you can write code in your custom form that accesses the Outlook object model. Two objects that represent the main windows you commonly see in Outlook can be accessed from the Outlook Application object: the Explorer object and the Inspector object. The Explorer object, which is returned by the ActiveExplorer method of the Application object, represents the Outlook application frame that contains the views of your personal and public folders, as well as the list of all items within a folder.

The Inspector object, which is returned by the ActiveInspector method of the Application object, represents an Outlook item such as a mail message, meeting request, or journal entry that is currently open.

The Explorer returned by the ActiveExplorer is set to the Outlook application window that was most recently active. The same holds true for the object returned by the ActiveInspector. If multiple Outlook items, such as a number of mail messages, are open, the ActiveInspector method returns the most recent one to be opened. In the following example, the ActiveInspector always returns the Inspector object that is currently displayed and that contains your custom form.

TIP The Microsoft Outlook Visual Basic Help file is not installed by the Typical installation of Microsoft Office 97. For more information on how to install the Microsoft Outlook Visual Basic Help file, ask the Assistant for help, using the words "Visual Basic." Display the topic "Get Help for Visual Basic in Microsoft Outlook."

Add code to a custom Outlook form

1   On the Form menu, click View Code to display the Script Editor.

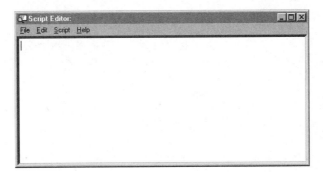

The Script Editor looks very similar to the Microsoft Notepad.

2   On the Script menu of the Script Editor, click Event.

The Events dialog box is displayed, listing the events that are supported by the form. The pane in the lower part of the Events dialog box describes the event selected in the list.

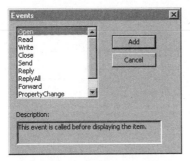

3   Select Open from the list and click Add.

As the description indicates, the Open event is called before the form is opened (displayed). When you click OK, Outlook adds the following lines to the contents of the Script Editor:

```
Function Item_Open()
End Function
```

4   Add the following line of code within the Item_Open function:

```
On Error Resume Next
```

The On Error statement indicates that if an error occurs while any of the lines in the Item_Open function are running, VBScript will ignore the line where the error occurred and continue with the next line.

 TIP While you are designing and testing your code, you should comment out the On Error statement by adding a single quotation mark (') at the beginning of the line. Thus, if any errors that you are unaware of occur, Visual Basic will alert you. When Visual Basic displays an error, the line number where the error occurred is displayed. To go to the line number in the Script Editor, click Go To on the Edit menu, and enter the line number in the Go To dialog box.

---

5 After the On Error statement, add the following Set statement in the Item_Open function:

```
Set oInspector = Application.ActiveInspector
```

The Set statement sets the object variable oInspector to the mail message form. The Application object represents Microsoft Outlook. The ActiveInspector method of the Application object returns the Outlook item that is currently the active window. If the form is open, the window displaying the form becomes the active inspector and will be the topmost Inspector object on your desktop.

 TIP If the Microsoft Outlook Visual Basic Help file is installed on your machine, you can access it by clicking Microsoft Outlook Object Library Help on the Help menu in the Script Editor.

---

6 After the Set statement, add the following line:

```
oInspector.SetCurrentFormPage ("Questionnaire")
```

The SetCurrentFormPage method of the Inspector object sets the page to be displayed. This line is not necessary in your custom form because you set only the Questionnaire page in the form to be visible. However, if you had more than one visible page, you could use the SetCurrentFormPage method to display a particular page. The PageName argument of the SetCurrentFormPage method corresponds to the tab name of the page in the form. When the form is in design mode, the name of the page you will set as the current page is "Questionnaire."

7 After the line using the SetCurrentFormPage method, add the following code:

```
oInspector.CurrentItem.To = "David Boctor"
oInspector.CurrentItem.Subject = "Energy Questionnaire"
```

The CurrentItem property of the Inspector object returns the Outlook item currently displayed in the inspector. In your custom form, the item returned is the MailItem object because you started with a mail message to create your custom form. If you started with an Appointment form, the AppointmentItem object would be returned. The To and Subject properties of the MailItem object are set in the Item_Open function.

8 Finally, add the following lines of code as the last four lines in the Item_Open function:

```
Set oPages = oInspector.ModifiedFormPages
Set mpgSteps = oPages("Questionnaire").Controls("mpgSteps")
mpgSteps.Value = 0
Call mpgSteps_Change
```

The first Set statement sets the variable oPages to the Pages collection for the item in the inspector. The second Set statement sets the variable mpgSteps to the MultiPage control named mpgSteps on the Questionnaire page in the form. Each Page object in a form contains a Controls collection object, which represents the controls available on a page.

Following the Set statements, the value of the mpgSteps MultiPage control is set to 0 so that the first page in the MultiPage control is displayed. The last line calls the mpgSteps_Change procedure, which you will create in the following steps.

Change pages in the MultiPage control

1 Place the cursor beneath the Item_Open function in the Script Editor and add the following event procedure:

```
Sub cmdNext_Click()
    Set oPages = Application.ActiveInspector.ModifiedFormPages
    Set mpgSteps = oPages("Questionnaire").Controls("mpgSteps")
    mpgSteps.Value = mpgSteps.Value + 1
    Call mpgSteps_Change
End Sub
```

The cmdNext_Click event procedure will be executed when the Next button is clicked. The four lines in the cmdNext_Click event procedure are the same as the last four lines in the Item_Open function except that the value of the MultiPage control is increased by a value of 1 rather than being explicitly set to 0.

2   Place the cursor beneath the cmdNext_Click event procedure and add the following cmdPrevious_Click event procedure:

```
Sub cmdPrevious_Click()
    Set oPages= Application.ActiveInspector.ModifiedFormPages
    Set mpgSteps = oPages("Questionnaire").Controls("mpgSteps")
    mpgSteps.Value = mpgSteps.Value - 1
    Call mpgSteps_Change
End Sub
```

The code in the cmdPrevious_Click event procedure is the same as the code in the cmdNext_Click event procedure except that the value of the MultiPage control is decreased by a value of 1 rather than increased by a value of 1.

3   Beneath the cmdPrevious_Click event procedure, add the following Sub mpgSteps_Change procedure:

```
Sub mpgSteps_Change()
    Set oPage = Application.ActiveInspector _
        .ModifiedFormPages.Item("Questionnaire")
    Set mpgSteps = oPage.Controls("mpgSteps")
    Set cmdNext = oPage.Controls("cmdNext")
    Set cmdPrevious = oPage.Controls("cmdPrevious")
    Set cmdFinish = oPage.Controls("cmdFinish")
End Sub
```

The Set statements within the mpgSteps_Change procedure set variables to the Next, Previous, and Finish navigation controls.

4   Below the last Set statement added in the previous step, add the following Select Case block:

```
Select Case mpgSteps.Value
Case 0
    cmdNext.Enabled = True
    cmdPrevious.Enabled = False
    cmdFinish.Enabled = False
Case mpgSteps.Pages.Count - 1
    cmdNext.Enabled = False
    cmdPrevious.Enabled = True
    cmdFinish.Enabled = True
Case Else
    cmdNext.Enabled = True
    cmdPrevious.Enabled = True
    cmdFinish.Enabled = False
End Select
```

The Select Case block is the same as the code added to the wizard created in Lesson 11. The value of the mpgSteps MultiPage control is evaluated to determine the enabled state of the Next, Previous, and Finish navigation controls.

5   Switch to the custom form. On the Tools menu, click Design Outlook Form to take the form out of design mode.

This action compiles the code in the Script Editor.

 IMPORTANT   If a compiling error occurs, switch to the Script Editor, go to the indicated line, and correct the error. Switch to the custom form, place the form in design mode, and then take it out of design mode to recompile the code.

---

6   Click the Previous button and then click the Next button.

You should see the different pages of the mpgSteps MultiPage control being displayed as you click the Next and Previous navigation buttons. The enabled state of each button should be set to True or False, depending on which page in the MultiPage control is currently displayed. The last thing to do is to add the code that runs when the questions in the MultiPage control are answered and the Finish button is clicked.

Send the form

1   On the Tools menu, click Design Outlook Form to put the form back in design mode, and then switch to the Script Editor for the form.

2   Beneath the mpgSteps_Change procedure, add the following cmdFinish_Click event procedure:

```
Sub cmdFinish_Click
    Application.ActiveInspector.CurrentItem.Send
End Sub
```

Within the cmdFinish_Click event procedure, the ActiveInspector object of the Outlook Application object will represent the inspector that contains your custom form because this inspector will be the active one when the cmdFinish button is clicked. The CurrentItem property of the Inspector object returns the item contained with the inspector.

The item you are working with is the MailItem. The MailItem object is thus returned by the CurrentItem property. The Send method of the MailItem object indicates that the item should be sent, which triggers the Item_Send event function, which will be added in the next step.

3   Place the cursor beneath the cmdFinish_Click event procedure and, on the Script menu, click Event. In the list of events, select Send and click Add. The following lines are added:

```
Function Item_Send()
End Function
```

As the Events dialog box indicates, the Send event is called before the item is sent and before the inspector is closed. In the Item_Send function you can determine whether certain conditions are met in the form. If the conditions are not met, you can set the return value of Item_Send function to False, which prevents the Send action from being completed and the item's inspector from closing.

4 Within the Item_Send function, add the following lines of code:

```
Item_Send = True
Set oPages = Application.ActiveInspector.ModifiedFormPages
Set mpgSteps = oPages("Questionnaire").Controls("mpgSteps")
```

The Item_Send function is explicitly set to True in the first line. The subsequent two Set statements are used to retrieve the mpgSteps MultiPage control and set it to the variable mpgSteps.

5 Below the two Set statements within the Item_Send function, add the following:

```
sQues1 = Trim(mpgSteps.Pages(0).txtQues1.Text)
sQues2 = Trim(mpgSteps.Pages(1).txtQues2.Text)
sQues3 = Trim(mpgSteps.Pages(2).txtQues3.Text)
```

The variables sQues1, sQues2, and sQues3 are set to text entered in the text boxes within the pages of the mpgSteps MultiPage control. The Trim function is used to remove any leading or trailing spaces from the text so that if only spaces are added to a text box, the user will be prompted to enter a comment in the text box. Note that the Trim function used here is not followed by a dollar sign ($) to indicate a function that returns a string, as it was in Lesson 11. Visual Basic, Scripting Edition, supports only string manipulation functions that return a Variant data type.

6 Add the following If...Then...ElseIf condition block below the lines setting the variables sQues1, sQues2, and sQues3:

```
If Len(sQues1) = 0 Then
    MsgBox "Please enter your comments for Question 1."
    Call SetPage(0)
    Item_Send = False
ElseIf Len(sQues2) = 0 Then
    MsgBox "Please enter your comments for Question 2."
    Call SetPage(1)
    Item_Send = False
ElseIf Len(sQues3) = 0 Then
    MsgBox "Please enter your comments for Question 3."
    Call SetPage(2)
    Item_Send = False
End If
```

Through the Len function provided by Visual Basic, Scripting Edition, the If...Then...ElseIf condition block evaluates the length of each string representing text entered in the text boxes in the mpgSteps MultiPage control. If the value of the Len function is 0, a message box is displayed asking the user to enter comments for the specific question.

The line following the message box statement calls the SetPage procedure and passes a value to the SetPage procedure that represents the page in the MultiPage control where the question was not answered. The Item_Send function is then set to False so that the Send action is not completed and the form is left open.

7   After the If...Then...ElseIf condition block, add the following lines of code:

```
If Item_Send = False Then Exit Function
Application.ActiveInspector.CurrentItem.Body = _
    sQues1 & Chr(13) & sQues2 & Chr(13) & _
    sQues3 & Chr(13)
```

The If...Then condition statement evaluates the current value of the Item_Send function. If the function is False, Visual Basic, Scripting Edition, exits the function, and the line below the If...Then condition statement is not executed. If the function is True, the Body property is set to the text stored in the variables sQues1, sQues2, and sQues3, each separated by a carriage return. The Edit Read Page view of the current item, which represents a MailItem object, contains the message text box (the body of the mail message).

8   Place the cursor beneath the Item_Send function and add the following SetPage procedure:

```
Sub SetPage(iPage)
    Set oPages = Application.ActiveInspector.ModifiedFormPages
    Set mpgSteps = oPages("Questionnaire").Controls("mpgSteps")
    mpgSteps.Value = iPage
    Call mpgSteps_Change
End Sub
```

The SetPage procedure is used to change the value of the MultiPage control so that it displays the page containing the question that was not answered. The value of the MultiPage control is set using the value of the variable iPage, which is passed as an argument to the SetPage procedure.

9   On the File menu, click Close to close the Script Editor.

Your custom form is now functional. In the next section, you will learn how to make your custom form available to yourself or to your users.

Saving, Publishing, and Managing Custom Forms

Once you have created a custom Outlook form, you can save it as a template, or you can publish your form to a *forms library*. When you publish a custom form to a forms library, you can make the form available to others, depending on which forms library you have permission to publish your custom forms in. Outlook also provides you with a way to manage the content of a forms library so that you can update, delete, or copy custom forms from a library.

Save your custom form as a template

1   On the File menu of your custom form, click Save As.

2   In the Save As dialog box, change to the folder C:\Program Files\Microsoft Office\Templates\Outlook.

Close Window

3   Type the filename **MyEnergyQuestionnaire** and click Save. Click the Close Window button to close the custom form, and do not save changes.

4   To display your custom form, on the File menu in Outlook, point to New and then click Choose Template on the submenu.

5   In the Choose Template dialog box, select MyEnergyQuestionnaire and click OK.

The Warning dialog box will appear, asking if you want to disable or enable the macros in the form. Click Enable Macros because you created the form.

 NOTE   If you have difficulty running or debugging your code, you can examine a completed working version of the template. Open the Energy.oft file in the Lesson 13 practice folder.

Publish your custom form to a forms library

Rather than saving your custom form as a template, you can easily make your form available to others by publishing your form to a forms library.

1   On the Tools menu of your custom form, click Design Outlook Form to put your form in design mode.

2   On the File menu of your custom form, click Publish Form As to display the Publish Form As dialog box.

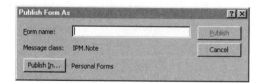

3   In the Form Name text box of the Publish Form As dialog box, type the name **Energy Questionnaire**.

4   Click the Publish In button to display the Set Library To dialog box.

Depending on whether your computer is connected to a network and whether public folders exist on your network, the folder list displayed below the Folder Forms Library option button may differ from the illustration. The Personal Folders item is listed in most cases.

5   Select the Forms Library option button, select Personal Forms in the drop-down list, and click OK.

For now, you will save the form locally. If you have permission to publish forms to other folders on your network, you can publish it to a public folder.

6   In the Publish Form As dialog box, click Publish.

The form is now published to your personal forms library.

7   Close the form from the File menu without saving changes.

Manage forms in your personal forms library

If you want to delete a custom form in a forms library, you can use the Forms Manager in Outlook.

1   In the Outlook application window, on the Tools menu, click Options.

2   In the Options dialog box, click the Manage Forms tab. In the Manage Forms tab, click the Manage Forms button.

The Forms Manager dialog box is displayed, allowing you to delete custom forms from a particular library or copy forms from one library to another.

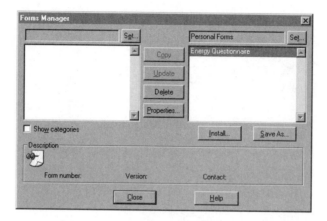

3   To display the list of custom forms in your personal forms library, click either one of the Set buttons. In the Set Library To dialog box, click the Forms Library option button, select Personal Forms from the drop-down list, and click OK.

4   In this lesson, you added custom properties to your form, so you may not want to remove your custom form. (If you want to remove any custom form in your personal forms library, select the form in the list and then click the Delete button. Do not delete your form now, however, so that you can continue the lesson.)

5   Click Close to close the Forms Manager dialog box, and click OK to close the Options dialog box.

Setting Custom Form Properties and Password Protection

When you publish your form and then display the list of forms in a forms library, you will see a description of the form in the bottom frame of the New Form dialog box. This helps you and your users know what the custom form represents, what its version number is, and who to contact about the form. You can also specify an icon for easy association to the form. You can easily set all of these attributes as well as add password protection to your form while a form is in design mode.

320

Add custom information to your form

1 On the File menu in the Outlook application window, point to New and click Choose Form on the submenu.

The Description frame in the lower part of the New Form dialog box often displays information about the dialog box, but no information has been specified for your form.

2 Click OK to close the New Form dialog box. Display your custom form in design mode.

3 Click the Properties tab, and then in the Properties page, add a description of the custom form in the Description text box.

4 If you want, add a contact name to the Contact text box. If you want to search for an e-mail name in your Outlook Address Book, click the Contact button.

5 If you want, set the version and form numbers in the Version and Form text boxes.

Once you have finished setting the custom properties of your form, you can republish it back to a forms library. However, you may want to password-protect your form so that the layout or functionality cannot be modified.

Password-protect your custom Outlook form

1 With your custom form in design mode, click the Properties tab and select the Protect Form Design check box.

When you do this, the Password dialog box is automatically displayed.

2 Enter a password in the Password text box and repeat it in the Confirm text box. Click OK.

3 If you want to change the password, in the Properties tab, click the Set Password button to display the Password dialog box.

 IMPORTANT   Remember your password because Outlook forms do not provide a method for retrieving the contents of password-protected forms. Your password is case-sensitive, so be sure to note the exact syntax you use.

4 On the File menu, click Publish Form As, and, in the Publish Form As dialog box, click Publish.

5 Close your form without saving changes.

If you try to display the form again in design mode, you'll be prompted for a password.

Your custom form is complete. If you want to share your custom form with others and you have permission to place your form on a public folder in your organization, publish your form to a public forms library.

 TIP If you are connected to an e-mail network, you can test your form and code by sending the results of the questionnaire to yourself. On the File menu, point to New, and click Choose Form. Select Energy Questionnaire and click OK. The questionnaire appears as you designed it in the Edit Compose Page view. In the To line of the form, type your e-mail address. Answer the questions and click Finish to send the form to yourself. Check your mail. The completed questionnaire appears as you designed it in the Edit Read Page view.

Lesson Summary

To	Do this
Display the Outlook Forms Designer	On the Tools menu of an Outlook item, click Design Outlook Form.
Display or hide a page in a form	On the Form menu, while in the Outlook Forms Designer, click Display This Page.
Rename a page in a form	On the Form menu, click Rename Page.
Add predefined fields provided by Outlook	In the Field Chooser dialog box, click the field and drag it to the page of the form where you want to place the field.
Add a control from the Toolbox	Click the Control Toolbox button to display the Toolbox, click a control in the Toolbox, and then click in your custom form.
Display different controls, depending on who is viewing the form	When your custom form is in design mode, toggle between the views by clicking either Edit Compose Page or Edit Read Page on the Form menu.
Write Visual Basic script in the form	On the Form menu, click View Code to display the Script Editor.
View the list of events supported by a custom form	On the Script menu of the Script Editor, click Event to display the Events dialog box.

To	Do this
Access the controls on a custom form using Visual Basic, Scripting Edition, and the Outlook object model	Set a variable to the Pages collection of the custom form and then set a variable to a control in the Controls collection of the page.
Save a custom form as an Outlook template	On the File menu of the custom form, click Save As and save the form in the folder C:\Program Files\Microsoft Office\Templates\Outlook. Outlook will list the form template in the Choose Template dialog box.
Make your form available to others	On the File menu of your custom form, click Publish Form As. In the Publish Form As dialog box, choose a public forms library folder.
Manage forms in a forms library	On the Tools menu in the Outlook application window, click Options. In the Options dialog box, click the Manage Forms tab. In the Manage Forms tab, click the Manage Forms button to display the Forms Manager dialog box.
Add a description of your form	When your form is in design mode, in the Properties page, add a description of the custom form in the Description text box.
Password-protect your custom form	In the Properties page of a custom Outlook form, select Protect Form Design and enter a password in the Password dialog box.

For online information about	Ask the Assistant for help, using the words
Outlook forms	"About forms"
Saving, publishing, and distributing forms	"Save and distribute forms"
Security in Microsoft Outlook and in forms	"Password protection"

Where Do I Go Next?

Congratulations! You have learned a lot about creating custom solutions using Visual Basic for Applications in Microsoft Office. Now that you have the basics, you may want to learn even more. Following are some information sources you can consult to create more advanced solutions.

Microsoft Office Developer's Forum   On the Internet, navigate to the Microsoft Office Developer's Forum at http://www.microsoft.com/officedev/. Here you will find a number of articles about automating Microsoft Word, Excel, PowerPoint, Access, and Outlook, and about building integrated Microsoft Office solutions.

Mastering Microsoft Office 97 Development   This CD-ROM–based tool provides interactive, in-depth training for developing solutions using Microsoft Office 97 and Visual Basic for Applications. Mastering Microsoft Office 97 Development is a logical step beyond *Microsoft Office 97/Visual Basic Step by Step* because it provides intermediate and advanced samples, techniques, and tips for creating and distributing Microsoft Office solutions.

Microsoft Press   Microsoft Press provides a number of quick-and-easy and self-paced training guides as well as desktop references, technical resources, and programming titles. To locate your nearest source for Microsoft Press products worldwide, visit the Microsoft Press Web site, or contact your local Microsoft office. In the United States, call (800) MS-PRESS. In Canada, call (800) 667-1115.

Index

Take
productivity
in stride.

Microsoft® Excel 97 Step by Step
U.S.A. $29.95 ($39.95 Canada)
ISBN 1-57231-314-5

Microsoft® Word 97 Step by Step
U.S.A. $29.95 ($39.95 Canada)
ISBN 1-57231-313-7

Microsoft® PowerPoint® 97
Step by Step
U.S.A. $29.95 ($39.95 Canada)
ISBN 1-57231-315-3

Microsoft® Outlook™ 97 Step by Step
U.S.A. $29.99 ($39.99 Canada)
ISBN 1-57231-382-X

Microsoft® Access 97 Step by Step
U.S.A. $29.95 ($39.95 Canada)
ISBN 1-57231-316-1

Microsoft® Office 97 Integration
Step by Step
U.S.A. $29.95 ($39.95 Canada)
ISBN 1-57231-317-X

Microsoft Press® *Step by Step* books provide quick and easy self-paced training that will help you learn to use the powerful word processor, spreadsheet, database, desktop information manager, and presentation applications of Microsoft Office 97, both individually and together. Prepared by the professional trainers at Catapult, Inc., and Perspection, Inc., these books present easy-to-follow lessons with clear objectives, real-world business examples, and numerous screen shots and illustrations. Each book contains approximately eight hours of instruction. Put Microsoft's Office 97 applications to work today, *Step by Step.*

Microsoft Press® products are available worldwide wherever quality computer books are sold. For more information, contact your book retailer, computer reseller, or local Microsoft Sales Office.

To locate your nearest source for Microsoft Press products, reach us at mspress.microsoft.com, or call 1-800-MSPRESS in the U.S. (in Canada: 1-800-667-1115 or 416-293-8464).

To order Microsoft Press products, call 1-800-MSPRESS in the U.S. (in Canada: 1-800-667-1115 or 416-293-8464).

Prices and availability dates are subject to change.

Microsoft® Press

Authoritative information.
Impressive results.

MICROSOFT® PROFESSIONAL EDITIONS

Covers Microsoft Office 97 for Windows® 95, Windows NT,™ and the Apple Macintosh®

Master the
Powerful
Development
Platform Within
the World's Most
Popular Office Suite

Microsoft®
Office 97
Visual Basic®
Programmer's Guide

Microsoft Press

U.S.A.	**$34.99**
U.K.	£32.49
Canada	$46.99

ISBN 1-57231-340-4

With this guide and a basic knowledge of Microsoft® Visual Basic® for Applications or any Microsoft Office programming language, you'll learn to do everything from automating individual tasks to creating full-fledged custom applications. You'll explore Microsoft Visual Basic for Applications version 5.0, the common programming language shared by applications in Microsoft Office 97. And always, you'll get the authoritative, inside story from the people who actually developed Microsoft Office 97.

Create ActiveX™ controls and Internet-enabled applications— fast!

U.S.A. **$44.99**
U.K. £41.99 [V.A.T. included]
Canada $60.99
ISBN 1-57231-436-2

MICROSOFT® VISUAL BASIC® 5.0 DEVELOPER'S WORKSHOP, Fourth Edition, is a one-of-a-kind book-and-software package that gives you the recipes to build powerful, full-featured graphical applications for Windows® 95 and Windows NT® This book demonstrates everything from creating a screen saver to building ActiveX controls that can be used in a Web page. You'll learn by example how to:

- Build 32-bit applications for Windows 95 and Windows NT
- Develop reusable objects to enhance your productivity
- Extend the language by calling Windows API functions
- Take advantage of ActiveX technologies
- Access data on an Internet server
- Install applications over the Internet

Create full-featured Windows 95 and Windows NT–based applications faster than ever before with MICROSOFT VISUAL BASIC 5.0 DEVELOPER'S WORKSHOP!

***Microsoft*Press**

IMPORTANT—READ CAREFULLY BEFORE OPENING SOFTWARE PACKET(S). By opening the sealed packet(s) containing the software, you indicate your acceptance of the following Microsoft License Agreement.

MICROSOFT LICENSE AGREEMENT

(Book Companion CD-ROM)

This is a legal agreement between you (either an individual or an entity) and Microsoft Corporation. By opening the sealed software packet(s) you are agreeing to be bound by the terms of this agreement. If you do not agree to the terms of this agreement, promptly return the unopened software packet(s) and any accompanying written materials to the place you obtained them for a full refund.

MICROSOFT SOFTWARE LICENSE

1. GRANT OF LICENSE. Microsoft grants to you the right to use one copy of the Microsoft software program included with this book (the "SOFTWARE") on a single terminal connected to a single computer. The SOFTWARE is in "use" on a computer when it is loaded into the temporary memory (i.e., RAM) or installed into the permanent memory (e.g., hard disk, CD-ROM, or other storage device) of that computer. You may not network the SOFTWARE or otherwise use it on more than one computer or computer terminal at the same time.

For the files and materials referenced in this book which may be obtained from the Internet, Microsoft grants to you the right to use the materials in connection with the book. If you are a member of a corporation or business, you may reproduce the materials and distribute them within your business for internal business purposes in connection with the book. You may not reproduce the materials for further distribution.

2. COPYRIGHT. The SOFTWARE is owned by Microsoft or its suppliers and is protected by United States copyright laws and international treaty provisions. Therefore, you must treat the SOFTWARE like any other copyrighted material (e.g., a book or musical recording) except that you may either (a) make one copy of the SOFTWARE solely for backup or archival purposes, or (b) transfer the SOFTWARE to a single hard disk provided you keep the original solely for backup or archival purposes. You may not copy the written materials accompanying the SOFTWARE.

3. OTHER RESTRICTIONS. You may not rent or lease the SOFTWARE, but you may transfer the SOFTWARE and accompanying written materials on a permanent basis provided you retain no copies and the recipient agrees to the terms of this Agreement. You may not reverse engineer, decompile, or disassemble the SOFTWARE. If the SOFTWARE is an update or has been updated, any transfer must include the most recent update and all prior versions.

4. DUAL MEDIA SOFTWARE. If the SOFTWARE package contains both 3.5" and 5.25" disks, then you may use only the disks appropriate for your single-user computer. You may not use the other disks on another computer or loan, rent, lease, or transfer them to another user except as part of the permanent transfer (as provided above) of all SOFTWARE and written materials.

5. SAMPLE CODE. If the SOFTWARE includes Sample Code, then Microsoft grants you a royalty-free right to reproduce and distribute the sample code of the SOFTWARE provided that you: (a) distribute the sample code only in conjunction with and as a part of your software product; (b) do not use Microsoft's or its authors' names, logos, or trademarks to market your software product; (c) include the copyright notice that appears on the SOFTWARE on your product label and as a part of the sign-on message for your software product; and (d) agree to indemnify, hold harmless, and defend Microsoft and its authors from and against any claims or lawsuits, including attorneys' fees, that arise or result from the use or distribution of your software product.

DISCLAIMER OF WARRANTY

The SOFTWARE (including instructions for its use) is provided "AS IS" WITHOUT WARRANTY OF ANY KIND. MICROSOFT FURTHER DISCLAIMS ALL IMPLIED WARRANTIES INCLUDING WITHOUT LIMITATION ANY IMPLIED WARRANTIES OF MERCHANTABILITY OR OF FITNESS FOR A PARTICULAR PURPOSE. THE ENTIRE RISK ARISING OUT OF THE USE OR PERFORMANCE OF THE SOFTWARE AND DOCUMENTATION REMAINS WITH YOU.

IN NO EVENT SHALL MICROSOFT, ITS AUTHORS, OR ANYONE ELSE INVOLVED IN THE CREATION, PRODUCTION, OR DELIVERY OF THE SOFTWARE BE LIABLE FOR ANY DAMAGES WHATSOEVER (INCLUDING, WITHOUT LIMITATION, DAMAGES FOR LOSS OF BUSINESS PROFITS, BUSINESS INTERRUPTION, LOSS OF BUSINESS INFORMATION, OR OTHER PECUNIARY LOSS) ARISING OUT OF THE USE OF OR INABILITY TO USE THE SOFTWARE OR DOCUMENTATION, EVEN IF MICROSOFT HAS BEEN ADVISED OF THE POSSIBILITY OF SUCH DAMAGES. BECAUSE SOME STATES/COUNTRIES DO NOT ALLOW THE EXCLUSION OR LIMITATION OF LIABILITY FOR CONSEQUENTIAL OR INCIDENTAL DAMAGES, THE ABOVE LIMITATION MAY NOT APPLY TO YOU.

U.S. GOVERNMENT RESTRICTED RIGHTS

The SOFTWARE and documentation are provided with RESTRICTED RIGHTS. Use, duplication, or disclosure by the Government is subject to restrictions as set forth in subparagraph (c)(1)(ii) of The Rights in Technical Data and Computer Software clause at DFARS 252.227-7013 or subparagraphs (c)(1) and (2) of the Commercial Computer Software — Restricted Rights 48 CFR 52.227-19, as applicable. Manufacturer is Microsoft Corporation, One Microsoft Way, Redmond, WA 98052-6399.

If you acquired this product in the United States, this Agreement is governed by the laws of the State of Washington.

Should you have any questions concerning this Agreement, or if you desire to contact Microsoft Press for any reason, please write: Microsoft Press, One Microsoft Way, Redmond, WA 98052-6399.

The
Step by Step
Practice Files Disc

The enclosed CD-ROM contains timesaving, ready-to-use practice files that complement the lessons in this book. To use the practice files, you'll need Office 97 and either the Windows 95 operating system or version 3.51 Service Pack 5 or later of the Windows NT operating system.

Almost all of the *Step by Step* lessons use practice files from the disc. Before you begin the *Step by Step* lessons, read the "Installing and Using the Practice Files" section of the book. There you'll find a description of each practice file and easy instructions telling you how to install the files on your computer's hard disk.

Please take a few moments to read the license agreement on the previous page before using the enclosed disc.

Register your Microsoft Press® book today, and let us know what you think.

At Microsoft Press, we listen to our customers. We update our books as new releases of software are issued, and we'd like you to tell us the kinds of additional information you'd find most useful in these updates. Your feedback will be considered when we prepare a future edition; plus, when you become a registered owner, you will get Microsoft Press catalogs and exclusive offers on specially priced books.

Thanks!

I used this book as
- ● A way to learn the software
- ● A reference when I needed it
- ● A way to find out about advanced features
- ● Other_____

I consider myself
- ● A beginner or an occasional computer user
- ● An intermediate-level user with a pretty good grasp of the basics
- ● An advanced user who helps and provides solutions for others
- ● Other_____

I purchased this book from
- ● A bookstore
- ● A software store
- ● A direct mail offer
- ● Other_____

I will buy the next edition of the book when it's updated
- ● Definitely
- ● Probably
- ● I will not buy the next edition

The next edition of this book should include the following additional information:

1•_____

2•_____

3•_____

The most useful things about this book are_____

_____

This book would be more helpful if_____

_____

My general impressions of this book are_____

_____

May we contact you regarding your comments? ● Yes ● No

Would you like to receive a Microsoft Press catalog regularly? ● Yes ● No

Name_____

Company (if applicable)_____

Address_____

City_____State_____Zip_____

Daytime phone number (optional) (_____)_____

Please mail back your feedback form—postage free! Fold this form as described on the other side of this card, or fax this sheet to:
Microsoft Press, Attn: Marketing Department, fax 425-936-7329

FOLD HERE

NO POSTAGE
NECESSARY
IF MAILED
IN THE
UNITED STATES

BUSINESS REPLY MAIL
FIRST-CLASS MAIL   PERMIT NO. 53   BOTHELL, WA

POSTAGE WILL BE PAID BY ADDRESSEE

MICROSOFT PRESS
MICROSOFT® OFFICE 97/VISUAL BASIC®
STEP BY STEP
PO BOX 3019
BOTHELL   WA   98041-9946